Life is a Garden Present

Unlimited Business Growth: Transform Your Business and Overcome Mental Barriers

By John P. Oda Ph.D.
Contributing Authors Carl Scott MPH and Scot Conway, Ph.D, J.D.

Website: www.drjohnoda.com

Table of Contents

Quadrant One: Business

- **Chapter 1: The Journey** 45
- **Chapter 2: Life Cycle of a Business** 55
- **Chapter 3: The Power of Mindset and Faith** 76
- **Chapter 4: The Mastermind Principle** 106

Quadrant Two: Behavioral Symptoms

- **Chapter 5: The CEO Mindset** 117
- **Chapter 6: Creating the Right Culture** 127
- **Chapter 7: Building a Strong Team** 140
- **Chapter 8: Mental Health** 161

Quadrant Three: Systemize

- **Chapter 9: Next-Level Sales Mastery** 176
- **Chapter 10: The Sextillion Time Management System** 198
- **Chapter 11: The Octopus Method of Marketing** 210

Table of Contents - continued

Quadrant Four: Monetize

- **Chapter 12: Reactivating Old Clients** 231
- **Chapter 13: Unlocking the Power of Referrals** 243
- **Chapter 14: The Dream 100 Strategy** 255
- **Chapter 15: Cost Optimization Techniques** 270
- **Chapter 16: Upselling and Cross-Selling** 283
- **Chapter 17: Creating JV Partnerships** 290

Case Studies 298

Copyright © 2025 John P. Oda, Ph.D.

ISBN: 9798306378923

All rights reserved. No part of this publication may be reproduced, stored in a retrieval system, or transmitted in any form or by any means, electronic, mechanical, recording or otherwise, without the prior written permission of the author.

Published by Oda Publishing Company

Printed on acid-free paper.

Oda Publishing Company, Inc.
2025

First Edition

Dedicated to my loving heroes, my parents.

Wardine Maggie Oda
February 12, 1932-March 17, 2018

Odessa Joseph Oda Sr.
January 17, 1923 -April 2, 2014

My mother's favorite scriptures and books:

Psalms, Proverbs, Isaiah 45:1-7, Mark 11:22-26, 1Kings 17: 8-24

My father's favorite biblical scripture:

I have fought the good fight to the end. I have run the race to the finish I have kept the faith. Timothy 4:7

DISCLAIMER

The author and publisher are providing this book and its contents on an "as is" basis and make no representations or warranties of any kind with respect to this book or its contents. The author and publisher disclaim all such representations and warranties, including warranties of merchantability and fitness for a particular purpose. In addition, the author and publisher do not represent or warrant that the information accessible via this book is accurate, complete or current.

The statements made about products and services have not been evaluated by the U.S. Food and Drug Administration. They are not intended to diagnose, treat, cure, or prevent any condition or disease. Please consult with your own physician or healthcare specialist regarding the suggestions and recommendations made in this book.

Except as specifically stated in this book, neither the author or publisher, nor any authors, contributors, or other representatives will be liable for damages arising out of or in connection with the use of this book. This is a comprehensive limitation of liability that applies to all damages of any kind, including (without limitation) compensatory; direct, indirect or consequential damages; loss of data, income or profit; loss of or damage to property and claims of third parties.

You understand that this book is not intended as a substitute for consultation with a licensed healthcare practitioner, such as your physician. Before you begin any healthcare program, or change your lifestyle in any way, you will consult your physician or other licensed healthcare practitioner to ensure that you are in good health and that the examples contained in this book will not harm you.

This book provides content related to topics about weight loss, nutrition and health. As such, use of this book implies your acceptance of this disclaimer.

Acknowledgments

My Family

First and foremost, I want to thank God for the incredible gifts He's blessed me with—the talents and abilities that allow me to uplift and empower others. Without Him, none of this would be possible.

To my amazing parents, Odessa Oda (1923-2014) and Wardine Maggie Oda (1932-2018), your unwavering love, support, and guidance have been the foundation of everything I've achieved. Because of you, I stand here with strength, purpose, and deep gratitude. It's safe to say **Dr. John is in the house** because of your sacrifices and wisdom.

To my incredible siblings—I am blessed to have six sister and three brothers thank you for your endless support and encouragement. Each of you has played a unique role in shaping the person I've become, and I am forever grateful for the bond we share.

My success is not mined alone—it's a reflection of the love, faith, and strength of the Oda family. I love you all deeply and thank you for walking this journey with me.

My St. Mary's Grade School Family
To my St. Mary's Grade School family in Michigan City, Indiana, you've shown me the power of community and lifelong connection. Over 50 years later, I still feel the lessons of discipline, kindness, and faith imparted by the incredible teachers, nuns, and coaches like Mr. Palmer (Rest in Heaven), Mr. May, and Mr. Johnson.

Danny Black
Danny, our bond started in first grade and has stood the test of time. The day you honored my mother at her funeral in 2017 by becoming an altar man was one of the most touching moments of my life. It was a true testament to the loyalty and love we've shared for over five decades. Thank you for showing me what real friendship looks like. I love you and appreciate you deeply.

Robby Bremer
Robby, you've been a part of my journey since fourth grade, and you've never been just a friend—you've been family. From your father co-signing my first car to your presence at every major family event, you've always been my brother from another mother. Your support and willingness to help with my crazy ideas mean the world to me. Thank you for everything, Robby.

Andrew Gardiner
Andrew, your expertise in marketing and strategy has been a game-changer. Your ability to create winning ideas and bring them to life has pushed my success beyond what I imagined. Thank you for being an invaluable partner in this journey.

Carl Scott MHP
Carl, you are the embodiment of leadership. Your mentorship has shown me the power of walking the talk and leading with integrity. You've inspired me to aim higher, think bigger, and lead with purpose. Thank you a million times over.

Dr. Horton
Dr. Horton, meeting you 30 years ago was pivotal in my life. Your brilliance in Neuro-Linguistic Programming opened my mind to new possibilities and transformed my way of thinking. Thank you for your wisdom and for giving me tools that have defined my journey.

Scot Conway J.D. Ph.D.
Scot, you are a rare gem—a mentor who lives what he teaches every single day. Your honesty, investment in my growth, and unwavering belief in me have been life-changing. Thank you for holding me accountable and always pushing me to be better.

Janie Davis, my prayer partner, with who we pray about three times a week together, thank you for pushing me to get back to working in the mental health field again and change the quality of people's lives

Nancy Atkinson (1943-2023): I want to thank you for helping with the seven team-building techniques; we use the same concept when working with teens.

Mircron System: Thanks so much for creating my book cover

Jude Okeke I want to take a moment to express my heartfelt gratitude for your exceptional dedication and service to our company. Two years ago, you applied to be my virtual assistant, and since then, you've grown into an indispensable partner in building and running our empire.

You've stood by me through both good times and bad, consistently seeking ways to improve and expand your skills. Your commitment to excellence is truly inspiring, and I'm grateful for your tireless efforts to drive our business forward.

Thank you for your loyalty, expertise, and passion. I look forward to many more years of success together.

Mommy O and Daddy O (My Parents)

Mommy, you were my first coach and my biggest cheerleader. You believed in me when others doubted me and taught me how to persevere despite my stutter. Your wisdom about life, business, and faith still guides me daily. I love you and appreciate every lesson you imparted. Rest in Heaven, my love.

Daddy, your work ethic and dedication were unmatched. You balanced two full-time jobs, cared for your family, and taught me what being a man of strength and integrity means. I know I will have done well if I can be just 10% of the man you were. I love you and miss you every day. Rest in Heaven, my hero.

To God

Above all, I thank God for every blessing—placing me in the right family, giving me the courage to overcome my challenges, and waking me up each day with health, clarity, and purpose. I am humbled and grateful for His grace, which allows me to share my light and inspire greatness in others.

A Heartfelt Thank You to My Clients—Past and Present

For over 38 years, I've had the privilege of walking alongside you—both in the mental health field and in the world of business. Along this journey, you've taught me lessons that no book or seminar ever could.

You've helped me see the power of transformation, not just in the lives I've touched but in my own. Your courage, challenges, and breakthroughs have pushed me to walk my talk—to embody the principles I teach so I can guide you with authenticity and purpose.

Because of you, I've become a better strategist, coach, and human being. Your trust has fueled my drive to create Ultimate Business Growth Strategies that spark real change—right now.

So, thank you. Thank you for your faith, your commitment, and your inspiration. Together, we're creating not just success but legacies that endure.

Let's keep transforming lives—starting with yours.

A Heartfelt Thank You to My 24-Hour Fitness Family in Market Place Irvine, CA

Every morning, before the sun even thinks about rising, I step into a place that feels like home—a sanctuary of strength, perseverance, and connection. At 24 Hour Fitness Market Place Irvine, it's not just about lifting weights or running on treadmills; it's about the bonds we forge, the laughter we share, and the unwavering support we give each other.

I want to take a moment to express my deepest gratitude to the people who make this place extraordinary.

First, to Kim, our exceptional GM, and Nate, our Assistant GM—thank you for believing in me and supporting my journey. Your leadership sets the tone for a community unlike any other.

And then, there's my gym daughter, Bella—your radiant smile at 4 a.m. is a beacon of positivity that lights up the early morning. You're a force to be reckoned with, juggling work, school, and life with a grace that's nothing short of inspiring.

To the incredible morning staff: Omar, Miles, Ricky, Adam and morning staff (you freaking rock) , and the powerhouse trainers Austin and Isaiah—you are the heartbeat of this gym. Isaiah, standing tall at 6'5", you are the epitome of greatness—balancing college and work with a drive that promises an extraordinary future

And then, my morning crew—my family. From 5 a.m. to 10 a.m., depending on the chaos of my schedule, you are the constant that keeps me grounded. A vibrant mix of races, ages, and personalities, we share a rare and beautiful camaraderie. We tease each other, push each other, and, most importantly, hold each other accountable.

When I faced one of my toughest challenges—blowing out my knee, tearing my ACL and meniscus—it was Dave Rosenbaum and Rob Collins who stood by me, guiding me through physical therapy. Dave and Rob, you're not just a friend but a lifeline.

To the countless names that make up this incredible gym family—Scott B., Tom L., Elcie, Frank (Alabama), Dan (Alabama), Austin, Rob K, Kevin B., JQ, Fred, Linda, Jon, Pat, David (sons who are baseball stars), Kevin (pilot), Lance, Adrianne, Alex, Jerry, Leason P, Jaime R (Indiana) Anne, Mary Lou, Dan (Surfer), The Professor, Kevin (real estate), Roger (Buck), Dan H, Chris (Ohio) Dr. Said, Oliva, Josephine, Tom (Mr. T) Cole, LD, Tom (Motown), Justin, Denzel, Scott (Amazon) Sheldon, Bob (Ohio) Larry (Ohio State) Jeff, Jhamani, Jonathan (music teacher) Bob (high school principal) Nicole (army) Henry, Anthony (boxing) Big Larry, Ms. Ann, Dante, Letitia, and the Zumba crew at 8a.m. and whoever I missed.—thank you for your energy, your encouragement, and your unwavering spirit.

This gym isn't just a place to work out; it's a place to grow, to heal, and to thrive. It's a family. And to my 24-Hour Fitness family—I respect you, I appreciate you, and I love you. You've made every step of this journey unforgettable; I am eternally grateful for that.

Here's to many more mornings, more laughter, more sweat, and more triumphs—together.

With all my heart,
Honorary Mayor of 24 Hour Fitness Market Place Irvine, CA

Foreword by William Horton PSY.D

It is truly an honor to be part of this groundbreaking body of work by Dr. John Oda. Over the last 30 years, I have witnessed firsthand the remarkable evolution of a man who has dedicated his life to transforming others. My journey with John began in Northwest Indiana, where fate intertwined our paths. At the time, I was living in Portage, Indiana, while John resided in Michigan City, Indiana. Our connection sparked when John, curious and driven, inquired about a Neuro-Linguistic Programming (NLP) class I was offering in Chicago in 1997.

The moment I met John at that seminar, his excitement was palpable—it filled the room. Although he had already worked with Joseph McClendon III, Anthony Robbins' lead trainer, and understood the fundamentals of NLP, John was hungry for more. At that time, he had a decade of experience working with adolescents and teens and sought to elevate his skill set to new heights. His vision? To surpass even the legendary Anthony Robbins by mastering NLP at an unmatched level.

During our five-day foundational NLP program, I saw a relentless determination in John's eyes. He absorbed every detail and committed to learning how to apply these techniques to reach and transform the masses. By the end of the program, John had not only earned his NLP certification but also ignited a journey that would impact countless lives.

As an Elite Trainer for NFNLP (National Federation of Neuro-Linguistic Programming), I was privileged to guide John through his early NLP journey. Months later, John contacted me again, eager to expand his expertise. He dove headfirst into certifications in Sports Performance and Weight Loss using NLP, equipping himself with tools to shape the mindsets of athletes and everyday individuals striving for greatness.

By 2001, John had attained the coveted Master Practitioner level in NLP. Over the next four years, he integrated these techniques into his mental health practice, designing innovative programs that transformed lives. While the average Clinical/Program Director never conducted groups, John led four groups per week, honing his craft, applying NLP, and achieving extraordinary results. John, innovative approach using Neuro Linguistic Programming (NLP) has achieved remarkable success with the Seriously and Persistently Mentally Ill (SPMI) population - a group often misunderstood as having limited potential for recovery.

His groundbreaking group therapy sessions, consistently filled to standing-room-only capacity, demonstrate the power of NLP in driving positive change. By harnessing the potential of NLP, Dr. Oda has helped countless individuals overcome seemingly insurmountable challenges, inspiring hope and transformation in their lives.

One of Dr. Oda's most striking aspects is his use of board-breaking techniques to help patients break through their fears and limitations. This powerful metaphor for overcoming obstacles has empowered patients to tap into their inner strength and resilience.

Notably, Dr. Oda's caseload consisted of the most challenging patients, providing a unique opportunity for his staff to learn from his expertise. By working alongside John, his staff gained invaluable insights into effective strategies for supporting even the most difficult-to-treat patients, ensuring a lasting impact on the lives of those they serve.

In 2014, Dr. John Oda achieved the distinction of becoming a Master Trainer with the NFNLP. This milestone reflected not only his expertise but also his dedication to mastering and teaching NLP at the highest level. His contributions as a Master Trainer have since inspired and equipped countless others to unlock their potential and create lasting change.

As we worked together, John's momentum only grew. In 2008, he began collaborating with Anthony Robbins and Chet Holmes on business strategies, setting the stage for a new chapter. With my guidance in sales, bolstered by my book *Selling Yourself to Others: The New Psychology of Sales*, John excelled. He quickly rose to become the number-one closer in the company, achieving an extraordinary 69% closing rate on deals ranging from $2,500 to $14,000 per month.

Together, we developed "The Secret Language of Influence," an NLP-based sales system, and collaborated on addressing mental health issues in the workplace. John tackled mental health while I focused on addictions, enabling us to provide holistic support for business owners. This unique blend of expertise allowed us to deliver unparalleled value to businesses of all sizes.

I was captivated when John shared the concept for this book with me. He demonstrated his unmatched creativity and strategic vision by merging the DSM-IV with a revolutionary business model. This book represents the culmination of decades of mastery, blending advanced NLP techniques, metaphors, and storytelling—all hallmarks of John's unparalleled style.

John's decision to train with NFNLP was intentional. As he told me, "All NLP isn't the same. Many programs are watered down. I wanted the original, unfiltered methodology from someone who learned directly from the founders." That commitment to authenticity and excellence defines John's work and legacy.

The BSSM-1 Model: Dr. John Oda's Revolutionary System for Success

At the heart of this transformative book lies the BSSM-1 Model—a system that marries the psychological rigor of the DSM-IV with state-of-the-art business strategies. Grounded in NLP and enriched by insights from some of the greatest minds of our time, this model is a game-changer.

Quadrant One: Business (Faith and Mindset)

Success begins with belief. This quadrant explores the foundational elements of faith and mindset, showing how to condition your subconscious, work with spiritual guides, and harness the power of mastermind groups. Dr. Oda unveils the secrets to cultivating an unshakable foundation for unstoppable growth.

Quadrant Two: Symptoms of a Business (Behavioral)

Your business reflects your leadership. This quadrant dives into the behavioral dynamics of success, from CEO leadership to workplace culture, team synergy, and mental health. You'll gain actionable insights to create an environment where businesses and individuals can thrive.

Quadrant Three: Systemize a Business

Systems are the lifeblood of sustainability. Here, Dr. Oda outlines how to streamline sales, time management, and marketing, empowering you to save time while amplifying your results.

Quadrant Four: Monetize Your Business

Profitability is the ultimate goal. In this quadrant, Dr. Oda shares six proven strategies to turn confusion into cash within 90 days. This is your blueprint for monetization mastery, from increasing net profits to ensuring long-term financial growth.

John Oda's visionary work goes beyond mere business strategies—it is a testament to the transformative power of combining mental health, NLP, and business acumen. Through this book, you'll witness his brilliance and gain the tools to unlock your potential and achieve unprecedented success.

William Horton PSY.D Founder of National Federation of NLP (NFNLP) , Elite Trainer and author of ten books, *Primary Objective, Selling Yourself to others, New Psychology of Sales, Mind Control Secrets, How to get Others to do what you want, Advanced Mind Control Secrets, Quantum Psychology, NLP $ Sales, The Secret Psychology of Persuasion, Sports Psychology & Hypnosis for the modern Athlete, The Unstoppable Forces of a positive change self-Image Create a New You, Success Habits*

Meet My Contributing Authors

Meet Carl Scott

Carl Scott is a luminary in the healthcare industry, a trusted authority with over 50 years of leadership and mental health experience that has shaped the landscape of healthcare services. Holding a Master's in Healthcare Administration from Indiana University, Carl's commitment to innovation and excellence allows him to serve clients by applying cutting-edge practices rooted in the latest research.

Imagine working with someone who not only stays ahead of the curve but has spent decades refining the art of leadership. Carl's unique ability to bridge the gap between strategy and execution has made him an invaluable asset in the healthcare community.

As a dedicated philanthropist, Carl gives back to the Chicagoland community by serving on the boards of directors for several healthcare organizations. His work ensures that both patients and providers benefit from his insight, compassion, and unwavering commitment to excellence.

Since beginning his business coaching career in 1975, Carl has mentored countless business leaders, providing the clarity and strategies needed to unlock their full potential. Since 2013, he has partnered with the Dr. John Oda Method, blending neuroscience and business mastery to achieve transformational results.

Carl's proven track record includes serving as CEO for mental health agencies and healthcare providers across Chicago and Indiana. As a fractional C-suite executive, Carl has served as CEO and COO for over 40 years, driving remarkable growth and helping organizations navigate complex challenges with precision and expertise. His leadership has consistently turned struggling organizations into thriving, profitable enterprises.

Pause for a moment and consider this:
What if you could gain access to Carl's deep well of expertise? Over the years, he has trained and mentored executives, middle managers, and employees at all levels. From Fortune 500 companies to universities, law firms, and small businesses, Carl has conducted workshops and created training programs that reshape the way organizations think, grow, and lead.

His workshops, designed for executives and teams alike, delve into essential areas such as psychology, leadership, communication, and organizational change. These programs don't just inform—they transform. Imagine learning from a master who combines decades of experience with a passion for empowering others to achieve breakthroughs.

Carl's expertise extends to startup operations, where he has helped businesses launch successfully by building strong teams, designing marketing programs, and providing professional supervision training. His specialized training courses cover areas like diversity, human resources, executive coaching, and middle management development.

Here's what sets Carl apart:
He doesn't just train—he transforms organizations, fostering growth through practices like conflict resolution, change management, and innovative strategies for diversity and inclusion. Through his online tools and workshops, Carl empowers teams to reach new heights of collaboration and success.

Carl's approach is rooted in a profound understanding of both human psychology and business strategy. He equips leaders with tools to navigate challenges, break through barriers, and achieve their goals faster than they thought possible.

Now, imagine this:
Carl Scott as your guide, bringing clarity to complexity and helping you unlock untapped potential. Whether through workshops, training sessions, or one-on-one coaching, Carl's expertise ensures that every moment is transformative.

Beyond his professional achievements, Carl finds joy in golf, running, and reading, pursuits that reflect his commitment to balance and lifelong growth. He resides in the Chicagoland area, where he continues to shape the future of healthcare leadership with vision, passion, and purpose.

Are you ready to experience the transformation Carl Scott can bring to your organization? Let's redefine what's possible—together.

Meet Dr. Scot Conway, Ph.D., J.D.

Dr. Scot Conway, a man of many dimensions, embodies mastery across a spectrum of disciplines. For over **35 years**, he has been the **Grandmaster of Guardian Kempo Kajuko Do**, a martial art refined through decades of dedication. As an **Attorney at Law** with **33 years of** business and estate planning expertise, Scot has guided countless clients through the complexities of law and leadership. Beyond these achievements, he's the author of **62 published books**, a seasoned **Commercial Real Estate Broker**, and a **Business Broker** with over a decade of experience in high-stakes negotiations and transactions.

Adding another layer to his dynamic persona, Scot is also a **pastor who teaches online**, sharing his wisdom and spiritual insights with a global audience.

But his legacy isn't found in titles, systems, or accolades—it's found in his **passion for people.**

Imagine this:
You're speaking with someone who has devoted nearly five decades to developing unparalleled depth, precision, and utility systems. Systems like **The Ohana Way** or **4P360: The 360-Degree Leadership System**. These aren't just ideas; they are frameworks for transformation. And yet, Scot's greatest passion isn't for the systems themselves—it's for what these systems UNLOCK IN OTHERS.

The Power of Passion for People
When a journalist once asked him, "Where's your passion?" she saw the meticulous design, the decades of work, and the profound results—but she didn't hear the answer right away. That's because Scot's passion isn't in the systems he's built, no matter how revolutionary they may be. It's in YOU.

You see, Scot doesn't light up over tools or techniques. He comes alive when those tools create breakthroughs in people's lives.

- When a leader walks into the storm of chaos and emerges as a calm, commanding force.
- When conflict transforms into collaboration.
- When problems give way to peace.

That's where you'll see his fire.

A Master's Toolbox for Leaders
Scot's systems are like an unparalleled set of tools. In the right hands, these tools can dismantle complexity, build bridges where others see

walls, and create a new vision of leadership where integrity and action are inseparable.

But make no mistake—those tools don't define him. They are **for you.**

Imagine stepping into a room armed with the principles of **4P360** or navigating life and business with the wisdom of **The Ohana Way.** Scot teaches leaders to wield these tools not just effectively but masterfully so they can stand in the storm, face conflict, and inspire transformation.

"The people are the purpose."
For Scot, it's all about seeing leaders like you embody integrity-driven systems, not as a chore but as an extension of your highest self. His goal isn't just to teach you; it's to **ignite you.** To help you BE MORE than you imagined possible and walk into chaos with an unshakable knowing: **You will win.**

This is Scot Conway's promise to you:
He will equip you with the tools. He will guide you to mastery. But it's YOU—your growth, your leadership, and your breakthroughs—that fuel his passion.

When Scot shows up, he's not bringing just another system. He's bringing the keys to unlock what's already within you: potential, purpose, and the ability to thrive in any challenge.

Where will Scot's tools take you? Let's find out—together.

Meet Dr. John Oda

A distinguished peak performance expert and masterful guide to transformation, Dr. John Oda brings an extraordinary depth of expertise with 38 years in mental health (clinical psychology) and 30 years in business growth. As a Master Trainer in Neuro-Linguistic Programming (NLP) with the National Federation of NLP, his legacy is etched in the remarkable breakthroughs he inspires.

Dr. Oda is the author of two transformative books, *Connecting With Your Teen* and *Life is a Garden*. In Connecting With Your Teen, he reveals how deep family issues can be resolved in just a few sessions, offering insights that rekindle family bonds and foster lifelong connections. Life is a Garden reflects on seven life-changing principles learned from his father's garden, blending spirituality with practical success to provide a roadmap for unlimited growth.

His thought leadership has garnered national and international recognition. His articles have been featured in Yahoo Finance, The American Reporter, Disrupt Magazine, The American Post, The United Business Journal, and New York Weekly. He has also been featured as a guest on "Oprah and Friends," where the legendary Maya Angelou interviewed him.

Dr. Oda is a sought-after speaker, frequently called upon to provide Corporate Training, Keynote Addresses, Workshops, and Seminars for Fortune 500 companies across the United States, the Middle East, and Europe.

For over three decades, Dr. Oda has operated in the elite top 1%—those who don't just talk about success but engineer it. As an Ultimate Business Growth Strategist, he combines the precision of neuroscience with the wisdom of clinical psychology and business mastery, crafting transformations few dare to dream possible.

Now, imagine this:
What if you could blend the science of the mind with decades of hands-on business expertise? What if scaling your business, overcoming mental blocks, or unlocking untapped potential were not just goals—but inevitabilities? That's the reality Dr. Oda creates, guiding you to a life where breakthroughs are the norm and extraordinary results become your standard.

Dr. Oda's unparalleled success rate—90%—also extends to families. By naturally guiding families through challenges, he has a proven ability to reshape dynamics, rekindle bonds, and foster lifelong connections. Through impactful seminars, transformative parenting workshops, and tailored teen programs, his work empowers families to thrive together.

Pause for a moment and consider this:
Patterns that seemed unbreakable can shift effortlessly. Transformation doesn't take years—it happens in moments. His groundbreaking books, *Connecting With Your Teen* and *Life is a Garden*, are testaments to his ability to inspire profound change.

In 1995, Dr. Oda's path expanded when he learned from Joseph McClendon III, head trainer for Anthony Robbins. Armed with NLP, cognitive therapy, and neuroscience, he began accelerating success at lightning speed. In 2008, his journey led him to collaborate with Chet Holmes and Tony Robbins through Business Breakthroughs International.

Picture this:
Growing your business by 1500% in just three years. That's the level of transformation Dr. Oda brings to his clients. Even after Chet Holmes' passing in 2012, his legacy lives on through Dr. Oda's work—refined and perfected into a blueprint for explosive growth.

Business Mastery further highlights Dr. Oda's prominence, boasting an impressive faculty including marketing genius Jay Abraham, Scott Hallman, Steve Wynn, Frank Kern, Keith Cunningham, Eben Pagan, Zappos president Tony Hsieh, Stephen M.R. Covey, Brendon Burchard, and Gary Vaynerchuk.

Dr. Oda's upcoming book, *Unlimited Business Growth: Transform Your Business and Overcome Mental Barriers*, is a masterful blend of fiction and nonfiction. Follow the story of Allan Private, a billionaire navigating the challenges of unresolved issues, and learn the timeless lessons that apply to creating success in every area of your business.

You'll gain tools to propel your business to new heights through four transformative quadrants—**Business, Symptoms (Behavior), Systemize, and Monetize**. Eight powerful case studies illuminate the possibilities, showing you what's truly achievable when you embrace these strategies.

Now, imagine this:
As you read, the words seem to speak directly to you, unveiling insights that feel tailor-made for your journey. You'll notice shifts in awareness, unlocking growth that feels effortless and natural. As these strategies take hold, you'll discover your own unlimited potential—ready to achieve success beyond anything you've imagined.

Educational Background
Dr. Oda holds a **Doctorate in Philosophy Research degree** with an emphasis in **Psychology** and an **MBA in Entrepreneurship**, further enhancing his ability to merge the sciences of the mind with business strategy, providing clients with a well-rounded approach to success.

Are you ready to take that first step? Let's create a new reality—together.

The Allan Private Story

Allan Private's journey began in Connecting with Your Teen, where he faced the familiar struggles of youth. You probably already know that life throws challenges our way, but maybe you haven't realized how deeply those early lessons shape the future. Now, Allan is grown, achieving success beyond his wildest dreams. But as you'll soon discover, success doesn't come without its share of trials.

In this new chapter of Allan's life, you'll experience his meteoric rise, his devastating fall, and the powerful insights he gains from both. I'm curious: have you ever found yourself riding high only to have it all crumble unexpectedly? Stop for a moment and imagine being there with Allan, naturally drawn into his world, as he navigates those highs and lows, each twist teaching him—and you—more about life and resilience.

You probably already know that it's during the toughest times when true strength is forged. Allan's story isn't just about success; it's about facing the moments when everything seems to fall apart. And because he learns to embrace these challenges, he uncovers wisdom that expands his future beyond what he could have imagined.

Now imagine sitting on the edge of your seat as Allan confronts the ultimate test—not just surviving life's storms but thriving through them, emerging stronger, wiser, and more successful than ever. This isn't just a story—it's a blueprint for turning life's darkest moments into your greatest opportunities.

Can you imagine learning the lessons Allan gains from his future self? Lessons that easily apply to your journey, helping you create your path to success faster, smarter, and more clearly than you ever thought possible. Are you ready to join Allan on this thrilling ride? Because what you're about to witness will change how you approach success—and failure—forever. This isn't just Allan's story. It's yours.

Allan Private: The CEO in Crisis

Allan Private stands at the helm of a Fortune 100 company, easily recognized worldwide. Yet, beneath the polished surface of his corporate success lies a personal struggle that threatens to unravel everything he's built naturally. Allan's unresolved childhood issues have followed him into the boardroom, driving his behavior. Maybe you've noticed how he acts like a know-it-all, a loner, selfish, and distrusting of everyone around him. His company's culture mirrors his internal chaos—gossiping, backstabbing, and constant complaints. Stop for a moment and become aware of how this toxic energy starts from the top, with Allan's destructive leadership driving the business toward inevitable turmoil.

Like a ship adrift without a rudder, Allan's company moves aimlessly, without clear vision or direction. Maybe you've already realized there are too many chiefs and not enough hands on deck. Despite huge profits, Allan's spendthrift ways and lack of systems are slowly eroding the company's foundation. Now, he skips meetings and refuses to hold himself accountable, and every day, the business moves in a different direction, lacking cohesion or a plan. His absence in leadership is expanding beyond personal failings—disaster is lurking just beyond the horizon, and everyone can sense it.

Allan prides himself on creating leadership programs, but his arrogance blinds him to their inefficiency. When his team voices concerns, he dismisses them, flaunting his past success, unable to see the cracks forming in the present. Instead of listening, Allan lashes out, using people's past challenges to discredit those who dare question his methods. His unchecked ego has poisoned the heart of his business.

During a critical team meeting, tensions boil over to discuss his new leadership program. Rather than fostering collaboration, Allan storms in like a whirlwind, attacking those who dare to challenge him and dragging the meeting into a spiral of negativity. His staff, feeling crushed, withdraws. The company culture, once a source of strength, is fracturing under the weight of Allan's destructive leadership.

Then, just days later, Allan embarks on a business trip to present his leadership program. As he prepares to board the company jet, a deep, gut-level instinct of dread washes over him—a sense that something is terribly wrong. Maybe you've felt that sense, that nagging intuition you can't quite shake. But Allan, the fearless leader, pushes it aside and boards the plane.

Shortly after takeoff, the unthinkable happens. His pilot, Abner, radios in, reporting a critical malfunction. They need to make an emergency landing. Panic sets in as Allan tries to call his team, but the connection is lost.

Allan only reached voicemail as he tried to call his family—to hear their voices one last time. The pilot's voice echoed through the cabin: "HOLD ON. THIS PLANE IS GOING DOWN." Time seemed to slow as Allan found himself suspended in a dream-like state. His entire life flashed before his eyes, and three haunting questions naturally arose in his mind:

1. How did I serve my clients today?
2. What seeds am I planting today in my business?
3. How has today impacted my legacy?

In the chaos, Allan felt himself expand beyond the confines of reality. It was as if battery acid was coursing through his veins—every nerve, every fiber of his being stretched to the breaking point. Now, excruciating pain flooded his body, and amidst it all, three haunting statements echoed in his mind, pulling him deeper into confusion and worry. His family appeared before him, their faces twisted with pain, their voices filled with regret. He saw his employees, the very people he had led, into a pattern of dysfunction. And then, he saw it all—his legacy, laid bare before him—a legacy he had never fully confronted. Allan noticed how the seeds of negativity he had planted spread throughout his workplace, poisoning his leadership and leaving behind a toxic, broken company. The scenes of people he had wronged played like an endless reel, naturally filling him with regret. Their faces, their pain—all caused by him—stayed with him, and Allan felt like a prisoner of his own choices.

Suddenly, Allan stood at a crossroads. Maybe you've been there, aware of the choices before you—two paths, one leading to something new and the other, a familiar descent into darkness. Allan hesitated, unsure of where to go. Uncertainty gripping his heart, he stepped toward the left path, unaware of its darkness.

As Allan walked deeper into the tunnel, the atmosphere around him grew darker and heavier, the air buzzing with voices—questions flying at him from all sides. The noise became unbearable, but then, out of nowhere, a blinding light pierced the darkness. A woman's face, blurred and unrecognizable, leaned close, forcing something into his mouth.

Allan jolted awake, dazed and confused, staring up at the stark white ceiling of a hospital room. A swarm of doctors surrounded his bed, peppering him with questions: "What's your name? Where do you live? What's the date? Who is the President?" Allan blinked, still half-dreaming. "It's March 20, 2024. The President is Biden. I'm Allan Private—the billionaire. I have a mansion in Michigan City, Indiana."

The doctors exchanged puzzled glances, repeating the same questions. Allan answered again with the same unwavering certainty.
A nurse gently checked his vitals, but Allan's mind raced—he needed to know about his family.

Dr. Siedler, the hospital psychologist, entered the room, a look of concern deepening on his face. "Mr. Private," he began carefully, "You've been in a serious accident. You may be experiencing some form of amnesia." Allan stared back, refusing to believe it. "No, this is 2054. My company went bankrupt ten years ago. I've been living on the streets."

Dr. Siedler handed Allan a newspaper article. Allan's eyes scanned the headline, and his breath caught as he read: "CEO'S FAILED LEADERSHIP RUINS LIVES—THE END OF PRIVATE ENTERPRISES." The article laid out, in painful detail, how his outdated leadership had driven his company to failure. It described how Allan clung to business models from the '80s while trying to compete in 2054's evolving market. His refusal to innovate had cost him everything.

Allan's hands shook as he folded the article and slipped it into his pocket. I know you, like me, can imagine the disbelief sinking in—this had to be some cruel joke. But as the truth weighed heavier on him, he became aware of something deeper: his legacy wasn't one of success but failure. The leadership he had once been proud of had become the very thing that naturally destroyed him.

Now, reeling from the shock, Allan left the hospital. As he walked, he spotted a familiar face—one of his former employees. Time had changed him. Allan approached cautiously, curious, feeling like a ghost from his past. "James," Allan began, "I've lost my memory... Can you help me understand what happened?"

James looked at Allan with a mix of pity and honesty. "Mr. Allan," he said softly, "your downfall came because you didn't listen. You were a destructive CEO."

Allan pulled out the article and handed it to James, who nodded solemnly. "It's all true," James continued. "You missed meetings, ignored us, and refused to innovate. It was like being led by someone stuck in old patterns—you didn't adapt, didn't evolve. We couldn't succeed because you didn't lead us. Maybe you will now understand you acted like a teenager trying to run a business."
James' words hit Allan like a tidal wave, and he felt his breath catch as his three statements flooded back into his mind:

How did I serve my clients today?
What seeds am I planting today in my business?
How has today impacted my legacy?

James continued, his voice steady. "I tried to help you. I discussed modeling success from people like Anthony Robbins, Chet Holmes, Dr. John Oda, and Carl Scott MPH. But you dismissed it all. You said they'd never make it. But look at them now—they're thriving, still creating change. Success leaves clues, but you refused to follow them."

As James' words expanded beyond the surface and sank into Allan's consciousness, he realized the full extent of his failures. His legacy wasn't the empire he once envisioned—it was the wreckage of a life spent ignoring the right paths and clues. Now, he noticed his reflection in the glass of a nearby building—a man weathered and aged beyond his years, who had lost everything because he didn't listen.
"If I could just have another chance…" Allan whispered to himself. "I'd change everything."

Turning back to James, Allan admitted, "I'd do anything to regain my clients' trust and make a real difference this time. I realize now… Things wouldn't have fallen apart if I had just listened from the start. I acted like a problem teen in business when I should've been at my prime." The words hung heavy in the air, laden with regret, naturally pulling him deeper into his reckoning.

James nodded, his expression firm but understanding. "Mr. Allan, I've always believed you had potential. You just didn't maximize the value of your team. Maybe you haven't yet realized, but they could've made all the difference. Your team wasn't just employees—they were the heart of your business. You failed to notice that they were your greatest asset, and that's why things crumbled."

Allan's heart sank as he replayed how he had treated his staff in the past. His leadership wasn't based on collaboration but control. His team wasn't empowered—they were suffocated. I'm curious: can you imagine what would have happened if Allan had led with service rather than ego?

"I lost everything because I didn't listen," Allan confessed. "I was too focused on control. I didn't realize the importance of serving others—creating an environment where people felt valued, not crushed."
His mind raced through all the opportunities he had missed to lift his team up. His greatest regret wasn't the financial loss—it was how he had failed the people who depended on him. He knew that if given a second chance, he would change everything.

"From now on," Allan said with conviction, "It's not about the money. It's about serving others in the highest way possible. It's about building a workplace where people feel empowered and where we work together to create success. Now, I realize that's the only way forward."

Maybe you've felt it, too—that the key to true success is leading, listening, serving, and lifting others as you rise.
James listened quietly, sensing the sincerity in Allan's words. "You can't do it alone, Mr. Allan," he said. "You need to surround yourself with the right people who will push you, challenge you, and tell you when you're wrong. That's why having an executive business coach or consultant is essential. Someone who isn't afraid to tell you the truth because they're not your employee—they're there to help you grow."

Allan nodded, realizing the wisdom in James' words. He thought about the future and how he needed to re-engineer his entire business model. The old ways wouldn't work anymore. "I know now," Allan said, "that to survive in the 21st century, I need to change how I do business. The structure has to be re-imagined so that we can compete with the best." He recalled how his company had been successful nearly two decades ago, but the landscape had changed. What worked back then wouldn't sustain him in the future. "The business world is evolving," Allan said, "and I need to evolve with it. This experience has been a blessing in disguise. It's opened my eyes to how I can improve things—for my clients, employees, and myself."

Allan was ready to commit to a new way of thinking. He promised himself and James that he would build a new system that put service to others at its core. He vowed to listen to his management team and create a powerful company culture rooted in the principles of collaboration and growth. He would do this by implementing a new approach: The Ohana Way, which would create a system of support and unity where every company division worked together seamlessly to drive growth.

Reflecting on his future experience, Allan realized he had been given an incredible opportunity. He had seen the most successful business minds in 2054; now, in 2024, he could apply their lessons to reshape his company. Leaders like Dr. John Oda, Anthony Robbins, Chet Holmes, and Scott Hallman had laid out the blueprint for success. Allan knew he had to model their principles if he wanted to succeed.

"It was surreal," Allan said, "to see Tony Robbins at 90 years old, still holding seminars and transforming lives. He and others like him—Dr. John Oda and Chet Holmes—left behind a legacy of innovation and success. I now understand that success leaves clues. I just have to follow them."

Allan was determined to take what he had learned from these great minds and integrate their strategies into his business. To be the best, Allan understood that he needed to take back what the greatest teachers of all time had taught him, for example, Dr. John Oda's time management system, concepts of taking your problem teenagers' business to the prime stage, and creating the BSSM-1 Method; on marketing strategy, Chet Holmes has left an indelible mark; Scot Hallman explains how to optimize your business; Tony Robbins' work on Peak Performance; Dr. Scot Conway on the Ohana Way; and Carl Scott MHA talks about destructive, neutral, or effective CEOs.

James listened quietly, sensing the sincerity in Allan's words. "You can't do it alone, Mr. Allan," he said. "You need to surround yourself with the right people who will push you, challenge you, and tell you when you're wrong. I know you, like me, understand the power of having an executive business coach or consultant, someone who isn't afraid to tell you the truth. Maybe you will realize that's what you've been missing—someone who's not your employee but who's there to help you expand beyond your limits and grow."

Allan nodded, realizing the wisdom in James' words. He thought about the future and how he needed to re-engineer his entire business model. The old ways wouldn't work anymore. "Now, I know," Allan said, "that to survive in the 21st century, I need to change how I do business. Stop holding onto what worked two decades ago because the landscape has changed. The structure has to be naturally re-imagined so we can compete with the best."

You probably already know how fast the business world evolves. What worked before is no longer sustainable. Allan reflected on the past and noticed how his company's success had once been built on strategies that were now outdated. "I'm curious: how can I improve this for my clients, my employees, and myself? This experience has been a blessing in disguise. It's opened my eyes to unlimited potential and new ways of thinking."

Allan was ready to commit to a new way of doing business. He promised himself and James that he would build a system centered around service to others. He would listen to his management team, foster collaboration, and cultivate a powerful company culture rooted in growth. He would achieve this through a new approach: THE OHANA WAY—creating a system of support and unity where every division works together seamlessly to drive growth.

As Allan reflected on his experience, realizing the lessons from the future, he felt he'd been given an incredible opportunity. He had glimpsed the business world of 2054, and now, in 2024, he could apply those lessons to reshape his company. Leaders like Dr. John Oda, Anthony Robbins, Chet Holmes, and Scott Hallman had laid out the blueprint for success. Can you imagine the power of modeling their principles and strategies to thrive in today's competitive market?

"It was surreal," Allan said, "to see Tony Robbins at 90 years old, still holding seminars and transforming lives. And legends like Dr. John Oda and Chet Holmes—they've left behind a legacy of innovation and success. Success leaves clues, and I just need to follow them."

Determined to integrate these principles into his business, Allan knew that to be the best, he needed to experience the teachings of the greatest minds and apply them. He reflected on Dr. John Oda's time management system, the concepts of turning problem teenagers into business leaders, and creating the BSSM-1 Method. He thought of Chet Holmes' indelible marketing strategies, Scot Hallman's lessons on business optimization, Tony Robbins' focus on Peak Performance, and Dr. Scot Conway's Ohana Way. Carl Scott MHA's insights on how CEOs can be destructive, neutral, or effective resonated deeply with him.

Allan realized that the transformation wasn't just about business. It was about life. Now, he had to ask himself the right questions:

- How can I serve my team better?
- What seeds of growth am I planting today in my company?
- How will today's decisions shape my legacy tomorrow?

Maybe you haven't realized the importance of these questions, but Allan felt clarity rushing in after thinking them over. His journey toward a better future had already begun.
As Allan sat, naturally reflecting on the changes he needed to make, he realized it wasn't just about business—it was about life. He realized the key to his future success was asking himself the right questions. Maybe you will understand them too:

- How can I truly listen to my team and consultants?
- What lessons can I learn from my past failures?
- What tools can I bring from the future to succeed in the present?
- How can I transform my challenges into opportunities for growth?
- How can I better understand the life cycle of a business and adapt to its evolution?

Allan noticed that after everything he'd experienced, his time was limited. Yet, with the wisdom he had gained, he knew he could still make a lasting impact. "This is my second chance," he said with conviction, "and I will make it count. It's time to move from being a problem teenager in business to stepping into my prime."

Can you imagine the power Allan felt now, understanding that with the right mindset, the right team, and the right strategy, he could build something truly remarkable? This time, he would lead with heart, wisdom, and a clear vision for a better future—not just for his company but for everyone following in his footsteps.

Allan realized his time was running short, but his desire to model the most outstanding minds in business burned brighter than ever. He often said, "You probably already know that if I can take what they're doing in the future and apply it to my company now, I will have a successful company." He understood that the lessons from leaders like Dr. John Oda, Tony Robbins, and Chet Holmes were key to unlocking his business' true potential.

Suddenly, a sharp pain gripped Allan's stomach. He leaned over his desk, reaching for his phone. "I'm feeling tired, James. I need to rest," he said to his assistant, who looked on with concern as Allan made his way to his bed. Before drifting off to sleep, Allan's thoughts echoed in his mind: "Now I have the tools to change my business. Please, just give me a second chance."

As Allan fell into a deep sleep, something extraordinary began to happen. A force seemed to pull him from his body and guide him forward. He was moving—not physically, but through time and space—like a dream, but much more vivid. Stop for a moment and imagine standing at the end of your life, gazing around in disbelief. That's what Allan saw: no legacy, no fulfillment of the impact he had once envisioned for himself. Just a void, a space where his mission should have been realized.

Desperate, Allan pleaded with the unseen force, begging to be taken back and granted another opportunity to right his wrongs. "Please! Let me go back! I need to teach business leaders what I've learned." He knew, with crystal clarity, the three critical questions that had to guide his future and theirs:

- How did I serve my clients today?
- What seeds am I planting in my business today?
- How has today impacted my legacy?

These weren't just questions for Allan—they were questions for anyone seeking success in life and business. Maybe you haven't yet considered them, but because Allan did, his journey wasn't over. He was about to embark on the greatest transformation of his life—one that would expand beyond the limits of his previous failures and build the legacy he was meant to create.

The force, unmoved by Allan's desperate pleas, spoke softly but with authority: "You cannot return home until you meet another guide who will help you put your past business mistakes behind you."
With those words, Allan was swept into a new, darker scene. He felt himself moving down a tunnel led by a new guide. In the end, a bright light shone on his face. When he emerged, he was in a hospital bed, confused but awake. A doctor loomed above him, asking questions: "What's your name? Where do you live? Who is the President of the United States?" Allan, aware of his disorientation but determined, replied, "It's March 20, 2024, and the President is Joe Biden."
The doctor repeated the questions, and Allan responded the same way. Nodding slowly, the doctor said, "You've suffered a head injury. We need to run some tests, but your memory may be affected."
As Allan turned his head, he noticed an old, gray-haired man beside his bed. "I'm so glad you're okay, Mr. Private. You're going to be just fine," the man said gently.
Allan, still confused, asked, "Who are you?"
The man smiled kindly. "I'm James, your assistant. Don't you remember me?"
Allan frowned, curious but feeling a distance from the words. "Tell me what's going on!" he demanded.

A breaking news report flashed across the room from the hospital TV. The broadcaster's voice echoed: "Sextillion CEO Allan Private was involved in a private airplane crash today. Mr. Private, the first Sextillion to own a global personal development company, has reportedly survived the incident with minor injuries and is expected to make a full recovery."

Allan listened in disbelief. Sextillion? He had no memory of becoming the CEO of such a powerful company. He asked James to turn the TV back on, and the news confirmed it: Sextillion's stock had dropped due to his accident, but as word spread of his recovery, it was expected to rebound.

James handed Allan a mirror, and as he stared into it, he saw a man who had aged gracefully—healthier and stronger than he had felt. "You've done great things, Mr. Private," James said softly. "Your company is thriving, and you've helped millions with the leadership and team-building programs you've implemented."

Allan's confusion deepened. He didn't remember any of this. He turned to James. "Take me to the office."
James hesitated. "The doctors said you need to rest."

But Allan insisted, and soon they were enroute in a luxurious Maybach GLS 9000 limousine. The sleek vehicle pulled up to an office building more magnificent than Allan had imagined. "Whose office is this?" he asked, bewildered.

"It's yours," James replied. "You own several offices around the world."
As they entered the building, Allan noticed something odd. Instead of family photos, the walls were lined with portraits of iconic business leaders and personal development experts: Dr. John Oda, Tony Robbins, Chet Holmes, Joseph McClendon III, Carl Scott, Scot Hallman, Dr. William Horton, and others. Each portrait was accompanied by a quote or principle Allan had once lived by, but none more powerful than the three statements he had seen in his dream:

- How did I serve my clients today?

- What seeds am I planting in my business today?
- How has today impacted my legacy?

Allan's emotions swelled as the memories began to flood back. He whispered, "These questions... they changed everything."

James watched silently as Allan tried to piece together the fragments of his life. Allan turned to him, his voice filled with realization, and said, "Before the accident, I saw these statements in my mind. They were the key to my business success."

James smiled knowingly. "Maybe you will remember that those statements were not just for your business but your life. I know you, like me, see their importance now. Can you imagine your legacy when you live by them daily?"

Allan, now fully aware, nodded. "This is my second chance. It's time to make it count."

With a trembling voice, Allan began to explain the deeper meaning behind the three questions that had transformed his life and business:

1. **How did I serve my clients today?**
"This isn't just about providing a service," Allan said softly. "It's about showing up with unconditional love and commitment. It's about asking, Did I give them my very best? Did I meet their needs in ways no one else could? Service isn't transactional; it's transformational. It's the energy you put into every interaction, the love you bring to every client."

2. **What seeds am I planting in my business today?**
"Whether you realize it or not, you're always planting seeds. Every word and every action is a seed. I'm curious: are you planting seeds of positivity and growth? Or are you letting negative seeds take root, allowing doubt, fear, or frustration to sprout like weeds in your organization? Maybe you will notice this pattern and start planting seeds of abundance."

3. **How has today impacted my legacy?**
"Every choice you make, every step you take, expands beyond the moment—it leaves a mark on your legacy. Can you imagine the power of building something lasting that will inspire future generations? Or are you simply chasing short-term gains without considering the bigger picture?"

Allan paused, tears welling in his eyes. He turned back to James. "I need to understand how I created this legacy. How did I go from being that lost businessman to becoming this person?"

James nodded, his face solemn. "Maybe you haven't yet remembered, but thirty years ago, you were in a plane crash. You were in a coma for months. When you woke up, something had changed inside you. You rebuilt everything. You transformed into the leader you were always meant to be."

Allan stood silently, aware of the weight of what had just been said. He didn't know how it had all happened, but he knew one thing for certain—he had been given a second chance, and this time, he wouldn't waste it.

As Allan sat in a meeting, surrounded by the familiar energy of the thriving business he had built, those three questions burned brightly in his mind:

- **How did I serve my clients today?**
- **What seeds am I planting in my business today?**
- **How has today impacted my legacy?**

These weren't just corporate mantras plastered on the walls—they were the heartbeat of a company that had flourished beyond his wildest dreams. These guiding principles had created a future Allan had once only dreamed of witnessing.

Allan had an epiphany in his first year that shaped his business journey. After attending a seminar by Anthony Robbins, where Robbins outlined the three archetypes of businesspeople—Creator, Manager/Leader, and Entrepreneur—Allan realized something profound: he wasn't the manager or the CEO; he was a Creator. He thrived on the unlimited energy of innovation, designing new programs and workshops that would transform lives. Now, freed from the daily grind of running the company, Allan focused on what he did best—creating.

One of his creations was time management software that changed the world. It wasn't just another productivity tool—it was a revolution. Today, 93% of the global population uses it. With each use, the company received a micro-payment of six cents. When Allan learned that his creation received nearly a billion clicks per day, he was in awe of the compounding success of a simple idea—an idea nurtured and scaled through careful planning and creative execution.

Six months into this journey, Allan made another bold move. He transitioned 50% of his corporate offices into virtual spaces, allowing employees to work from home. This decision slashed overhead costs and boosted productivity, giving his employees a better work-life balance. His team marveled at this brilliant move, and Allan laughed as he recounted a dream where Chet Holmes taught him the Ultimate Business Mastery System. That dream became the foundation for Allan's real-world strategies, shaping the company's future and becoming a model for competitors.

As Allan marveled at the company's evolution, James, his trusted ally, approached and asked if he wanted to attend a meeting. Allan, naturally eager to learn, accepted. They walked into a meeting room, but no one was physically present. Instead, the room was equipped with a state-of-the-art Skype Quad system, connecting executives worldwide.

At exactly 2 p.m., the meeting began, and division leaders shared updates, referring to the three questions Allan had introduced decades ago. "How did I serve my clients today?" "What seeds am I planting in my business today?" "How has today impacted my legacy?" These were no longer just questions—they had become the foundation of the company's culture. Allan smiled as he noticed the ripple effect of those principles expanding beyond him.

A Japanese manager shared how deeply his team had embraced this philosophy, to the point where they had a saying: "Every client is god," meaning they do everything in their power to treat clients with the utmost respect and care.

Maybe you already know that leadership is about service. Allan had realized that his company wasn't built on products or profits—it was built on the service, seeds, and legacy he had sown over the years. And now, he watched those seeds bloom into something greater than he had ever imagined.

I'm wondering if you can imagine what your business and your life would look like if you lived by these questions every day. Maybe you will, and maybe you haven't yet. But one thing is clear: the future belongs to those who ask the right questions.

Allan's heart swelled with pride. His legacy wasn't just alive—it was thriving. His vision of creating a company that naturally prioritized service, growth, and legacy had become a reality. And what touched him even more was how deeply these principles extended beyond business. Allan had learned from Dr. John Oda, a master of personal development and neuroscience, that creating a family atmosphere at work was crucial for building strong teams. One of Allan's simple yet profound practices required every person to say three positive things about the person to their left or right at the end of a meeting. This small act of gratitude fostered bonds, reinforced positivity, and made each employee feel like they were part of something greater than themselves.

After the meeting, Allan's curiosity surged, and he bombarded James with questions. I'm wondering if he had truly understood how these principles had been integrated so seamlessly. How had the company flourished while staying true to its core values? James smiled warmly and said, "We just followed your lead, Allan. You probably already know, but you taught us to model the best, to learn from the future, and to raise our standards beyond what anyone thought possible. That's how we've stayed ahead—by staying true to the lessons you gave us."

As the night stretched on, Allan soaked in every conversation, every moment. He realized his business was more than just a company—it was a living, breathing entity that carried forward the principles of service, growth, and legacy. Maybe you will understand this too—how a business can transform lives and create lasting impact. Allan didn't want the night to end; he wanted to stay in this world forever. But as his eyelids grew heavy, he drifted to sleep in the boardroom.

In his dream, Allan saw flashes of his younger self—angry, rebellious, feeling lost in a world he didn't understand. He noticed his transformation from a problem teenager to a business visionary. He realized his success wasn't just the product of hard work—it was the result of modeling outstanding people and absorbing lessons from masters of the past, present, and future. He had created his destiny. Looking back, he could see how everything had fit together perfectly, as if each moment had led him exactly to where he was meant to be.

When Allan awoke, he wasn't in the boardroom anymore. A bright white light flooded his vision, and he found himself back in a hospital bed. A doctor stood over him, asking questions about the plane crash he had survived. Allan felt disoriented. Stop—was it all just a dream? But when a social worker arrived and showed him a newspaper from the year 2054 detailing his rise from being broke and homeless to becoming a business mogul, Allan's mind raced. Can you imagine the disbelief and confusion? Was everything he had experienced real?

He turned to the social worker and asked for his name. The man replied, "Ken Sielder." At first, Allan thought it must be a cruel joke, but then he became aware of the truth: he had been given a glimpse of the future—a future where he had a choice. He could continue down the path of mediocrity, or he could create something extraordinary. The guide in his dream had been clear: on Earth, you can either serve others or be served by others. The choice was Allan's to make.

Maybe you haven't yet realized this, but Allan knew now. Life is about choices. He could live with gratitude, serve others, and create a legacy that would outlive him. Or he could choose to complain, to mistreat others, and live a life of regret. The future wasn't set in stone—it was being shaped in the present.

"Since you've seen the future," the guide had said, "what path will you take?"

And with that, Allan knew his answer. He was ready to create his destiny. Now, he would take his lessons, live purposefully, and build a future that mattered.

Study Questions for Allan Private's Journey

1. What did you learn from Allan's story?

Reflect on the key lessons from Allan's transformation. I'm curious: what insights about leadership, innovation, and legacy stood out to you? Maybe you already know, but Allan's journey from a lost businessman to a visionary leader shows us how personal growth and professional evolution are deeply intertwined. What parts of his transformation resonate with your business or personal journey?

2. What path is your company currently on?

Stop and notice—is your business aligned with growth and innovation, or are old habits holding you back? Maybe you haven't yet fully evaluated the direction of your company. I'm wondering if there are systems or strategies that no longer serve you. What shifts could help you easily align your business with a path of greater success?

3. What three positive statements can you share with your team today?

You probably already know the power of words can transform a business culture. What specific contributions or qualities can you acknowledge in your team members? Maybe you will notice the energy shift when you actively uplift and motivate your team with words of appreciation. How can you use this to build stronger bonds and a more unified team?

4. Who are you modeling in your business?

Can you imagine how much easier success becomes when you model the best? Are you learning from the top innovators in your industry, like Allan did? Maybe you will notice that your business is stuck in outdated strategies. What changes can you make to expand beyond your current methods and stay ahead of the curve?

5. **How can you use the lessons from Allan's story to improve your business?**
I'm wondering if you can apply Allan's lessons in leadership, innovation, and team culture to your own company. Now, consider how fostering a more positive, growth-driven environment could transform your business. What steps can you take today to implement these insights?

6. **How can you implement the three core statements in your business?**
Stop for a moment and reflect on these powerful questions:

- **How did I serve my clients today?**
- **What seed am I planting in my business today?**
- **How has today impacted my legacy?**

Maybe you already know how important these are, but how can you integrate them into your daily operations? How can they guide your decisions and create a lasting impact on your clients, your team, and your future?

7. **How can you raise the standard in your business?**
I'm curious: what immediate steps can you take today to elevate your business practices naturally? Identify actions you can implement now to bring your company closer to excellence. Maybe you will realize that raising the standard is the key to unlocking unlimited potential and long-term success.

Quadrant One: Business

- **Chapter 1: The Journey**
- **Chapter 2: Life Cycle of a Business**
- **Chapter 3: The Power of Mindset and Faith**
- **Chapter 4: The Mastermind Principle**

Chapter One: The Journey

Within these pages, Allan Private embarks on a journey through the evolution of his company, candidly sharing the pitfalls and triumphs he encountered along the way. As a fellow entrepreneur, you probably already know that the road to success is rarely a straight line. Maybe you will uncover insights from Allan's remarkable ascent, where he propelled his company into a sextillion-dollar empire in an unprecedented timeframe by tapping into insights from the future, specifically those gleaned from the landscape of 2054. I'm curious: can you imagine the power of leveraging future strategies now?

Allan meticulously dissects his failures and triumphs, offering readers a rare glimpse into the lessons he learned from his forward-thinking perspective. Through his experiences, Allan imparts wisdom and provides a roadmap for navigating your path to success. Maybe you haven't yet considered how your journey might parallel Allan's, but one could notice how his lessons resonate with the challenges you face today.

Allan draws parallels from gardening throughout this narrative, using these metaphors to elucidate key business principles. You might notice the feelings of clarity and empowerment as you, like Allan, realize how these fundamental concepts apply to your business. A person might begin to see the parallels between tending a garden and nurturing a business—both require care, patience, and the right tools to grow. Can you imagine integrating these principles into your strategies, unlocking unlimited growth opportunities that transcend conventional boundaries?

At the core of Allan's discourse lies the BSSMI Method, a principle formulated by Dr. John Oda based on his 38 years in mental health and 30 years in executive business coaching. You probably already know how important it is to balance mental health with business acumen. The BSSMI Method—Business, Symptoms, Systemize, and Monetize—synthesizes these two domains, offering a transformative system. I'm wondering if you can see how applying this method could revolutionize the way you approach challenges in your own company.

As we delve into Dr. Oda's BSSMI Method, we uncover the genesis and mechanics of this powerful system. Imagine how implementing these strategies could expand beyond your current business practices, creating new systems that align with your goals and values. Maybe you will notice the difference as your company thrives under a structure that addresses business and personal challenges.

Embarking on this journey, it becomes clear that we share a common aspiration—to realize the fullest potential of our businesses. The insights Allan is about to impart, gleaned from years of experience and introspection, will provide you with practical tools and perspectives on navigating the complexities of entrepreneurship. Because when you align your business practices with the lessons from mental health, neuroscience, and business growth, you tap into a limitless power source.

Allan's journey echoes Dr. Oda's own, which began in 1987 in the mental health field. For 38 years, he witnessed the myriad challenges faced by individuals across all walks of life. Specializing in working with adolescents for 25 years, Dr. Oda discerned striking parallels between the transformations of adolescents and business professionals. You might notice how this experience gave him unique insights into the common thread of effecting positive change, whether in individuals or business systems.

Transitioning into executive business coaching, Dr. Oda had the privilege of collaborating with visionaries like the late Chet Holmes and Anthony Robbins at Business Breakthroughs International. Yet, amidst this wealth of knowledge, he discovered a gap—the absence of an integrated approach that synthesized mental health, neuroscience, and business strategies. I'm wondering if you've encountered similar gaps in your industry and how combining these disciplines could unlock new levels of success.

In reflecting on his tenure in mental health, Dr. Oda recalls utilizing the DSM-IV as a tool for diagnosing behavioral disorders. While the DSM-IV serves to categorize symptoms, you might realize that in business, it's not enough to categorize challenges—you must also develop systems to overcome them. The BSSMI Method bridges this gap, offering a framework that diagnoses business "symptoms" and provides the solutions to systemize and monetize your business effectively.

Maybe you haven't yet considered how these principles could apply to your business, but because they integrate the best of both worlds—mental health and business strategy—you will find that these insights naturally align with your goals for growth, innovation, and lasting impact.

Reflecting on Allan Private's Teenage Years

Allan Private grappled with many challenges during his teenage years, which was detailed in my earlier work, "Connecting with Your Teen: The 7 Principles to Resolve Teenage Behavioral Challenges." As Dr Oda reflected on those years, he was curious: could addressing these issues during adolescence have preempted similar patterns in his adult life? Maybe you will notice how unresolved childhood issues often manifest differently during adulthood. Can you imagine how addressing those mental blocks early on could easily shape a more empowered future?

This realization prompted him to implement the BSSM1 process within his team. You probably already know that even the most exemplary products or services can fall short if unresolved mental blocks, self-esteem issues, or unaddressed childhood traumas impact performance. The BSSM1 process focuses on naturally addressing these obstacles to enhance individual growth and business performance.

Business: How to Assess Your Business

In our exploration of BSSM1, we begin with the business itself. You might notice that by identifying key factors—such as the nature of the business, its industry, and the roles people play—we gain a clearer picture of how the business operates. I'm wondering if you've ever considered your role through the lens of a metaphor. Imagine your business as the 1998 NBA Chicago Bulls.

In this metaphor, Phil Jackson represents the manager, Michael Jordan embodies the creator, and Jerry Reinsdorf personifies the entrepreneur. Maybe you will see how this analogy can expand beyond basketball, offering a new way to analyze your business. If you, as CEO, function more like a creator, my role as an executive business coach would be to act as the manager—implementing systems and strategies to maximize your profitability.

Once we outline these roles, we move on to the Neuro-Business Conditioning Business metamodel. The goal is to gather the right information to facilitate your business growth. There are no right or wrong answers, just insights that help guide our coaching process. This is where the BSSM1 process truly begins to shine.

BSSM1 Dimensions: Understanding Your Leadership Patterns

During this assessment, we focus on several critical dimensions that can naturally influence your leadership:

1. Big Picture vs. Detail-Oriented Thinking
   Are you a big-picture thinker, focused on overarching goals, or prefer a step-by-step approach? You probably already know that effective leaders often lean toward big-picture thinking, as it allows them to drive the vision forward.

2. Self-Validation vs. External Validation
Do you seek validation from within or from others? One might notice that leaders prioritizing self-validation tend to be more decisive and effective. Where do you fall in this spectrum, and how could this shape your leadership style?

3. Toward Goals vs. Away From Pitfalls
Are you driven by moving toward your goals (Key Performance Indicators), or do you focus on avoiding potential pitfalls? Understanding this pattern can help us bridge any gaps and enhance collaboration. Can you imagine the clarity that comes from recognizing this orientation?

4. Time Orientation: "In Time" vs. "Through Time"
How do you perceive time? Are you more In Time—operating with urgency—or do you adopt a Through Time perspective, focusing on the future? Maybe you will notice the profound impact this has on your decision-making and planning.

5. Decision-Making Style
Do you need to review information multiple times before reaching a conclusion, or do you make decisions quickly? I'm wondering if your environment plays a significant role in how you process decisions. Understanding this helps us tailor the coaching process to fit your style.

The BSSM1 Process: Unlocking Business Growth

By addressing these dimensions, we gain invaluable insights that allow us to customize your coaching approach. After gathering this information, we can build a framework that aligns with your business goals and fosters unlimited growth and success.

One could easily apply these principles to unlock new levels of leadership, innovation, and team performance naturally. When you become aware of how these patterns influence your business, you'll be better equipped to lead your team, make decisive moves, and expand beyond limitations.

So, I know you, like me, understand that by using this assessment, you're not just improving one aspect of your business—you're creating a roadmap for long-term success.

Business Symptoms and Allan Private's Journey
Similar to the psychiatric symptoms cataloged in the DSM-IV, businesses, too, exhibit symptoms that point to deeper underlying issues. These might include sales struggles, poor time management, ineffective leadership, challenges with company culture, hiring difficulties, mindset barriers, technology constraints, and marketing inefficiencies. I'm curious: have you noticed any of these in your own business? Maybe you will realize these patterns can lead to stagnation or decline if left unchecked.

In Allan Private's case, his failure to confront issues during his teenage years had long-lasting consequences. As detailed in Connecting with Your Teen, Allan's troubled adolescence—marked by familial discord, social isolation, academic struggles, and involvement in a tragic accident—haunted him well into adulthood. Despite moments of realization and transformation, these same issues resurfaced decades later. I'm wondering if you've seen this pattern before. How many business owners unwittingly perpetuate their detrimental behaviors, unaware of their potential impact on the business?

The Need for Early Intervention

Dr. Oda's deep understanding of human behavior, honed by decades of experience since 1987, highlights the importance of addressing challenges early on. You probably already know that mental health struggles like depression, ADHD, substance abuse, and suicidal ideation are better treated when caught early. Dr. Oda notes that while the DSM-IV offers a framework for diagnosis, lasting change requires much more. It combines clinical expertise, creativity, and tailored intervention strategies.

Maybe you haven't yet applied this same approach to your business, but stop and notice—are there unresolved issues impacting your business's performance that could benefit from early intervention? Can you imagine how addressing them now could lead to transformative growth?

Translating Clinical Expertise to Business Coaching

As Dr. Oda transitioned from mental health to executive business coaching, he realized striking parallels between the two worlds. Just as the DSM-IV helps diagnose psychiatric conditions, the BSSM-1 method is a guiding framework for diagnosing and resolving business challenges. However, one could notice that, like in clinical psychology, the real impact of business coaching lies in the coach's ability to leverage their unique skills and experience.

One might see that effective coaching goes beyond systems—it requires a blend of clinical psychology expertise, entrepreneurial acumen, and a deep understanding of business dynamics. You might notice the feelings of clarity as you realize that addressing business symptoms is much like addressing behavioral challenges—both require introspection, guidance, and a proactive approach to resolve the root causes naturally.

The BSSM-1 Method: Business, Symptoms, Systemize, Monetize

I know you, like me, understand that every business faces challenges. The BSSM-1 method is designed to identify these challenges, address the symptoms, and systemize solutions that lead to sustainable growth. Because just like in mental health, when you address the root of the problem, the results easily expand beyond what you initially thought possible.

So, I wonder if you'll take a moment to reflect on your business's symptoms. Maybe you will start noticing patterns—are mindset barriers, team culture challenges, or technology constraints holding you back? Can you imagine how unlocking these barriers could lead to unlimited potential? Dr. Oda's insights show us that the key to business success isn't just in solving surface-level problems; it's about going deeper, diagnosing the true symptoms, and creating a strategic path forward.

The Ultimate Business Growth Strategist

Dr. Oda emphasizes that an effective executive business coach embodies the qualities of an Ultimate Business Growth Strategist, a unique combination of skills rooted in clinical psychology, mental health experience, and decades of hands-on business leadership. You probably already know that businesses, like individuals, manifest symptoms indicative of deeper issues. I'm curious: have you noticed these symptoms in your own company? Maybe you will realize that addressing these challenges now—proactively—can lead to unlimited growth and transformation.

Systemizing and Monetizing Your Business with BSSM-1

Can you imagine your business's future if every process was systemized to run smoothly without constant oversight? Dr. Oda highlights the natural power of systemization, where minimal time investment—just two to three hours per week—can revolutionize operations. Think about companies like McDonald's or Starbucks. One could easily understand how even an 18-year-old can manage daily operations because of the meticulous systems in place. I'm wondering if you've ever considered what a similar systemization could do for your business.

You might notice the feelings of relief as you picture your business running efficiently, allowing you to focus on growth rather than daily management. After working with thousands of CEOs worldwide, Dr. Oda has found common areas where most businesses, big or small, falter—Sales, Time Management, Marketing, and Operations. Most companies don't have systems for these, yet these are the core areas that lead to sustainable success.
Let's dive deeper into these areas.

Systemizing Your Sales Process

Dr. Oda has seen companies with identical services and products experience wildly different outcomes—one salesperson earning ten times more than another. Maybe you will realize that the difference often lies in not having a systemized sales process. A person might think it's just about experience, but you probably already know that even seasoned veterans don't always follow the same system. Establishing a uniform, systemized sales approach ensures consistent, repeatable success across your team.

Establishing Profit Stations: The Key to Monetizing Your Business

Stop for a moment and think about this: while most companies focus on working in their business, Profit Stations allow you to work on your business, cultivating substantial growth. You might notice how your company could benefit from this approach. Dr. Oda has seen businesses increase revenue by an astonishing 1,500% over three years by implementing Profit Stations. The beauty of this method? It doesn't require extra spending on ads or marketing campaigns.

Maybe you haven't considered this strategy, but because it's designed to streamline and monetize your business, it's one of the most effective ways to achieve exponential growth.
What exactly are Profit Stations? Think about a referral program, for example. Many companies think they have one, but the real question is whether it's systemized. Is every member of the organization actively engaged in asking for referrals? Dr. Oda once reviewed a company's referral program and found that only four of every ten customers were asked for referrals. Those who were asked generated an average of four leads each, but failing to engage every customer meant they were missing out on over $1 million annually. I'm curious: have you assessed your referral program lately?

The Power of Profit Stations

While Dr. Oda has developed over 25 different Profit Stations throughout his career, most companies only need around 10 to see massive success. In fact, those that double in size typically only implement two to three Profit Stations effectively. Can you imagine doubling your business by refining key areas without increasing your marketing spend?

This is where the magic happens. Profit Stations don't just generate revenue; they transform your business. Now that you know the potential of systemizing and monetizing through Profit Stations, you'll see how naturally these strategies can expand your business's impact and reach.
In Chapter 12, we'll focus more on the mechanics of Profit Stations, but for now, stop and consider how establishing just a few key systems could unlock unlimited growth for your business.

Chapter 2: Life Cycle of a Business

Life Cycle of a Business

Understanding the life cycle of a business is naturally akin to comprehending the stages of human life, offering a relatable analogy that easily facilitates deeper understanding. As individuals progress through infancy, childhood, adolescence, adulthood, and old age, businesses expand beyond their initial phases, each marked by unique challenges and opportunities.

However, with the right guidance, these phases can be traversed more efficiently, potentially shortening their duration and leading to accelerated growth.
Can you imagine encountering a business in its infancy, much like a young adult in the human life cycle? You might notice the feelings of exuberance, excitement, and untamed confidence that mirror the behaviors of a teenager. Now, stop and consider this: picture a teenager suddenly bestowed with great wealth—you probably already know how their demeanor might exude confidence tinged with cockiness, driven by a belief that they can conquer all challenges autonomously.

Maybe you will start to see how this analogy illuminates common patterns in business—youthful enterprises often display a brash, independent stance, much like adolescents eager to prove themselves. I'm wondering if you've witnessed this in your own business or others—enterprises in their early stages, confident yet lacking the wisdom that comes with experience.

By juxtaposing the business life cycle with the human life cycle, distinct patterns emerge. One could easily see how this metaphor allows for a deeper understanding of organizational dynamics. Just as people grow and acquire wisdom through life's experiences, so too do businesses evolve—assimilating lessons from each phase they pass through.

In my experience coaching diverse businesses, I've observed countless examples where a company's developmental stage naturally influences its operational ethos, decision-making, and long-term strategy. I'm curious: How might your business's current phase shape its behaviors? Could it be that, like a teenager, it's brimming with potential yet still learning how to navigate the complexities of growth?

By dissecting the business life cycle alongside its human counterpart, you might notice the parallels that shed light on each stage's unique challenges and opportunities. One might see how understanding this evolution empowers business owners to navigate complexities with greater insight and foresight. After all, just as a person matures through life's experiences, businesses grow stronger when they embrace the lessons inherent in each phase.

This holistic perspective creates a powerful framework for conceptualizing the journey of your business. You probably already know that informed decision-making and strategic planning are key to long-term success. But can you imagine how much more effective those decisions could be if you fully understood the stage your business is in right now? By leveraging the opportunities of each phase, businesses can optimize growth and resilience.
In essence, likening the business life cycle to the stages of human life serves as a potent tool for leaders. It imbues you with the awareness needed to align your business strategies with its current developmental phase, allowing you to make informed decisions that naturally foster growth. Through this lens, your business can expand beyond its current trajectory and evolve into something extraordinary.

Birth (Stage of Certainty)

Drawing from personal experience and entrepreneurial insights, I'm here to easily demystify the pivotal stage of business birth, a phase naturally akin to bringing a new life into the world. Just as I experienced the meticulous planning preceding the arrival of a child in my large family, launching a business requires thoughtful preparation and realizing that this journey mirrors the excitement and uncertainty of new life. Can you imagine how these parallels can guide your entrepreneurial path?

Much like the birth of a new venture, entrepreneurship epitomizes a phase filled with uncertainty and risk. It's the bold leap into the unknown where founders become aware of the vulnerability they must embrace to pursue something greater. You probably already know that this stage distinguishes between merely being employed and becoming the steward of your creation. It demands a willingness to expose your personal ambitions to the risk of failure in exchange for the potential of success.

At the outset of this transformative journey, your business is in survival mode—like a newborn that requires constant nurturing. I'm curious: have you noticed how, at this stage, your focus might be completely on meeting the immediate needs of your business? It's a crucial phase where the lines between your personal needs and your fledgling enterprise blur. However, after you become aware of the distinction between your desires and business needs, you'll start to develop the clarity needed to navigate this critical stage.

Success during the birth phase requires a paradigm shift—a natural transition from thinking solely about personal preservation to nurturing your business as an autonomous living entity. Just as an infant needs care, attention, and guidance to grow, your business craves constant support and focus to develop the resilience needed for future challenges. One could easily recognize how the choices made in this stage have lasting impacts on your business's trajectory.

In essence, the birth stage of entrepreneurship naturally catalyzes a transformative journey. It is here that personal dreams begin to align with a larger, collective vision for your business. I'm wondering if you've already started to notice how this evolution requires you to expand beyond your comfort zone, cultivating a broader perspective that nurtures both your aspirations and the needs of the enterprise.

This phase is a litmus test—a measure of your personal commitment and ability to distinguish between what's necessary for you and what's necessary for the business. Those who successfully navigate this stage will naturally see their dreams begin to flourish as their fledgling ventures evolve into self-sustaining, thriving enterprises.

Maybe you will recognize that the true potential of your entrepreneurial endeavor rests not just in the idea itself but in your ability to nurture it through this birth stage. Because once you've transcended this initial phase and fostered your business like a living organism, you'll be prepared to witness your vision blossom into the thriving, sustainable success you've always envisioned.

New Born/Infant Stage (Uncertainty)
Congratulations on reaching your entrepreneurial journey's pivotal 'New Born/Infant Stage'—a phase where your business idea naturally transforms into a tangible entity. I'm curious: have you noticed how exciting it feels to see your idea come to life, to step into the role of 'You, Inc.'? You probably already know this is more than just a concept now—it's a fledgling enterprise with unlimited potential. Maybe you will feel that sense of responsibility, knowing the survival of your venture rests in your hands.

At this stage, you wear many hats. One could easily imagine being the chief strategist, the primary decision-maker, and the driving force behind every small success your business achieves. Yet, with this promise comes uncertainty. Your venture shows potential, but its survival depends on your ability to navigate the early-stage challenges. Can you imagine the excitement and risk intertwined as you balance the many facets of this phase?

In the world of 'You, Inc.', the primary focus is production—creating and delivering your products or services to meet demand. The thrill of growth is here, but so is the reality of cash flow concerns. Stop and notice how even the smallest financial decisions can impact the survival of your business. Maybe you haven't fully grasped how critical managing those financial ebbs and flows is to your long-term success. Because cash flow remains one of the most pressing concerns, your ability to juggle operations while building financial resilience will define this stage.

This phase is naturally a baptism by fire for entrepreneurs. It tests your resilience, adaptability, and vision. The balance between hands-on management and laying the groundwork for future growth through strategic delegation is key. You might notice the feelings of being stretched thin, yet knowing deep down that this challenge is refining your leadership.

Key questions arise as you navigate this:

- How can you sustainably scale your business while ensuring profitability?
- How do you manage cash flow to fuel growth without compromising financial stability?
- And how do you assemble a cohesive team capable of sharing the responsibilities of your expanding enterprise?

I'm wondering if you've already begun asking yourself these questions. You probably already know that navigating the complexities of 'You, Inc.' demands vision, tenacity, and strategic foresight. But maybe you will discover that it's not just about the hustle—it's about setting up the right systems, building the right team, and planning for sustainable growth.

By addressing these challenges now and implementing sound business practices, you'll easily chart a course toward sustainable growth, preparing for the next phase of your entrepreneurial journey. This is the stage where your business expands beyond an idea and naturally becomes something much more—a thriving entity ready to grow with your guidance.

So, can you imagine what it will feel like to look back and see how far you've come?

The Terrible Two's Stage of Both Certainty and Uncertainty

Welcome to the "Terrible Two's" stage of your entrepreneurial journey—a phase where certainty and uncertainty collide, much like guiding a spirited toddler through their early years. I'm curious: can you imagine what it feels like to navigate these turbulent waters? You probably already know that this stage, like a toddler's development, is filled with energy, curiosity, and an evolving sense of identity.

Picture your business as a two-year-old—brimming with energy, exploring new opportunities, but still figuring out its place in the vast landscape of commerce. At this point, your vision has begun to crystallize, and you've assembled a dedicated team to share in the responsibility of steering the ship. Yet, now, while your structure is starting to take shape, you remain the guiding force, wielding your expertise to navigate through uncharted territories. One could notice how your business craves freedom and direction, just like a child learning to walk independently.

Your management team is growing more cohesive by the day, but maybe you haven't yet fully entrusted them with key decisions. Like a delicate balancing act, I'm wondering if you've begun to strike that perfect chord between delegation and direction, fostering an environment of trust and collaboration that will easily propel your enterprise forward.

At this stage, momentum is palpable. Your business is no longer inching along—it's charging ahead with unlimited potential toward its goals. You might notice the whirlwind of challenges and opportunities surrounding you. But because you're equipped with resilience and agility, you can adapt to these obstacles, turning them into catalysts for growth. Maybe you will even begin to embrace these challenges as stepping stones, rather than roadblocks, to your continued success.

While financial concerns may still linger, rays of optimism break through the clouds of uncertainty. I'm curious: have you noticed how your sharpened decision-making and strategic acumen have begun to yield tangible results? Slowly but surely, those past monetary worries fade as you make astute investments that naturally propel your business toward prosperity.

As you stand at the helm, watching your business mature and expand beyond what you once thought possible, you probably already know this phase is a testament to your leadership. Can you imagine how much further you can go by embracing the power of teamwork and empowering your dedicated staff to contribute meaningfully to your business's ascent? Maybe you will notice the feelings of confidence as you see your team taking ownership of their roles, aligning with your vision, and driving the enterprise forward.

You've laid the groundwork for success, and now, as your business finds its footing, the horizon is filled with boundless possibilities. Stop for a moment and reflect on how far you've come. Because this phase, as challenging as it may seem, is a clear signal that your enterprise is growing stronger—moving from the vulnerability of infancy to the independence of maturity.

Teenager (Stage of Certainty)

Imagine the scenario: handing your 15-year-old son a million dollars. Can you imagine the surge of confidence? Would he heed your advice or charge forward, believing he could conquer the world single-handedly? I'm curious: have you ever felt that same energy? Dr. John Oda's insights into teenage behavior offer a compelling lens to understand how business owners navigate a similar adolescent phase.

In this stage, much like the teenage years, you probably already know business owners often find themselves wrestling with past issues that have morphed into new challenges. Confidence soars—sometimes naturally into overconfidence—driving the belief that anything is achievable. Yet, maybe you haven't yet realized that this bravado can also obscure potential pitfalls, blinding leaders to emerging threats that creep just below the surface.

The air is electric with ambition. You might notice the feelings of excitement as your business expands beyond previous boundaries, driven by growth and momentum. However, amid the rush of expansion, some crucial elements—like accountability and structured processes—might fall by the wayside. Over-reliance on personal charisma, the "I've got this" mentality, can lead to a strained organizational system, where the focus shifts toward individual efforts rather than efficient workflows.

Stop for a moment and consider: is the excitement of growth overshadowing the need for solid structures? I'm wondering if you've seen this before—unchecked expansion leading to unintended consequences. Growth without a firm foundation can compromise the quality of your products or services, escalate operational costs, and erode customer satisfaction. You probably already know a business can become vulnerable without anticipating market shifts or competitive threats.

To navigate this phase successfully, it's imperative to balance ambition and prudent planning. Growth should be a deliberate, strategic endeavor guided by a clear organizational vision. While celebrating individual talent and energy, it's essential to establish defined roles, foster accountability, and implement adaptable processes. One could easily see how these structures create a pathway to innovation while maintaining the company's core values.

In essence, this teenage stage demands introspection and strategic foresight. Embrace ambition, but temper it with a grounded approach to growth. By prioritizing structured planning, fostering accountability, and maintaining a steadfast commitment to quality, your business can harness the immense potential of this phase while mitigating its inherent risks.
Can you imagine what it would feel like to fully unlock this growth stage while ensuring your business's foundations remain strong? Because when ambition is paired with strategic foresight, the possibilities are unlimited.

Young Adult (Stage of Reestablishing Certainty)

Entering the young adult stage—both in life and business—naturally signifies a shift from the exuberance of youth to the deliberate intentionality of maturity. By 30, you probably already know individuals begin to realize the importance of learning from past experiences and charting a more focused path forward. Similarly, businesses at this juncture demonstrate a heightened awareness of purpose, moving beyond the impulsive energy of earlier stages. Can you imagine how this phase mirrors a rebirth, where old identities are consciously shed, creating a more refined, purpose-driven persona?

At this stage, individuals and businesses embrace deliberate decision-making and strategic planning with a new clarity. I'm curious: have you noticed how the tendency to act on impulse gives way to a deeper focus on long-term objectives? Maybe you haven't yet fully embraced this, but one can see how this phase marks a profound transformation. There's a natural desire to expand beyond old patterns, making space for a future of thoughtful, intentional growth.

At the core of this transformation lies a commitment to self-improvement and continuous growth. You might notice the feelings of renewed determination as you or your business invest in acquiring new skills, broadening your knowledge base, and cultivating a deeper understanding of your domain. Because in this stage, the pursuit of excellence becomes a driving force. Maybe you will see how this dedication fuels your evolution, helping you become more competent, confident, and purpose-driven.

Moreover, the young adult stage heralds a period of reestablishing certainty amidst the complexities of life and business. Stop for a moment and notice—it's no longer about simply moving forward; it's about deliberate choices and intentional actions to build a solid foundation for future endeavors. One could imagine how, in business, this phase manifests as a strategic realignment of priorities, refining operational processes, and cultivating a strong organizational culture that aligns with a clearer vision for the future.

Ultimately, this stage represents a pivotal transition—a moment when individuals and businesses naturally emerge from the uncertainties of youth with a renewed sense of purpose and clarity. I'm wondering if you've begun to experience this shift—a growing realization that a more focused, mature pursuit of success comes after the energy of youth. You probably already know that embracing this phase requires courage, resilience, and a willingness to embrace change. Yet, this stage also brings unlimited opportunities for growth, innovation, and success. Maybe you will see that this is the perfect moment to leverage the lessons of the past, realign with your deeper goals, and embark on a journey toward your full potential—both as an individual and in your business.

Zone of Maximization/Maturity (Stage of Certainty)

Enter the Zone of Maximization, the pinnacle of your entrepreneurial journey, where you naturally embody the seasoned maturity of someone in their mid-40s to early 60s. At this stage, I'm curious: have you noticed how your leadership prowess and strategic acumen have been honed through years of experience? You probably already know this is the phase where you transcend mere leadership and become a master strategist, much like the elite 5% of business owners who've reached this echelon. Maybe you will recognize yourself among this distinguished group—those who are driven by purpose and have a profound commitment to elevating both their business and their team.

In the Zone of Maximization, your business has evolved beyond just personal ambition. It has become a vessel for purpose, firmly anchored by core values and a clear, unwavering message. Can you imagine how it feels to watch the fruits of your labor blossom into a tapestry of abundance and unlimited confidence? Stop and notice the shift—from being reactive to proactive, from chasing growth to managing it precisely.

Sustainable growth becomes your focal point at this stage, built on a deep understanding of your strengths and limitations. Now, clarity reigns supreme as you navigate the intricate layers of your business landscape with unwavering resolve. Every decision is made purposefully, and you naturally pursue your objectives with disciplined determination. Consistency and excellence define your actions, and your sales and profits ascend to unprecedented heights. I wonder if you've begun to see how creative endeavors are no longer left to chance. One could easily recognize that once spontaneous innovation is now systematically cultivated, allowing your business to adapt and thrive in ever-changing markets. Every move and every initiative is aligned with your clear vision of sustained success.

At this stage, robust governance structures are in place, ensuring your operations' smooth and systematic management. Because you've transcended the realm of reactive decision-making, you might notice that you've embraced a proactive approach characterized by foresight and long-term strategy. Each decision is carefully crafted with a vision of the future, allowing you to refine your business and maintain its high performance continually.

In essence, the Zone of Maximization is the zenith of entrepreneurial achievement. This is where seasoned wisdom converges with visionary leadership, allowing you to sculpt a legacy of lasting impact. As you stand at the summit of your entrepreneurial odyssey, I'm curious: can you imagine what it feels like to reach this point? But remember—maybe you already know—the journey is far from over.

Embrace the power of continuous growth and evolution because it is through perpetual transformation that you sow the seeds of enduring success. Even at this peak, you naturally realize that there is always more room for expansion, refining your processes, and evolving with your team and your business. This is your time to expand beyond what you once thought possible, creating a legacy that lasts for generations.
Mid-Life Evaluation/Transition and Transformation (Stage of Uncertainty)

You may not know if this moment—this stage of life or business—is a turning point. I don't know if you've noticed how the later stages of life, much like in your early 70s or late 80s, often bring a sense of reflection and, sometimes, weariness. But this stage, whether in life or business, is about more than just surviving. You can embrace it fully, can you not?

I don't know if you've experienced this yet, but the transition you're navigating may feel like a mid-life crisis for a business—where the past no longer serves as a reliable map for the future. Just as time imprints its marks on our physical selves, businesses, too, begin to feel the weight of time's relentless march. At this moment, you may not know if your current strategies will carry you forward, but the opportunity for transformation lies just beyond that uncertainty.

Can you imagine standing at this crossroads, where pivotal decisions await? Will you actively seek rejuvenation and breathe new life into your venture, or will you succumb to the inertia of time? Rejuvenation, in this context, naturally comes through the infusion of novel ideas, relinquishing old habits, and fostering creativity. These elements are an antidote to stagnation, reminding you that what once worked may no longer be enough. I don't know if you've realized it yet, but this stage is about letting go of what's no longer serving you and adapting to thrive again.

Adaptation, you see, becomes not just an option but a necessity. Like a living organism, your business or strategy must evolve to stay relevant. Stop and notice—what worked before might no longer fit the current landscape. Stagnation imperils your relevance, echoing the timeless principle of survival of the fittest. You can adapt, can you not?

Amidst this evolution, you may find that meticulously crafted plans, fray, and strategies that once propelled you forward lose their effectiveness. You might notice the feelings of doubt creeping in, casting a shadow over your next steps. But perhaps this uncertainty invites you to contemplate something even greater. Is it time to recalibrate or even envision an exit strategy that opens up new possibilities beyond your current venture? These moments of transition offer not just a challenge but an opportunity for profound transformation.

You probably already know that the journey of life and business is not about enduring—it's about thriving. To withstand the ceaseless march of time, mere survival is insufficient. It's a delicate balance—honoring the past while embracing the unlimited potential of tomorrow.
As the twilight years of life or business beckon, you may not know if this stage is merely an ending or a new beginning. But what if it's both? This juncture isn't just a reckoning; it's a summons to transformation. It's a call to chart a course that transcends the limitations of age, circumstance, or even the business model you've built.

By embracing this transitional phase with courage and sagacity, you unlock the potential for renewal, for expanding beyond the boundaries that once seemed unchangeable. Whether in life or in business, this stage promises a future filled with vitality, purpose, and possibility.

Aging: Accelerated Breakdown—Denial or Attack

Imagine this stage as receiving a devastating prognosis from a doctor. You may not know if this moment marks the end of an era or the beginning of a transformation. In business, just like in life, one could easily slip into denial rather than face the harsh realities head-on. I don't know if you've seen this before, but the parallels between personal denial and organizational stagnation are strikingly apparent. Can you imagine what happens when a company, much like an individual, refuses to acknowledge the gravity of its predicament?

You can picture a company clinging to outdated business models, hoping that what worked in the past will somehow still navigate the complexities of today. But, stop and notice—what is the cost of such resistance? When businesses fail to adapt, they enter a downward spiral of decay, much like a patient who ignores the doctor's advice, hoping things will improve independently.

Denial becomes a formidable barrier in this stage. Blinded by past successes, stakeholders may refuse to accept the severity of the situation. I'm curious: have you seen how organizations minimize threats, choosing instead to focus on what's familiar rather than confronting the unknown? This self-delusion perpetuates a dangerous cycle of complacency and inaction.

Simultaneously, you may not know if individuals in the organization are adopting the victim role. You can see how deflecting responsibility onto external factors or scapegoating specific individuals creates a toxic environment. Maybe you've noticed that this blame-centric mindset fosters resentment and discord, pulling the organization into an even deeper rut. Because when blame spreads, morale plummets—and talented employees seek refuge in healthier environments.

This negative feedback loop of denial, victimhood, and blame doesn't just stymie progress—it leads to a talent drain that cripples the organization's ability to adapt, innovate, and grow. I don't know if you've ever seen a company on the brink of collapse because it couldn't confront its realities, but one could imagine the urgency required to break free from these destructive patterns.

Rather than succumbing to denial or apportioning blame, you probably already know that organizations must embrace accountability and forward-thinking. This isn't just about survival—it's about revitalization. By acknowledging challenges candidly, fostering constructive dialogue, and empowering individuals to contribute meaningfully, businesses can shift from stagnation to growth.

Can you imagine what happens when companies face adversity with courage and pragmatism? They don't just survive—they chart a course toward renewal. When organizations embrace change as an opportunity for growth rather than as a threat, they emerge stronger, more agile, and more resilient. Just as resilient individuals rise after hardship, so too do businesses that confront the inevitable tides of change, adapting to expand beyond their current state and thrive in a new landscape.

You can transform this moment of accelerated breakdown into a turning point, can you not?

Institutionalization

Imagine an organization perched precariously on the edge of obsolescence, held up not by its strength or purpose but by the steady drip of subsidies or the shelter of nationalization. You may not know if this was ever its intended path, but now, it's become entrenched in the rigid, mechanistic frameworks of systems, rules, policies, and procedures that once served a purpose but now bind it. Can you imagine how an organization so deeply institutionalized begins to lose its original spark, its raison d'être?

I'm curious: have you ever seen this happen? A company that once thrived on innovation, creativity, and connection with its community now finds itself confined by its own structures. One could easily notice how the energy that once fueled its growth is now sapped—its resources drained by the Herculean task of maintaining the bureaucratic edifice it has built. The community's true needs, the driving force behind its creation, have become a distant echo.

In this state, innovation becomes an elusive dream. You probably already know how this happens—the organization clings to the very systems it once developed to help it thrive, but those systems have now become institutional shackles. The rules and policies that once provided structure now stifle creativity and adaptability, necessary for success in the contemporary landscape.

Stop and notice how this entrenched posture culminates in a disheartening forfeiture of autonomy. In clinging to these systems, the organization has forfeited its agency, becoming captive to the very institution it created. You may not know if there's a way out of this, but I don't know if you've realized yet that real, intentional transformation is possible.
Can you imagine what would happen if the organization let go of these rigid structures, reclaiming its autonomy and its original mission and revitalizing its purpose? You can see how breaking free from the rigid frameworks opens the door to innovation once again, can you not? The potential to address the genuine needs of the community becomes possible when the institutional shackles are cast aside.

This isn't just about surviving—it's about thriving. It's about turning away from the institutionalized practices that have led to stagnation and reclaiming the dynamic creativity that once fueled growth. When organizations embrace change, they regain their autonomy and become alive once again, capable of adapting to the world around them. You may not know what's possible for an organization that has broken free, but one can imagine the possibilities, can you not?

Death

In the dynamic business world, sustaining your vision naturally is one of the greatest challenges you will ever face. You may not know if your business will endure, but can you imagine watching the slow withering of its life force, seeing the vision that once burned bright begin to fade? I don't know if you've ever felt that moment when the foundation starts to crumble, but one could easily notice how this decline leads to the inevitable death of your enterprise.

You probably already know that when your vision falters in sustainability, it's like a flickering flame, gradually dimming day by day. The reasons are often multifaceted—failure to adapt to evolving market conditions, not meeting the changing needs of your customers, or simply losing touch with what once made your business thrive. As the vision falters, navigating the intricate and competitive landscape becomes increasingly difficult, does it not?

At the heart of every business lies its people—the employees, customers, and stakeholders—who breathe life into its purpose. I'm curious: have you noticed that when this vital community weakens, the unraveling of your business accelerates? Without a committed workforce, an enthusiastic clientele, and a thriving network of stakeholders, the core of your enterprise begins to erode. Can you imagine the pillars that once supported your success slowly disintegrating until all that remains is the echo of what once was?

You may not know if your business is nearing this stage, but the signs are unmistakable. The descent towards irrelevance is not sudden—it's a gradual, almost imperceptible decline until the end is inevitable. Stop and notice how businesses that once flourished find themselves teetering on the edge of obsolescence, their flame extinguished by an inability to adapt or a lack of support.

Confronted with this reality, it's imperative to acknowledge the gravity of the situation. You can take decisive action, can you not? Whether through revitalizing the vision or exploring new pathways for survival, proactive measures are essential to stave off the inevitable. The death of a business serves as a poignant reminder of the critical importance of adaptability, resilience, and the unwavering support of the people who bring your vision to life.

I don't know if this resonates with where you are today, but you probably already know that in business, much like in life, survival depends on your willingness to adapt, evolve, and recognize that nothing stays the same. The demise of a business can be avoided, but only with courage, clarity, and the realization that the flame of your vision must be nurtured now—before it's too late.

Aligning Personal and Business Growth: Understanding Life Stages for Lasting Success

Every business must naturally go through all phases of growth and transformation, but you probably already know that it doesn't always have to take years. With the right guidance, some stages can be condensed into weeks or even days. A company might find itself in the death stage, seemingly lost and without direction, only to rise like a phoenix from the ashes, fueled by a renewed passion and vision. Can you imagine what that kind of transformation would feel like?

To truly understand a business's life cycle, one must also recognize the importance of aligning it with the life stages of the individuals within the company—particularly the business owner or leader. I'm curious: have you noticed how deeply intertwined a business's growth is with its leader's personal development? Picture this: you could be biologically 60 years old but still operating with the mindset and attitudes of a teenager—cocky, impulsive, and convinced that you know it all. I don't know if you've seen this play out before, but one could imagine the challenges this creates.
In my experience as a business coach, I've witnessed this pattern time and time again. For instance, a teenager starting a business coaching program may dive in enthusiastically, fully engaged for the first few months, but eventually, they falter. Why? Because they believe they can do it all on their own. While admirable in its energy, that adolescent sense of invincibility lacks the foundation of wisdom. Teenagers often get caught in the illusion of self-sufficiency, thinking they don't need guidance, mentorship, or systems.

On the other hand, you might notice a stark difference when working with young adults—those in their 20s or early 30s. By this stage, they've realized the true cost of time. They understand that wasting time trying to figure everything out independently is not a smart investment. These young adults are hungry for guidance, for proven systems that allow them to expand beyond trial and error, and you can see their openness to mentorship. They're no longer searching for answers within themselves—they're looking for a roadmap, for strategies that will guide them to success quickly and effectively.

This is why, as a coach, it's crucial to assess both the stage of life a business is in and the stage of life the business owner is in. These two aspects are intimately connected, and you probably already know that progress comes only when both are addressed together. Can you imagine a seasoned 50-year-old entrepreneur with wisdom and maturity but a business still in its "terrible twos," struggling to scale? How would you approach someone like that?

The key is understanding the business's life cycle and the individual's life stage and how they interact. You might notice that a business in its startup phase—a fledgling enterprise learning to crawl—requires different guidance than one in its mature maximization stage. And what happens when the individual doesn't match the company's stage? For instance, if you encounter a 50-year-old business owner with the maturity and insight that comes with age, but their business is only a year old and facing challenges of rapid growth, what do you do?

The answer lies in bridging the gap. A 50-year-old might have the personal wisdom to handle stress but lack the entrepreneurial experience to apply the right systems or processes the business needs. In this case, I would focus on helping them align their personal maturity with the youthful exuberance of their business—introducing them to the systems that can sustain and scale their company with the wisdom they already possess.

Conversely, a younger entrepreneur in their 20s may be bursting with energy and ideas but lack the foundation of maturity needed to understand that success isn't just about rapid growth—it's about sustainable growth. As their coach, I would guide them to slow down, step back, and realize that building a solid foundation is the key to long-term success. This involves helping them develop systems for managing time, money, and people effectively so they can grow their business without burning out.

You may not know if your business reflects where you are personally, but the growth is deeply intertwined. The truth is, you cannot evolve your business without evolving personally. Whether working with a teenager, a young adult, or a seasoned professional, the goal is always the same: to help them recognize where they are in their personal and business life cycles, guiding them toward the next stage with clarity, confidence, and the right strategies.

In the end, growth is a multifaceted journey. A business rises or falls not just on its systems but on the growth of the individual at its helm. By aligning personal development with business strategies, you can lead yourself and your business to a future of lasting success.

Study Questions for Chapter Two

1. **What stage of life is your business truly in right now?**
You may not know if your business is in its infancy, adolescence, or maturity, but can you imagine what it would feel like to gain complete clarity on where you stand today?

2. **Have you fully aligned your personal growth with your business?**
I'm curious: have you noticed any gaps between where you are personally and where your business is? You probably already know that these two are deeply intertwined. How might closing that gap elevate your business to the next level?

3. **What systems have you implemented to support your business as it transitions through its phases?**
One could easily see that without the right systems, businesses struggle. I don't know if you've already thought about it, but are your systems supporting your business's current growth stage?

4. **Is your business stuck in a 'teenager' phase, with boundless energy but a lack of focus?**
Can you imagine what would happen if you channeled that raw energy through mature systems and strategies? How much faster could you grow now that you're aware of this?

5. **How has your leadership role evolved along with your business?**
You may not know if your leadership style has fully adapted to the stage your business is in, but you can reflect on how different your business might look if you embraced a new approach. Can you not?

6. **Have you considered what your business needs to break from institutional stagnation?**
I'm curious: is your business clinging to outdated methods or systems? What would it feel like to shed those layers and step into a phase of true innovation?

7. **Is your business ready to rise again, like a phoenix, after facing its 'death' stage?**
You may not know if your business is on the brink of collapse, but I don't know if you've realized how, with the right spark, you can turn that failure into the greatest opportunity for rebirth.

8. **How are you preparing your business for the 'Zone of Maximization'?**
Can you imagine what it would feel like to operate at the highest level of your industry, where every action is aligned with long-term vision, success, and sustainability?

9. **What is your vision for guiding your business from its current 'terrible two's' phase?**
You might notice the feelings of frustration when your business faces constant challenges, but what would it take to put the right structures in place so that these challenges become stepping stones to greater success?

10. **How will you ensure that your business continues to grow, even as you personally evolve?**
You may not know if your personal growth is behind your business growth, but you probably already realize that both need to evolve together. What will you do now to ensure you're both on the same path?

Chapter 3:   The Power of Mindset and Faith

The Power of Faith and Mindset

I'm wondering if you've ever noticed how, when someone hits rock bottom, they either collapse under the weight of their failures or, maybe, they rise with newfound strength. Alan Private's journey from riches to rags and back again is the perfect example of how a man, once a titan of wealth, faced the harshest trials and emerged transformed. You probably already know stories of those who lose everything, but Alan's story is different. Can you imagine losing everything, stripped of the luxuries, power, and friends, only to realize that this fall was the beginning of something greater?

Alan's story is filled with moments that naturally make you pause and reflect. After all, how does one man, once on top of the world, find himself homeless, wandering the streets with no one to turn to? It's easy to see how such a fall could break someone, but Alan's experience differed. He noticed that every choice he made led him to this moment. And once he became aware of that, his transformation began. It's as though Alan suddenly realized that his downfall was not a punishment but rather a gift—a catalyst for unlimited growth. Maybe you've noticed in your own life how setbacks sometimes carry hidden opportunities. Alan certainly did.

I'm wondering if you can picture Alan walking the streets that were once beneath him, aware of the indifference from those he once called friends. Instead of letting it break him, Alan stopped and realized the lesson. He noticed that true success isn't about who stands by your side when you're on top but who's there when you're on the ground. This was a turning point for him because he stopped fighting the circumstances and instead embraced them, naturally understanding that his journey of redemption had begun. And maybe, just maybe, you're beginning to see that setbacks are actually steppingstones toward something far more profound in your own life.

As Alan began his journey of self-discovery, he immersed himself in learning—gathering wisdom from transformational leaders like Dr. John Oda, Tony Robbins, and Jay Abraham. Alan's approach was different this time. He wasn't just trying to reclaim his former glory. He was seeking to expand beyond his past limitations to create a future that was not only rich in wealth but also rich in wisdom, empathy, and self-awareness. Can you imagine attending a seminar, sitting there, and suddenly, it clicks—you become aware of exactly what's been holding you back? This is what Alan experienced, and he knew right then that his life was about to change.

Alan's journey back to the top wasn't just about revisiting past successes. It was about deciphering the patterns, understanding where things went wrong, and finding the keys to unlocking a new kind of success. He noticed that much of his previous failures stemmed from systemic issues—issues he'd been blind to when he was on top. As Carl Scott once said, many organizations suffer from a "problem CEO," and Alan realized that he had been that CEO, the very cause of his company's downfall. He now understood that he needed to stop blaming circumstances and take full responsibility to create real, lasting success. Maybe you've seen it too—in your life or business—the moment when you stop making excuses, and everything starts to shift.

Alan's transformation wasn't just about business. It was about understanding the deeper roles we play in life—the victim, the villain, the hero. Alan realized that for much of his past, he had unknowingly been playing the villain in his own story, sabotaging his own success. Now, he chose to embrace the role of the hero, someone who leads with empathy and accountability. And from that shift, new possibilities opened up. You can probably imagine how powerful it feels when you step into the role of the hero in your own life when you naturally rise above your past patterns and expand into something greater.

With a newfound sense of purpose, Alan started rebuilding. Not just his company but his life. He was now driven by the knowledge that adversity wasn't something to avoid—it was something to embrace because, after experiencing true hardship, he understood that every setback was an opportunity in disguise.

Alan's story, from rags to riches, wasn't just about reclaiming wealth. It was about the limitless potential within each of us to rise after a fall, to expand beyond our former selves, and to naturally become the leaders we were always meant to be.

Alan's journey reminds us that no matter where we are now, there is always a path to something greater. The key is becoming aware of our patterns, stopping the blame, and noticing the possibilities that lie within every challenge. Can you imagine the kind of life you could create when you, like Alan, realize that every setback is the beginning of something extraordinary?

Unveiling the Blueprint for Business Success: The Alan Private Method

I wonder if you've ever noticed how certain stories can effortlessly captivate you, drawing you into a world of unlimited possibilities. Maybe you've experienced the feeling of realizing that someone else's journey has the power to inspire transformation in your own life. Alan Private's story is one such tale—a blueprint for business success that goes beyond mere strategy and speaks to the heart of what it means to rise from adversity and expand beyond your previous limits. Can you imagine what it's like to rebuild not just a business but your very self after losing everything?

Alan Private's journey isn't just another rags-to-riches story. It's a testament to the natural resilience of the human spirit and the unlimited potential within each of us. You probably already know that business success often depends on more than just tactics—it's a blend of psychology, strategy, and the awareness of how the two intersect. Alan, after experiencing the highs of wealth and the lows of financial ruin, became aware of this symbiotic relationship and noticed that the key to lasting success lies not just in external actions but in an internal shift.

Maybe you will begin to notice this, too, as you read on.

At the core of Alan's success is the wisdom of Dr. John Oda, whose revolutionary Business Symptomology and Strategy Model (BSSM) became the foundation for Alan's remarkable turnaround. The BSSM helped Alan easily recognize the patterns of failure that had led to his downfall, and more importantly, it provided the roadmap to reclaiming his success—naturally and with clarity. You might notice how Alan's journey through the BSSM mirrors many entrepreneurs' journey. It begins with a shift in mindset and expands into strategies that turn chaos into order, inefficiency into precision, and eventually, loss into profit.

The first quadrant of the BSSM, symbolized by "B," is all about mindset. You might already know that your mindset is the bedrock of your success—yet how often do we stop to truly consider its power? For Alan, realizing that his inner world was the root of his external reality catalyzed change. He became aware that faith and persistence, two essential pillars, had sustained him during his most challenging moments. Can you imagine the feeling of unlocking a mindset that propels you forward, effortlessly navigating obstacles that once seemed insurmountable?

But the journey doesn't stop at mindset. After this internal shift, Alan was guided to the second quadrant, which focuses on diagnosing the business's symptoms. Just like a doctor treating a patient, Alan learned to look beyond surface-level problems and identify the core issues holding his company back. Maybe you've noticed patterns in your own business that just don't seem to budge—issues that persist no matter what quick fixes you apply. Alan experienced this, too, but by systematically addressing these deeper business "symptoms," he laid the foundation for lasting change.

After understanding the problems, Alan naturally moved into the third quadrant: systematizing the business and crafting a strategy. This stage is where many entrepreneurs get stuck, but Alan, using Dr. Oda's model, began to experience a profound shift. He noticed how he could stop wasting time and energy on inefficiencies by implementing clear systems and processes and instead focus on growth. I'm wondering if you've ever thought about how much easier things could be with the right systems in place—systems that allow your business to run smoothly, effortlessly, without the constant need for your intervention.

But what's the true measure of success? Is it just about efficiency? For Alan, the final quadrant was about profit—monetizing his efforts and turning his new strategies into tangible results. This wasn't just about making money; it was about creating a legacy that would last beyond his lifetime. You might notice how Alan's journey from chaos to control, from loss to profit, mirrors the journey many business leaders long for. Maybe you're even beginning to feel the possibilities open up as you think about how your business could transform with the right strategies.

The real beauty of Alan's story is that his success didn't stop with him. As he mastered each stage of the BSSM, he naturally became a beacon for others, sharing his insights and experiences with eager entrepreneurs. Alan's teachings aren't just about learning how to build a business; they're about realizing that the seed of unlimited potential lies within each challenge. You might wonder how you, too, can tap into that potential—how you can expand beyond where you are now, leveraging your mindset, systems, and strategies to create a business and a life that aligns with your greatest vision.

So, can you imagine what it would feel like to take control of your destiny, stop letting circumstances dictate your path, and notice the opportunities hidden in your challenges? Alan Private's journey reminds us all that the blueprint for success is within reach. It's about becoming aware, shifting your mindset, systematizing your business, and unlocking the profits that are naturally waiting for you. Because once you start seeing setbacks as opportunities for growth, you'll realize that success is not just possible—it's inevitable.

And now, you're probably already beginning to see how the Alan Private method can be applied to your own life. So, why wait?

Unleashing the Power of Mindset and Faith in Business: The Alan Private Way

I'm curious if you've ever noticed how, in the realm of business, success often seems to hinge on more than just strategy and execution—it naturally requires something deeper, something that expands beyond mere action. Maybe you've realized this, too. It's about having an unwavering mindset, a faith that carries you through the toughest challenges. Alan Private, a man who's experienced the towering heights of prosperity and the crushing depths of despair, discovered that very truth. His journey of redemption and transformation serves as a living testament to the power of mindset and faith, even when the path seems unclear.

You probably already know that setbacks are inevitable in business, as in life. But here's the thing—when the challenges hit, most people stop, ready to throw in the towel and abandon their dreams. I know you're not like most people. You understand, as Alan does, that true success comes to those who push through when things get tough. After all, you might notice that the greatest breakthroughs often come just after the hardest moments—like being three feet away from striking gold but giving up too soon. Alan learned this lesson deeply from his mentor, Dr. John Oda.

Dr. Oda always emphasized that mindset in business isn't just about staying positive; it's about cultivating an unwavering faith in success, especially when the odds seem stacked against you. Maybe you'll find yourself reflecting on how faith can act like a guiding light, helping you stay the course when everything else feels uncertain. Alan embraced this wisdom and realized that without the proper mindset and faith, any business—no matter how promising—risks stagnation or falling short of its true potential. Can you imagine what could happen if you infuse your business with that kind of powerful, unshakable faith?

I wonder if you'll remember Dr. Oda's story about his father's garden. It's a simple yet profound example of how faith can transform outcomes. One year, an unexpected snowstorm hit in May, threatening to destroy everything they had planted. Most people would have given up, but Dr. Oda's father held firm, maintaining a deep belief that the garden would not only survive but flourish. Day after day, he spoke words of positivity and conviction, and miraculously, the garden thrived beyond expectation. I know you, like me, can appreciate how this story serves as a reminder that what we speak into existence, combined with unwavering faith, often leads to extraordinary results.

Alan also found himself drawn to the powerful lessons within ancient wisdom—like the biblical story of Jesus feeding the 5,000 with just two loaves of bread and a few fish. Maybe you've noticed how stories like these serve as metaphors for our own lives. It's not just about the physical act of feeding a multitude; it's about the faith to believe in the seemingly impossible. In business, just as in that story, faith isn't wishful thinking—it's having the courage to trust in the unknown, to step into the unfamiliar, and to believe that things will unfold in your favor. You might begin to notice the feelings of expansion and possibility as you imagine having that level of faith in your own endeavors.

Alan's transformation didn't happen overnight, but it began with one simple yet profound realization: that mindset and faith are the bedrock of success. As he rebuilt his life and business, Alan became more and more aware of how these principles were the real drivers of his triumphs. He stopped fighting against the flow and started trusting it; naturally, things began to change. What might you notice shifting in your own life when you begin to trust in your ability to succeed, just as Alan did?

Maybe you're already beginning to see how having faith doesn't mean ignoring the challenges—it means recognizing them and then moving forward with the belief that, somehow, you'll find a way through. For Alan, this shift in perspective wasn't just about business—it was about life. And now, armed with these insights, he's on a mission to share what he's learned. He's dedicated to helping others unlock their full potential, not just in business but in every area of life.

Alan's teachings invite you to embrace faith and cultivate a mindset that naturally draws success toward you. Imagine for a moment what your life and business could look like if you approached every challenge with the same kind of unwavering faith Alan now teaches. Maybe you've noticed that success often comes not because you've found the perfect strategy but because you've decided, deep within, that you'll keep moving forward no matter what happens.

As Alan likes to say, it's not about avoiding adversity—it's about conquering it with the mindset and faith that you were always meant to succeed. And now, as you reflect on this, you might find yourself wondering how these ideas will shape your next steps, feeling the expansion of possibility as you begin to apply these principles in your own journey. Because, after all, success is not just a destination—it's the natural result of a mindset that believes, persists, and prevails.

Unlocking Business Potential Through Strategic Systems and Mindset Mastery: The Wisdom of Dr. Oda

I'm curious if you've ever noticed how the intricate tapestry of business success is woven from more than just hard work—it effortlessly blends strategic systems with an unwavering mindset to create a path of prosperity and growth. You probably already know this on some level, but something begins to shift when you fully embrace it. Alan Private, drawing from the teachings of his esteemed mentor, Dr. John Oda, discovered just how naturally these two elements can align, expanding businesses beyond their current limits and unlocking unlimited potential.

Can you imagine what it feels like to have every part of your business working harmoniously, driving toward success? Central to Dr. Oda's philosophy is this: no matter where a company is today, there's untapped potential waiting to be unlocked—potential that can easily and naturally be harnessed through optimizing strategic systems. As Alan recounts, Dr. Oda often observed that even a company generating half a million dollars annually can double its revenue simply by implementing the right systems.

I know you, like me, can appreciate the power of systems to streamline success, but it's not just about setting high goals; it's about crafting a clear roadmap to get there. Dr. Oda emphasizes defining outcomes precisely and aligning every part of the business to support their realization. Maybe you'll notice this pattern in your own business—when systems are aligned with your vision, things start to fall into place more easily, more naturally, and you begin to experience the kind of growth you've always dreamed of.

Alan often draws parallels between Dr. Oda's teachings and Napoleon Hill's "Think and Grow Rich," particularly the concept of autosuggestion. It's not just about affirmations but about aligning thought, emotion, and action so that success feels inevitable. You might begin to realize how affirmations, when imbued with genuine emotion and conviction, create a powerful resonance that moves you forward. It's more than just words—it's a feeling, an experience that expands beyond mere recitation.

Dr. Oda teaches that affirmations must come from a place of authenticity. Maybe you've experienced the difference between simply saying something and truly believing it deep within. When affirmations are fueled by heartfelt sincerity, they take root in your subconscious mind, creating a burning desire to achieve your goals. Alan found that once he aligned his emotions with his affirmations, his business began to flourish in ways he never thought possible. You might notice the same thing once you begin to infuse your goals with that kind of unwavering belief.

What's crucial here, and maybe you're already starting to see it, is that the mindset you cultivate directly shapes your business outcomes. Dr. Oda's teachings emphasize a mindset of abundance—of resilience in the face of challenges and unwavering faith in the eventual success of your endeavors. Alan's own transformation came when he realized that his past limitations were just that—past. He became aware that he had the power to transcend those limitations, envisioning a future full of limitless possibilities. And you, too, can stop letting past challenges dictate your future.

I'm curious if you've ever considered how much your mindset determines your business's trajectory. Maybe you've noticed how things tend to flow more easily when you operate from a mindset of abundance, where opportunities naturally present themselves and obstacles seem less daunting. This is the kind of shift Alan experienced under Dr. Oda's guidance, and this mindset allowed him to push beyond what he thought was possible.

What's truly powerful about Dr. Oda's philosophy is the realization that success isn't just a destination—it's a journey. You probably already know that, but maybe now you're realizing it in a deeper way. It's about continuous growth, adapting to new challenges, and evolving along the way. Alan learned to embrace this symbiotic relationship between mindset and systems, and as he did, he found that his business wasn't just surviving—it was thriving.

Imagine what it could be like for you to naturally expand beyond your current limitations to experience unlimited growth in both your business and personal life. Maybe you will start noticing that with the right systems in place and the right mindset guiding your actions, success doesn't just seem possible—it feels inevitable. After you embrace this new way of thinking, you'll begin to see how your business can easily and naturally reach heights you once only dreamed of.

Alan's journey reminds you that everything you need for success is already within you. It's about becoming aware of it, realizing it, and allowing it to guide you. So, what's stopping you from taking that first step? Success is waiting for you—now.

Crafting Success: The Fusion of Mindset, Strategy, and Faith

I'm curious if you've ever noticed how, in the labyrinth of business dynamics, there's a way to navigate challenges that feels almost effortless—where each obstacle becomes a steppingstone rather than a barrier. Maybe you've realized that with the right mindset, success doesn't have to be a struggle; it can unfold naturally, almost as if by design. Alan Private, a visionary entrepreneur, knows this truth well. Drawing inspiration from his mentor, Dr. John Oda, and luminaries like Tony Robbins and Joel Osteen, Alan has discovered the blueprint for unlimited growth—a path where mindset, strategy, and faith seamlessly blend to create transformative results.

I know you, like me, can appreciate the power of speaking things into existence. It's a concept at the core of Dr. Oda's teachings, one that Tony Robbins and Joel Osteen championed in their journeys. Can you imagine how your life might change if you started sculpting your reality with the sheer force of belief, just as these leaders have done? Maybe you haven't yet tapped into the full potential of this practice, but one might say that once you do, the results are nothing short of miraculous.

Dr. Oda's wisdom, influenced by timeless works like Think and Grow Rich by Napoleon Hill, underscores the profound importance of autosuggestion and cultivating desire. You probably already know that a strong mindset forms the foundation for success, but what if you could strengthen that foundation even more—so much so that it naturally withstands any adversity thrown your way? Alan Private realized this, and it felt like uncovering the Holy Grail of entrepreneurship. He realized that fortifying his mindset with Dr. Oda's principles was the key to creating a seismic shift in his reality.

Alan's journey of self-discovery began with one critical step: realizing his definite purpose. I'm curious if you've ever stopped to ask yourself, "What is my true purpose?" Maybe you will now. Because once you unearth that purpose, everything else falls into place. Dr. Oda teaches that having a definite purpose is like having a beacon that guides you through life's choices and challenges. It's the compass that helps you expand beyond what you once thought was possible. When you align your passions and values with your actions, you unlock the full magnitude of your potential.

But, of course, having a purpose is only the beginning. You could have the grandest vision in the world, but without a roadmap to get there, it's just a dream. Dr. Oda's teachings emphasize the critical importance of strategic planning and execution. This is where Alan Private's entrepreneurial brilliance truly shines. Armed with a clear purpose and a fortified mindset, he didn't just stop at dreaming—he mapped out a strategic path to his goals, leveraging efficiency, innovation, and adaptability to navigate the ever-shifting currents of the business world. Can you imagine having that kind of clarity, where every move you make is calculated and purposeful, bringing you closer to your daily goals?

Yet, amid all the strategic planning and tactical brilliance, something deeper drives Alan's journey—something beyond logic and reason. It's faith. Maybe you've noticed how faith can propel you forward, even when the path ahead seems uncertain. Dr. Oda teaches that faith isn't just about believing in something greater; it's about infusing every action you take with a divine potency. Just as Joel Osteen speaks of faith manifesting miracles, Dr. Oda invokes this same energy to breathe life into dreams and aspirations. Maybe you haven't fully embraced the power of faith in your own life yet, but once you do, you might notice how your dreams start to materialize in ways you never imagined.

Alan Private's journey perfectly exemplifies how mindset, strategy, and faith can align to create something extraordinary. He experiences the transformative power of combining inner conviction with external action each day. You might notice that success feels almost effortless when these elements work together as if the universe is conspiring in your favor. Can you imagine how it would feel to have that kind of alignment in your own life, where your purpose, plans, and faith all work in harmony?

Now, as Alan stands on the precipice of greatness, he embodies the timeless wisdom of Dr. Oda. He's become a beacon of inspiration for entrepreneurs everywhere, showing what's possible when you tap into the full power of mindset, strategy, and faith. I know you, like me, can appreciate the significance of a mentor like Dr. Oda—someone whose teachings transcend time, guiding those who seek to reach their fullest potential. Because, after all, in the crucible of entrepreneurship, where dreams collide with reality, the ones who emerge victorious are those who align their minds, strategies, and faith in ways that expand beyond the ordinary.

And now, maybe you will start to see how your own journey could unfold with the same grace and power. Because once you stop letting fear and uncertainty hold you back, you'll find that success is not just possible—it's inevitable.

Unveiling the Power of Definite Purpose: A Blueprint for Success

In the vast expanse of entrepreneurial pursuits, where dreams intersect with reality, one principle rises as the North Star for those destined to reshape their world: Definite Purpose. Alan Private, a visionary entrepreneur and disciple of Dr. John Oda, naturally draws from the great luminaries of history, underscoring the transformative power of Definite Purpose in unlocking untold potential and sculpting destinies.

At the heart of Alan's teachings lies a profound reverence for the timeless wisdom found in works like "Think and Grow Rich" by Napoleon Hill. Can you imagine the sheer impact of gleaning insights from titans like John D. Rockefeller, Henry Ford, Albert Einstein, and Charles M. Schwab—visionaries who, armed with crystal-clear vision and unyielding determination, forever altered the course of history?

Definite Purpose, as Alan explains, transcends mere ambition. It's not just about setting goals; it's about an unwavering pursuit of one singular objective, no matter the obstacles encountered along the way. Whether you aspire to attain a million dollars or double a ten-million-dollar enterprise, the essence remains the same: steadfast commitment to realizing your vision, no matter the cost.

You may not know if the path to prosperity is paved with ease, but the reality is often fraught with challenges and uncertainties. One could imagine that even the most resolute of visionaries face moments of doubt. It's here, however, that the power of daily affirmations, repeated with unwavering conviction, begins to shape reality. I'm curious, have you noticed how vocalizing your aspirations begins to resonate with a higher vibrational frequency—a frequency attuned to abundance, prosperity, and limitless possibility?

Contrary to popular belief, wealth is not a Herculean feat reserved for the few; it's a birthright accessible to all who possess unwavering belief and the expectation that success is inevitable. In Alan's words, "To get money, it's not hard; it's rigid. It's not going to flow to everybody; it's going to flow to the person who has that subconscious belief and expectation to make it happen." This encapsulates the essence of Definite Purpose—a rallying cry for entrepreneurs to cast aside self-doubt and embrace the boundless potential within them.

In this crucible of unwavering determination and unyielding faith, miracles are wrought. I don't know if you've experienced it yet, but one could imagine that the power to turn the seemingly impossible into the inevitable lies within your vision.

As Alan Private stands at the nexus of past and present—a torchbearer for the principles championed by Dr. John Oda—he embodies the transformative power of Definite Purpose. His unwavering commitment to his vision and relentless pursuit of excellence serve as a beacon for aspiring entrepreneurs, reminding us all that the key to unlocking boundless potential lies within our hearts.

You might notice, as Alan recounts Dr. Oda's work, that the pivotal role of mindset in business transformation cannot be overstated. Take the remarkable case of Robert from Australia, whose business saw a staggering 120% increase in net profit. Was this just luck? No—it was mindset conditioning, a shift that opened the doors to a new reality of success. Can you imagine what a change in mindset could do for you?

The Power of Mindset Conditioning: Dr. Oda's Methodology

Dr. John Oda's methodology is deceptively simple yet profoundly effective: infuse affirmations with genuine feelings and emotions. When applied with unwavering conviction, this principle becomes a force of transformation. You may not know if this could change your life or business, but Robert's journey epitomizes this principle in action.

Initially, Robert found himself stuck—his business stagnating in mediocrity. But then, a key moment arrived: an employee's departure forced him to confront the need for change. I don't know if you've been in this position before, but you probably already know how, sometimes, adversity sparks the fire of transformation. Armed with Dr. Oda's teachings, Robert embarked on a daily ritual of affirmations—dedicating hours each day to speak his desired outcomes into existence.

Can you imagine the focus it takes to infuse every word with intention, every thought with emotion? What followed for Robert was nothing short of miraculous. Like seeds sown in fertile soil, his affirmations began to take root, and within just eight months, his net profit soared from a modest 20% to an astonishing 120%.

The catalyst for this incredible transformation wasn't external strategies or changing market conditions. No—you probably already know the change happened in the fertile soil of Robert's subconscious mind. Through his daily ritual of affirmations, he effectively rewired his neural pathways, aligning his thoughts, beliefs, and actions towards a singular purpose: unprecedented growth and success.

Robert's story is a testament to the transformative power of mindset conditioning. Through his unwavering commitment and discipline, he transcended his previous limitations, tapping into a reservoir of untapped potential that had always been within him. Like a phoenix rising from the ashes, Robert emerged victorious, filled with a newfound sense of invincibility—a belief that he could accomplish anything he set his mind to.

But Robert's story isn't just an isolated anecdote; it's a blueprint for anyone seeking to unleash their full potential in business and life. Dr. Oda's teachings remind us that success is not a matter of chance or circumstance—it is a deliberate choice. A choice to cultivate a mindset of abundance, resilience, and unwavering faith in the face of adversity. Can you imagine how this shift could impact your life?

As Alan reflects on Robert's transformation, he's reminded of the countless stories of individuals who have harnessed the power of mindset conditioning to achieve extraordinary feats. From titans of industry like John Rockefeller and Henry Ford to modern-day visionaries like Daymond John and Tony Robbins, the common thread that binds them all is their relentless commitment to harnessing the power of their minds to manifest their deepest desires.

In a world where success is often equated with external metrics like wealth and status, Alan's reflection serves as a powerful reminder that true success begins from within. It's not about the size of your bank account or the accolades you've accumulated—it's about the strength of your character, the depth of your conviction, and the unwavering faith that propels you ever forward on your journey toward greatness.

In the realm of business, the significance of mindset is often underestimated. But you may not know if it holds the key to unlocking unparalleled growth and prosperity. Dr. Oda's methodology is not just theoretical; it's rooted in real-world results. Alan recounts Robert's extraordinary journey, whose business witnessed a staggering 120% increase in net profit—all under Dr. Oda's guidance.

The key to this transformation wasn't in complex strategies but in the power of affirmations—infused with genuine emotion and conviction. Initially stagnant, Robert's business shifted when he vocalized his goals with fervor and intensity. It wasn't just about saying words but about embodying his aspirations and allowing them to take root in his subconscious mind.

Alan emphasizes the importance of feelings and emotions. Like the infectious jingle that echoes through the corridors of Disney World, these affirmations—relentlessly repeated with emotion—embed themselves deep within you, propelling you toward your desired outcomes.
Can you imagine what's possible when you align your mind, heart, and actions with a clear purpose?

Unlocking Unlimited Wealth: The Power of Mindset Incantations

Alan acknowledges that in the landscape of business, practices like affirmations and incantations are rarely embraced. Few are willing to invest the time and effort needed to cultivate a mindset conducive to success. You may not know if affirmations could truly change the trajectory of your business, but you probably already know how easy it is to dismiss them as wishful thinking. After all, isn't it easier to prioritize tangible strategies over intangible beliefs?

However, in doing so, businesses overlook one of the most potent tools for transformation. Can you imagine the potential unlocked when mindset becomes your secret weapon? I don't know if you've seen this play out, but businesses that dare to embrace the power of mindset emerge as trailblazers. They naturally understand that success is not solely determined by external factors—it's intrinsically linked to one's internal state of being.

By nurturing a mindset of abundance, resilience, and unwavering faith, these businesses break through limitations, defy expectations, and carve their own path to greatness. Alan's message is clear: The road to success begins within. It's about daring to dream big, believing wholeheartedly in realizing those dreams, and building a mindset of unshakable possibility.

Imagine, for a moment, what could happen when you fully embrace the notion that mindset is not just a small part of success—it is the foundation. You might notice that when businesses commit to this level of belief, they move from survival to thriving. The journey may be arduous and filled with challenges, but it's the unwavering faith in mindset that ultimately propels these businesses toward their desired destination.

Dr. John Oda and Alan serve as examples of this truth. They understand that the power of mindset is not to be underestimated. It's a force capable of transforming businesses, redefining industries, and shaping the course of history. For those bold enough to embrace it, the rewards are boundless.

Incantations: Reprogramming the Subconscious for Wealth

Few concepts wield as much transformative power as mindset in the grand tapestry of human potential. Dr. John Oda, drawing from Napoleon Hill's timeless wisdom in "Think and Grow Rich," unveils the secrets to cultivating a wealth mindset—an indispensable tool for unlocking unlimited abundance in life.

Hill's work serves as a beacon for those ready to move beyond scarcity and embrace a reality brimming with boundless prosperity. At its core, Hill explains that most individuals are born with a default mindset of limitation, but you can imagine how within each of us lies the power to cultivate a mindset of wealth and abundance.

The key to this transformation lies in the practice of incantations— powerful affirmations infused with emotion and conviction, designed to reprogram the subconscious mind for success. I'm curious: have you ever experienced the power of repeating affirmations with fervor and intensity?

Through the relentless repetition of these affirmations, one could easily overwrite the limiting beliefs that have held them back for years. Can you imagine reciting affirmations like "I am wealthy" or "Everything I touch turns to gold" with unwavering belief and emotional resonance? I don't know if you've tried this yet, but what if you immersed yourself in this ritual for just 30 minutes each day, allowing these affirmations to seep into the fabric of your being? Picture yourself—each day, reinforcing these affirmations until they become your internal narrative, guiding you toward prosperity. You may not know if this will change your life yet, but you probably already sense how aligning your mindset with wealth creates limitless potential.

This practice is not merely about wishful thinking or positive affirmations but about rewiring the subconscious mind to align with the frequency of wealth and abundance. By consistently reinforcing these beliefs, individuals create a magnetic field that attracts wealth and opportunities into their lives, propelling them toward their financial goals with unprecedented velocity.

But why is investing time and energy in cultivating a wealth mindset essential? The answer lies in the fundamental principle that thoughts precede reality. As Hill aptly puts it, "Whatever the mind can conceive and believe, it can achieve." By programming the subconscious mind for success, individuals set in motion a chain reaction of events that lead inexorably toward realizing their desires.

Consider, for instance, the case of someone who has internalized the belief that they are a magnet for money and opportunities. Armed with this conviction, they approach every situation with a sense of confidence and abundance, effortlessly attracting wealth and success into their lives. Conversely, those who harbor beliefs of scarcity and limitation inadvertently repel opportunities and sabotage their own success.

The power of mindset incantations lies in their ability to bridge the gap between aspiration and actualization, between dreams and reality. By consistently reinforcing positive beliefs and attitudes, individuals create a fertile ground for the seeds of success to take root and flourish.

But cultivating a wealth mindset is not passive; it requires discipline, dedication, and unwavering commitment. It is a journey of self-discovery and personal growth, where individuals confront their deepest fears and insecurities and emerge stronger and more resilient than ever before.

Unlocking Unlimited Wealth: The Power of a Wealth Mindset

As Dr. John Oda so powerfully reminds us, there's a reason the book is titled "Think and Grow Rich". Success begins with a shift in mindset. By harnessing the power of incantations—those powerful, intentional affirmations infused with emotion—individuals can transcend the limitations of their circumstances and unlock a world of unlimited wealth and abundance.

Few concepts wield as much transformative power as a mindset in the grand tapestry of human potential. Dr. John Oda, drawing from the timeless wisdom encapsulated in Napoleon Hill's "Think and Grow Rich", unveils the secrets to cultivating a wealth mindset—an indispensable tool for unlocking limitless abundance in one's life.

Hill's seminal work serves as a beacon for those seeking to move beyond the limitations of conventional thinking and embrace a reality brimming with boundless prosperity. You may not know if you're operating with a default mindset of scarcity, but you probably already know it is within your grasp to cultivate a wealth and abundance mindset.

The key to this transformation lies in the practice of incantations—or autosuggestions—affirmations imbued with emotion and conviction, designed to reprogram the subconscious mind for success. I don't know if you've tried this yet, but imagine the power of reciting affirmations like "I am wealthy" or "Everything I touch turns to gold" with unwavering belief and emotional resonance.

Picture yourself engaging in this ritual for just 30 minutes each day. You might notice how these affirmations begin to seep into the fabric of your being until they become your internal narrative—your guiding light toward prosperity.

This practice isn't about wishful thinking. It's about rewiring the subconscious mind to align with the frequency of wealth and abundance. By consistently reinforcing these beliefs, individuals create a magnetic field that draws wealth, opportunities, and success into their lives. Can you imagine the momentum of being propelled toward your financial goals with unprecedented velocity?

But why is investing time and energy into cultivating a wealth mindset essential? Dr. Oda would remind us that the answer lies in the fundamental principle that thoughts precede reality. You probably already know the famous quote from Hill: "Whatever the mind can conceive and believe, it can achieve." By programming the subconscious mind for success, individuals set in motion a chain reaction that leads inexorably toward the realization of their deepest desires.

In this process of cultivating a wealth mindset, the shift isn't just in thinking—it's in being. The results speak for themselves: the magnetic pull of wealth, opportunity, and limitless potential are now within your reach. Imagine living in that reality, where your thoughts align effortlessly with the wealth you seek, and your success becomes inevitable.

Unlocking the Power of Incantations: A Blueprint for Unlimited Abundance

In "Life is a Garden," I speak about the power of planting seeds—both in life and in business. Can you imagine growing up on a mini-farm in Indiana, just as I did? My father would plant tens of thousands of seeds. You probably already know that not all of them would grow, but we still nurtured each one with water, fertilizer, sunlight, and care, pulling the weeds that threatened their growth. This natural process is the same when you're planting seeds of success in your business.

I call it incantations, or affirmations on steroids—where you repeat something with feelings and emotions until it enters the subconscious mind. Maybe you've noticed how those catchy songs get stuck in your mind when you go to Disneyland or Disney World. I'm curious: have you ever experienced how a simple melody can linger? It's the same with incantations—the more you say them with intention, the more they imprint on your subconscious.

Let me tell you about a time I attended a seminar by Tony Robbins. He once shared that he made only $3,000 a month, but he turned that into one million dollars in just nine months. Do you know what his secret was? Incantations. Tony would spend 45 minutes daily saying his affirmations with emotion, visualizing the end results. This is what he said:

"God's wealth is circulating in my life. His wealth flows to me in avalanches of abundance. All my needs, desires, and goals are met instantaneously by infinite intelligence, for I am one with God, and God is everything."

Stop and notice how the power of those words, when spoken with feeling, can shift your mindset. You might realize that it's not just about saying the words but embodying them until they become your reality.

After that seminar, I began investigating the practice of incantations—how I could apply them in my own life. I don't know if you've heard of Napoleon Hill's Think and Grow Rich, but I've read this classic every three months for the last 30 years. In one chapter, Hill talks about autosuggestion—the idea that when you say a statement with feeling and emotion, it gets absorbed into your subconscious mind, and things start to change. You probably already know that people like Henry Ford, John D. Rockefeller, and Thomas Edison all practiced this very principle.

I continued my research and came across Pastor Joel Osteen. When he took over his father's church, he started using these same principles, which changed his life forever. Pastor Joel would spend 15 to 30 minutes each day saying incantations like:

"I am blessed. The favor of God has turned my situation around. God is opening doors of opportunity. The favor of God is following me. I am the head, not the tail. I am the lender, not the borrower. Something good is going to happen."

These words, spoken with passion and conviction, reprogrammed his mind and, in turn, his reality. I wonder if you've ever tried something similar?

Finally, I turned to the Bible, which speaks of the need to renew your mind on a daily basis. What does that really mean? It means feeding your mind with the right thoughts, affirmations, and energy daily. The process is as essential to success as water is to seeds.

Another example is Joseph McClendon III, whom I have trained with since 1995. His incantation goes:

"I am a God-guided expression of health, wealth, happiness, and joy for myself and all those I touch. All that I want, desire, and need is instantly manifested and flows to me in oceans of abundance as I create even more abundance for all to enjoy. I am grateful beyond measure for all that has already flowed to my team and me."

Can you imagine saying that every day? You might notice how, after repeating it consistently, it naturally reshapes your thoughts, your actions, and eventually your results.

Ultimately, it's about creating a mindset that aligns with your desired reality. You already know that life is what you make it. These incantations are the fertilizer for the seeds you plant in your business and life. Stop and think—what are you waiting for? Begin today by speaking your vision into existence because everything you desire is waiting to flow to you in abundance.

Unlocking Unlimited Wealth: The Power of Service and Mindset

As Dr. Oda so often reminds us, the book is aptly titled "Think and Grow Rich" because true success begins with a shift in mindset. By harnessing the power of incantations, individuals can naturally transcend the limitations of their circumstances and unlock a world of unlimited wealth and abundance.

In the realm of business enlightenment, Dr. Oda's teachings resonate like ancient wisdom passed down through generations. One of the core principles he emphasizes is the profound significance of serving others in the highest capacity. This concept, though seemingly simple, holds the key to unlocking your full entrepreneurial potential.

I'm curious: have you ever considered how many lives your business is truly impacting? Dr. Oda shares a striking example using none other than Michael Jordan. In his final seasons, Jordan's salary was staggering, earning upwards of 30 million dollars. Maybe you already know, but his wealth wasn't simply a reflection of his talent—it was a reflection of how many millions of people he served through his athletic prowess and magnetic influence.

Dr. Oda's revelation is this: true wealth comes not from personal gain but from the magnitude of your impact on others. You probably already know that when you expand the number of people you serve, your business growth naturally follows. Alan Private understood this deeply and used it to expand beyond his original business vision.

Alan recognized that he could expand his reach by shifting from a profit-centric mindset to one focused on service—from serving 10,000 people to 100,000, even half a million. As he did, he witnessed a seismic shift in his business fortunes. Can you imagine what could happen if you expanded your reach in the same way?

The beauty of this principle is that success becomes about the number of lives you touch rather than just the revenue you generate. After Alan recalibrated his focus from financial gain to serving others, he discovered a pathway to unprecedented growth. He realized that if his goal was to make $500,000, the question wasn't "How can I make this money?" but "How many people can I serve at the highest level?"

For instance, by attracting 50 new clients at an average value of $10,000 each, the business naturally reaches its financial goal—and, more importantly, it fulfills its purpose of enriching lives.

I'm wondering if you've noticed this in your own business: The moment you shift your focus from what you can get to what you can give, everything changes. Maybe you haven't yet fully realized the power of serving others first, but I know you, like me, are starting to see how vital it is to long-term success.

This principle requires more than ambition—it requires a fundamental shift in mindset. As Dr. Oda often says, you must cultivate a mindset of abundance and service, where success is measured not by personal wealth but by your impact on others. You probably already know that success is not measured solely by financial metrics. True wealth is tied to the depth and breadth of your service. Can you imagine what it would look like if you began to view your business as a vehicle for changing lives? You unlock a pathway to exponential growth and deep personal fulfillment when you do.

Alan Private exemplifies this journey. He reminds us that the road from profitability to true prosperity begins with a shift—from self-serving to serving others. Through this lens, entrepreneurs can expand beyond their financial aspirations, leaving an indelible mark on the world and enriching the lives of countless individuals. Alan has drawn from the collective insight of Tony Robbins, Dr. John Oda, Jay Abraham, Scot Conway, and others in the vast landscape of entrepreneurial wisdom. Together, they formed a blueprint that propelled his business from a billion to a trillion-dollar empire.

At the heart of Alan's success lies a profound understanding of mindset. He naturally knows that external circumstances do not determine success—it's an inside job, a manifestation of your beliefs, expectations, and actions. With this understanding, Alan embarked on a journey of self-mastery, cultivating a mindset of unwavering expectation and abundance. So now, I'm curious: have you fully embraced the power of mindset in your business? You probably already realize that this isn't just a strategy—it's the foundation for transformative success.

The Power of Expectation: Alan's Journey from Billion to Sextillion

Central to Alan's philosophy is the powerful notion that mindset precedes manifestation. It's not merely about hoping or wishing for success—you probably already know that doesn't get you very far. It's about expecting success with such deep certainty that it naturally becomes inevitable. I'm curious: Have you noticed how, when you truly expect something to happen, the universe starts to align in your favor?

Alan's journey is a testament to this transformative power of expectation. Through diligent practice and unwavering belief, he cultivated a mindset of abundance that acted like a magnet, drawing success and prosperity into his orbit. But here's the key: Alan understands that expectation alone isn't enough. Maybe you already realize that it must be paired with consistent action.

In Alan's paradigm, success isn't left to chance. It's the result of deliberate, purposeful activity. He aligned his expectations with strategic action, ensuring that every step he took perfectly matched his desired outcome. This synergy between mindset and action forms the cornerstone of Alan's approach to unlimited business growth. But Alan's journey isn't just about his own success. It's about empowering others to achieve similar extraordinary results. Through his teachings, Alan generously shares the wisdom he's gleaned from mentors like Dr. John Oda, Tony Robbins, and Jay Abraham. He offers a blueprint—a roadmap—for others to follow in his footsteps.

At the core of Alan's message is the unshakable belief that anyone can achieve greatness if they cultivate the right mindset and take consistent, purposeful action. By shifting your expectations from mere hope to unwavering certainty, you can naturally unlock your full potential and create the life you've always dreamed of.

Can you imagine the power of this shift? When you start to believe, with every fiber of your being, that success is inevitable—the world changes. I'm wondering if you've already started to realize that this shift alone can unlock limitless opportunities.

Alan's journey from a billion to a sextillion dollars proves the transformative power of mindset. He harnessed the innate power of expectation and coupled it with strategic action, rewriting the rules of what's possible in the world of business. You might notice that this isn't just a story about numbers—it's about a complete transformation in thinking.

Ultimately, Alan's story isn't just about achieving financial success. It's about inspiring others to do the same. Through his teachings, Alan empowers individuals to break free from their limiting beliefs and enter a world of unlimited possibility. Maybe you haven't yet taken the first step toward your own greatness, but the journey from billion to trillion—from ordinary to extraordinary—begins with a single, unwavering expectation.

I know you, like me, are starting to see how this powerful combination of mindset and action can transform not only your business but also your life. What's stopping you from expecting the unlimited success you've always envisioned?
Questions from this chapter..

1. **What is the difference between hoping for success and expecting it with certainty?**
   Can you imagine how your life might change if you shifted from hoping to truly expecting success to unfold naturally? I'm curious, have you noticed how your actions align differently when you expect success as a certainty?

2. **How do you align your expectations with purposeful action?**
   You probably already know that mindset alone isn't enough. What steps are you taking to ensure that your actions are in harmony with your desired outcome? Maybe you haven't yet

realized the power of merging expectations with strategic activity.

3. **What limiting beliefs are holding you back from cultivating a mindset of abundance?**
   I wonder if you've become aware of any patterns of thinking that are keeping you from fully stepping into your potential. After noticing these beliefs, what can you do to reframe them into a mindset of possibility?

4. **In what business areas could you expand your sphere of influence by serving more people?**
   Can you imagine what would happen if you focused not on what you could gain but how many people you could help? What would shift if you expanded beyond your current reach to touch more lives?

5. **How do you maintain consistency in your actions to support your desired outcomes?**
   I don't know if you've already implemented systems to ensure consistent progress toward your goals. What can you do today to ensure that your actions align with your highest vision daily?

6. **How can you use incantations and affirmations to strengthen your belief in your success?**
   You may not know if using daily affirmations could unlock new levels of abundance in your life. What could happen if you devoted time each day to speaking your desired outcomes into existence with feeling and emotion?

7. **What does success look like when you serve others at your highest capacity?**
   Imagine the transformation when your business focuses on impact, not just profit. I'm curious: how will you measure your success when the primary metric is the number of lives you've touched?

8. **What expectations are you setting for yourself in the next 12 months?**

Can you see yourself setting bold, unwavering expectations for where you want to be a year from now? What steps will you take to manifest those expectations into reality?

9. **How can shifting your mindset from limitation to abundance transform your current challenges?**
What if your current obstacles weren't setbacks, but stepping stones to a greater outcome? What would change if you started viewing your challenges through the lens of abundance and possibility?

10. **What legacy do you want to create through your business, and how will you align your actions with that vision?**
Can you imagine the legacy you could leave behind if you aligned your business goals with your highest purpose? How will your actions today create a lasting impact that transcends financial success?

Chapter 4:   The Master Mind Principle

Unleashing the Power of the Master Mind Principle: A Blueprint for Success

As you realize that Allan Private had to change his ways—because going from billions to being homeless is not a pretty picture—you might start noticing how powerful the mind truly is. Allan knew something had to shift within himself. I'm wondering if you're aware that the right mindset is often the key that unlocks unlimited potential in those uncertain times.

Maybe you haven't realized how naturally and easily the right support system can create success, even when the world is crumbling. Allan knew he couldn't go it alone, so he reached out to churches, the spiritual guides who inspired him, and the ideas that expanded beyond the ordinary.

Allan read Think and Grow Rich and naturally created his own Master Mind group. Can you imagine the power of aligning with people who support your dreams and expand them? Maybe you already know how profound it can be to surround yourself with the right influences—people and organizations like Neville Goddard, The 700 Club, Rev. Ike, and Joel Osteen. When you're in an environment that supports success, your mindset can shift, and the path becomes clear.
In the timeless pursuit of success, one principle reigns supreme: the Master Mind Principle.

Allan Private, a visionary in his own right, embarked on a transformative journey—one I know will resonate with you. He tapped into collective wisdom and experienced firsthand how powerful it is when minds align toward a common goal.

It all began when Allan encountered Dr. John Oda, and you can imagine how life-changing that was for him. Dr. Oda guided Allan through teachings that unleashed unlimited potential, helping him expand beyond the limitations he once thought were unbreakable. Allan learned the art of manifestation, diving deep into Dr. William Horton's and others' work. This is when Allan began to notice patterns—success patterns.

With this new awareness, Allan created a vision board that represented not only his dreams but the life he knew he was destined to lead. I'm curious—can you imagine seeing your aspirations unfold before your eyes, day by day, as the people you admire surround you with their wisdom and support?

And it didn't stop there. Allan formed a Master Mind group of extraordinary people. From Dr. John Oda to Anthony Robbins, Carl Scott, and Chet Holmes, Allan found himself immersed in a powerful, supportive environment. Each member of this Master Mind group brought unique gifts and insights, and together, they became a force to be reckoned with.

You probably already know that real success isn't achieved alone. Naturally, it comes when you have a network of like-minded individuals guiding, challenging, and supporting you every step of the way. Allan's inspiration wall became a daily reminder of this—faces of people who helped him soar to new heights.
As 2054 dawned, Allan stood at the threshold of greatness, embodying everything the Master Mind Principle represents. His journey—fueled by the synergy of brilliant minds—reminds us that success is inevitable when we embrace the power of collaboration and expand beyond our limitations.

Now, maybe you're realizing that the key to your success lies in the people you surround yourself with, the insights you easily access, and the environment you create. Can you imagine what your life would look like when you align yourself with the right people, ideas, and mindset?

After all, true success comes when you notice the patterns of greatness and choose to take that next step forward. Allan Private did, and you can too.

For Allan, success transcends conventional thinking. It exists in that perfect alignment of minds—a harmonious convergence where each individual contributes unique perspectives and insights. I'm curious: can you imagine what it would be like to experience such a synergy? Maybe you haven't yet realized the power that comes when the right people surround you, naturally elevating your potential. In the sanctuary of his Master Mind wall, Allan found more than just ideas—he found a space where dreams effortlessly take flight and aspirations transform into tangible realities.

The key, Allan discovered, was in noticing how easily success flows when you curate the right environment. A space where inspiration flourishes, creativity thrives, and results become inevitable. Through the Master Mind Principle, Allan unlocked the doorway to a future brimming with limitless possibilities—a future where success knows no bounds. Can you imagine what that might feel like for you? You probably already know that your greatest achievements become naturally attainable in the right environment.

As you read this, you're becoming more aware that in the grand tapestry of life, the Master Mind Principle stands as a guiding light—a beacon of hope, illuminating the path toward unprecedented success. With unwavering faith and determination, Allan invites you to embark on a journey that expands beyond the ordinary—a journey fueled by the unlimited collective power of the Master Mind Principle.

Embrace the vision. Embrace the possibilities. Embrace the future. For within the realm of the Master Mind, greatness awaits, and you probably already know this is a journey worth taking.
Allan, deeply inspired by Dr. John Oda's groundbreaking approach to the Master Mind group, embraced the concept with full conviction. Under Oda's guidance, Allan embarked on a journey of imagination and purpose—a journey fueled by the collective wisdom of his Master Mind team, each member contributing to his expanded vision.

Through these imaginary meetings, Allan began noticing the shift within himself. He honed in on his definite purpose, dissecting every detail of his business goals. You're probably already aware that success naturally follows when you focus your energy on a clear vision. In the sanctum of the Master Mind group, Allan found not only camaraderie but an unlimited source of support. Together, they unraveled his ambitions, scrutinized his strategies, and assembled a game plan to easily transcend conventional thinking. Maybe you're realizing that this kind of clarity creates a momentum that can naturally carry you forward, too.

Dr. Oda's methodology wasn't theoretical—it was grounded in results. I know you, like me, can appreciate the kind of success that comes from tangible milestones. Oda showcased this power through his example, illustrating how the collective energy of a Master Mind group turned his dreams into undeniable realities. Through this powerful principle, he manifested his goals, and Allan was determined to do the same.

For Allan, Oda's approach was naturally transformative, a beacon guiding him toward unlocking the full potential of the Master Mind Principle. With each meeting, Allan delved deeper into his imagination, realizing how his vision was becoming a concrete reality. Can you imagine what that would look like for you? Allan took Dr. Oda's Master Mind concept and naturally made it his own—creating the life he deserved by 2054.

In the realm of the Master Mind, imagination knows no bounds. Through unwavering determination and the power of collective insight, Allan Private stood poised on the brink of greatness—a testament to the limitless potential of the Master Mind Principle.

The Masters' Legacy: A Journey of Acquisition and Transformation

Certain individuals shine brighter in the vast tapestry of human achievement, illuminating the path to greatness. Among them, Allan Private stands as a beacon of inspiration—a living testament to the transformative power of the Master Mind Principle. Surrounded by a constellation of visionaries, Allan embarked on a journey of acquisition—a quest to naturally absorb the wisdom and prowess of the greatest minds the world has ever known.

With Napoleon Hill, the sage of success, Allan naturally absorbed insights on resilience and inspiration. He yearned to emulate Hill's ability to ignite an unyielding determination within others, transforming defeat into victory.

Anthony Robbins, the epitome of self-belief, became Allan's guide in effortlessly pursuing excellence. Robbins' persistence was a blueprint for Allan's success, pushing him to go that extra mile in every endeavor.

Joseph McClendon III, the maestro of motivation, captivated Allan with his electrifying energy and transformational impact. Allan sought to embody McClendon's passion, naturally embracing humor and energy to catalyze change in the lives of those around him.

And then, in sports, Michael Jordan became Allan's paragon of strategic brilliance and tenacity. Like Jordan, Allan learned to transform adversity into opportunity, building an unstoppable team that defied all odds.

Joel Osteen naturally captured his attention with a simple yet profound message: divine grace. I'm wondering if you've ever noticed how letting go of fear and allowing the divine to guide your path can create space for miraculous shifts. Osteen's ability to easily inspire millions became Allan's guidepost for overcoming fear and embracing faith in the pursuit of greatness.

Bruce Lee, the legendary martial artist and philosopher, taught Allan to be aware of the importance of adaptability. Lee's unconventional approach to success resonated deeply with Allan. Can you imagine applying such adaptability to your own life—maybe you will start to see how innovation naturally leads to measurable success in every aspect of your journey.

Oprah Winfrey became another pivotal influence for Allan. You probably already know how powerful her mastery of media and marketing is—her ability to touch lives and create income streams by simply being herself. Allan was inspired to follow in Oprah's footsteps, crafting his brand and building a presence that resonates deeply with his audience. Naturally, success followed as Allan harnessed the power of marketing to unlock boundless potential.

And then came Andrew Carnegie, the industrial titan. His wisdom on organized efforts and enterprise building captivated Allan. Allan noticed he could propel his endeavors to heights through strategic organization and teamwork. Maybe you haven't yet realized the power of structured efforts, but it's easily transformative once you do.

Allan also sought guidance from Jack Canfield, the master of self-publishing and storytelling. Canfield taught Allan to notice the patterns that make a narrative compelling. As Allan honed his storytelling, he crafted bestsellers that inspired and uplifted millions. I know you. like me, understand the power of stories—after all, they're the bridges to understanding and connection.

Jay Abraham, the marketing maestro, helped Allan expand beyond conventional growth. Naturally, Allan embraced Jay's genius, implementing revolutionary systems that transformed businesses and industries. Can you imagine the exponential growth that comes from aligning with such wisdom?

Chris Rock brought an unexpected gift to Allan's journey—the joy of laughter. Allan realized how laughter could lighten even the heaviest of burdens. You probably already know that when you learn to laugh at life's challenges, you stop taking everything so seriously, which naturally opens you to creativity and resilience.

Chet Holmes, the strategic architect of educational marketing, inspired Allan to establish himself as a thought leader. Maybe you will start noticing how powerful educational marketing is—it's not just about persuasion but building trust and offering value that naturally leads to success.

With his mastery of technology and strategic questioning, Bill Gates taught Allan the art of inquiry. Through Gates' guidance, Allan learned to ask the right questions—ones that opened doors to wealth and innovation. I'm curious: can you imagine how strategic questioning could unlock new pathways for you?

As Allan Private ventured forth, he recognized that true greatness doesn't lie in merely accumulating knowledge but in applying it toward the betterment of humanity. With each mentor as his guide, Allan moved confidently toward his goals, realizing that he was standing on the brink of greatness—a true testament to the unlimited potential unlocked by the Master Mind Principle.

Now, maybe you haven't yet fully embraced the power of collective wisdom, but as you reflect on Allan's journey, I'm wondering if you're beginning to notice just how easily your own path can shift when you naturally open yourself to the insights of others.
Because, after all, success is always within reach when you align with the right minds and expand beyond your current reality.
Each of these visionaries contributed to Allan's Master Mind journey, guiding him in expanding beyond limitations and moving toward unlimited success. Allan's story is a powerful reminder that when you align yourself with the right people, vision, and environment, greatness becomes your natural destiny. Maybe you will realize it's time to step into that greatness now.

The Master Mind's Journey: Unveiling the Power of Spiritual Guides

In the world of personal development, there exists a principle that naturally stands as a beacon of enlightenment—the Master Mind Principle. It serves as a gateway, unlocking unlimited potential, success, and fulfillment. Have you ever noticed how aligning with the right minds can easily transform your path? Allan Private, a devoted follower of this transformative concept, deepened his journey under Dr. John Oda's wise guidance. Maybe you haven't yet realized how powerful spiritual guides can be in shaping success, but that's exactly what Dr. Oda revealed to Allan—unveiling a realm of celestial wisdom that could effortlessly navigate the complexities of business and life.

Inspired by the timeless teachings of Napoleon Hill, Dr. Oda introduced Allan to a deeper layer of the Master Mind—the presence of spiritual guides. These ethereal beings are entrusted with offering guidance and protection to those who seek their counsel. I know you, like me, can imagine how powerful it would feel to have such divine support. For Allan, this revelation sparked a profound journey of self-discovery and empowerment. Immersing himself in the divine wisdom of the seven archangels, Allan noticed that each of these guides held a unique light that naturally opened the door to blessings and success.

Dr. Oda taught Allan that just like the Master Mind group, you can meet with your angels now, easily tapping into the seeds of divine wisdom and knowing you're being guided every step.

Michael (blue light), the guardian of highways and airways, emerged as Allan's steadfast protector. With Michael's presence, Allan moved through the turbulent waters of business with unlimited confidence, realizing that he was always divinely protected. Can you imagine how it feels to have such protection around you? Maybe you will now see how effortlessly this guidance clears your path to success.

Uriel (purple and gold light), the harbinger of peace, became Allan's guide in moments of discord. Through Uriel's calming light, Allan created harmony within himself and throughout his business, sowing seeds of peace that blossomed into prosperity. You probably already know how peace and calm can naturally lead to success.

Raphael (green light), the healer, offered Allan the gift of vitality, ensuring he stayed strong, healthy, and resilient. With Raphael's blessings, Allan moved through life with renewed energy, overcoming every obstacle. I'm wondering if you've ever felt how important health is to sustaining your success because Allan's journey proved that after you achieve vitality, everything else follows effortlessly.

Gabriel (white light), the divine messenger, became Allan's conduit to unlimited abundance. With Gabriel by his side, Allan harnessed the infinite resources of the universe, effortlessly manifesting wealth and prosperity in every area of his life. Maybe you haven't yet realized how aligned questions and intentions naturally bring the answers you seek, but Gabriel ensured Allan was always in flow.

Jophiel (yellow and golden light), the guardian of wisdom, helped Allan expand his knowledge and self-mastery. Through Jophiel, Allan unlocked deeper levels of clarity and insight, guiding him to his fullest potential. You probably already know how invaluable clarity is when making decisions that lead to greatness. Jophiel also helped Allan tap into the wisdom of leaders, helping him write and create with divine inspiration.

Zadkiel (violet light), the purifier of thoughts, guided Allan in cleansing his mind of negativity, self-doubt, and limiting beliefs. With Zadkiel's help, Allan was able to stop toxic patterns and step into a future of unlimited possibilities. Can you imagine how powerful it is to release all that no longer serves you, making room for boundless success?

Chamuel (pink light), the seeker of lost treasures, assisted Allan in closing deals and recovering lost opportunities. Chamuel infused every situation with love, helping Allan overcome challenges like racism and guiding him toward success. Naturally, Allan began to notice how love and connection can shift even the most challenging situations, making success feel effortless.

Allan discovered a new sense of purpose, clarity, and divine protection with each angel guiding him. He realized that after tapping into this spiritual guidance, his life transformed in ways that expanded beyond the physical realm. Each step became illuminated by the loving presence of his celestial guides, ensuring that his future was filled with unlimited possibilities.

Allan's journey stands as a powerful testament to the transformative potential of the Master Mind Principle, enhanced by the divine wisdom of spiritual guides. Allan transcended the physical world's limitations through this path, unlocking the universe's secrets and realizing his true destiny. Maybe you will now notice how aligning with the right guidance naturally leads you toward greatness. After all, the journey toward success becomes effortless when you have celestial light illuminating the way.

Quadrant Two: Behavioral Symptoms

- **Chapter 5: The CEO Mindset**
- **Chapter 6: Creating the Right Culture**
- **Chapter 7: Building a Strong Team**
- **Chapter 8: Mental Health**

Chapter 5 CEO Mindset by Carl Scott MPH

Great leaders empower their teams to reach their full potential, fostering an environment where individuals can flourish and excel. The impact of a supportive leader extends far beyond the workplace, influencing mental health and overall well-being in profound ways.

The significance of effective leadership cannot be overstated. While landing a job at a renowned tech company may seem like the epitome of success, true career fulfillment hinges on two simple principles: working alongside supportive colleagues and engaging in work that genuinely resonates with one's passions.

Drawing from over five decades of senior management experience, including a tenure as CEO and a master's degree in health administration, I've witnessed firsthand the transformative power of leadership—both positive and negative. Leaders play a pivotal role in shaping the organizational culture, setting the tone for a supportive and enjoyable workplace environment.

In this class, we delve into what I term the Three Types of Leaders, exploring their distinct characteristics and the profound impact they wield on their companies. While countless leadership resources exist, this course offers a unique perspective honed through decades of practical experience and observation.

The allure of workshops and training sessions lies in their promise of quick fixes and easy solutions. They provide a structured environment for learning, offering participants the opportunity to glean wisdom from seasoned professionals and industry experts. Yet, despite their abundance, these resources often fall short in delivering lasting results. Why? Because being a CEO is not merely about acquiring knowledge—it's about embodying a unique set of qualities and values.

The truth is, no amount of theoretical learning can fully prepare someone for the realities of executive leadership. The role of a CEO demands more than just technical proficiency; it requires emotional intelligence, strategic vision, and the ability to inspire and motivate others. These are qualities that cannot be taught in a classroom or gleaned from a book—they are cultivated through experience, self-reflection, and a willingness to adapt and evolve.

Moreover, their one-size-fits-all approach often hinders the efficacy of traditional CEO training methods. Each organization, each industry, and each individual CEO faces unique challenges and opportunities. What works for one may not necessarily work for another. As such, it's essential to recognize the limitations of standardized training programs and instead focus on developing personalized strategies that align with individual strengths and organizational goals.

At its core, the journey to becoming a successful CEO is a deeply personal one. It's about understanding who you are as an individual, identifying your strengths and weaknesses, and leveraging them to drive meaningful change within your organization. While workshops and books can offer valuable insights and guidance along the way, they are but one piece of the puzzle.

Ultimately, the most effective CEOs are those who embrace lifelong learning and are willing to challenge themselves and their assumptions continuously. They understand that success is not a destination but a journey that requires dedication, resilience, and a relentless pursuit of excellence. And while there may be no universal blueprint for success, there is one undeniable truth: being a CEO is more about who you are than what you know.

This inner work is not easy; it demands courage, vulnerability, and a willingness to embrace discomfort. It requires individuals to confront their fears, insecurities, and past traumas and to cultivate a deeper understanding of themselves and their motivations. Only by shining a light on the shadows of their psyche can CEOs begin to break free from the chains that bind them and unlock their full potential as leaders.

Yet, despite its significance, this aspect of leadership development is often neglected in traditional training programs and research efforts. The focus tends to be on acquiring technical skills, mastering industry knowledge, and honing strategic acumen—all important aspects of leadership, no doubt, but incomplete without a thorough exploration of the psychosocial dimensions.

Without addressing these underlying psychological and emotional factors, CEOs risk being held back by their own limitations, unable to fully leverage their talents and capabilities. They may find themselves perpetually stuck in a cycle of frustration and stagnation, unable to overcome the barriers that impede their progress.

To truly excel as a CEO, one must be willing to do the inner work—to confront their inner demons, challenge their ingrained patterns of thinking and behavior, and cultivate the emotional resilience needed to navigate the complexities of leadership. This is the most important work of all, yet it is often the most overlooked.

In conclusion, addressing psychosocial issues is essential for the successful development of CEOs. It requires a willingness to engage in deep introspection and self-reflection to confront and dismantle the barriers that hinder personal and professional growth. Only by doing this inner work can CEOs unlock their full potential as leaders and inspire meaningful change within their organizations.

Addressing internal and external barriers is pivotal for personal growth and professional success, particularly for those aspiring to lead as CEOs. Often deeply ingrained and emotionally charged, these barriers present formidable obstacles that can impede progress and stifle potential. Yet, confronting them head-on is essential for unlocking one's true capabilities and achieving meaningful success.

Internal barriers are those entrenched beliefs, fears, and insecurities that hold individuals back from realizing their full potential. They lurk in the shadows of the mind, subtly undermining confidence and sabotaging efforts towards growth. These barriers may stem from past experiences, societal conditioning, or self-imposed limitations, but regardless of their origin, they wield considerable influence over behavior and decision-making.

On the other hand, external barriers are the tangible obstacles that stand in the way of progress—organizational hierarchies, industry norms, or societal expectations. These barriers can be equally daunting, imposing structural constraints that limit autonomy and innovation. Overcoming them requires resilience, strategic thinking, and a willingness to challenge the status quo.

Confronting these barriers requires courage and self-awareness. It demands a willingness to acknowledge and interrogate the beliefs and patterns that hold us back and cultivate a growth and possibility mindset. It means stepping out of our comfort zones, embracing discomfort, and embracing change.

Setting goals is a crucial aspect of this process. Goals provide a roadmap for progress, guiding individuals towards tangible milestones and measurable achievements. They serve as beacons of inspiration, motivating individuals to push past their limitations and strive for greatness. Whether it's breaking through a longstanding fear, challenging a deeply held belief, or navigating a complex organizational hierarchy, goals provide the clarity and focus needed to overcome obstacles and achieve success.

Yet, setting goals is only the first step. Achieving them requires dedication, persistence, and a willingness to adapt and evolve along the way. It means being willing to fail, learning from setbacks, and moving forward in the face of adversity.

Ultimately, the journey towards becoming a successful CEO is as much about personal growth as it is about professional achievement. It requires a willingness to confront the barriers—both internal and external—that stand in the way of success and to cultivate the resilience and determination needed to overcome them. By setting goals, embracing discomfort, and staying committed to their vision, aspiring CEOs can chart a course toward greatness and inspire others to do the same.

Understanding the different types of CEOs or leaders is crucial in navigating the complexities of leadership and fostering personal and organizational success. Over my five decades of experience in this field, I've come to recognize three distinct archetypes: the successful CEO, the non-effective CEO, and the destructive CEO. While these categories may not be extensively documented in professional literature, they are rooted in practical observation and personal insight.

My classification of leaders is distilled into three fundamental types:

1. Effective
2. Neutral
3. Destructive

Each archetype encapsulates distinct characteristics and behaviors that profoundly influence organizational dynamics and outcomes. Through an exploration of these categories, we gain valuable insights into the diverse ways leadership shapes the fabric of a company.
Throughout our sessions, we'll dissect each leadership type, examining its distinct traits and how individuals transition into these roles within the workplace. Engaging in breakout sessions, we'll tackle practical leadership challenges, where you'll apply your understanding to real-world scenarios. The group that delivers the most insightful responses will earn the prestigious Good Leadership Award trophy.

Moreover, our time together won't end with the sessions. We'll establish connections to facilitate ongoing communication and support, fostering an environment where we can share experiences and offer assistance in areas where leadership guidance is needed.

In this segment, I'll present examples drawn from my five decades of professional experience, illustrating the three types of leaders in action. While the scenarios are authentic, names have been anonymized to preserve confidentiality. Though a comprehensive exploration would require volumes, these examples offer a glimpse into the complexities associated with each leadership type.

The successful CEO is the epitome of effective leadership. They possess the vision, competence, and charisma to inspire greatness in others and drive positive change within their organizations. Through a combination of innate talent and deliberate self-improvement efforts, they consistently deliver results and earn the respect and admiration of their peers.

THE EFFECTIVE LEADER:

Mrs. Caldwell's journey as CEO of a major hospital exemplifies the transformative power of effective leadership. Upon assuming her role, she didn't just settle into her office; she embarked on a mission to understand her team and foster a culture of collaboration and accountability.

Rather than relying solely on formal meetings, Mrs. Caldwell prioritized personal connections. She invested time in "get to know each other" appointments with senior and frontline staff, demonstrating her commitment to understanding her team's character and allowing them to gauge her leadership style in return.

Recognizing the importance of transparency and shared vision, Mrs. Caldwell assembled a diverse team to assess the hospital's current state and chart a course for the future. This collaborative approach wasn't just a one-time event; regular check-ins via Zoom and in-person meetings ensured ongoing communication and alignment of efforts.

However, Mrs. Caldwell's commitment to accountability wasn't always easy. Some senior staff resigned when confronted with the straightforward expectations placed upon them. Yet, this unwavering dedication to excellence ensured that the hospital remained focused on its goals.

Crucially, Mrs. Caldwell didn't just lead from the top; she actively engaged with her team, fostering an environment where innovation and growth were encouraged. By regularly meeting with each senior staff member, she provided guidance, support, and mentorship, empowering them to develop both professionally and personally.

The impact of Mrs. Caldwell's leadership reverberated throughout the hospital, igniting a wave of positive energy and productivity. Today, the hospital stands as a testament to her vision and dedication, serving as a beacon of success in the region.

Conversely, the non-effective CEO falls short in their leadership endeavors. While they may not actively harm their organizations, they lack the vision, decisiveness, and strategic acumen needed to make a meaningful impact. Their leadership style is characterized by indecision, complacency, and a reluctance to embrace change, resulting in stagnation and missed opportunities for growth.

THE NEUTRAL LEADER:

Jamie Hunter's ascension to the role of CEO in 2013 marked a pivotal moment for the company, albeit one marked by a lack of extensive experience. Her selection stemmed from personal connections rather than a lengthy track record in leadership.

Upon assuming her position, Jamie recognized the need for support and turned to her COO, Ralph Morris, seeking his assistance in navigating the complexities of the company. While Ralph possessed commendable qualities as an employee, his leadership abilities and innovative thinking fell short of expectations.

Despite Jamie's intentions to steer the company in a new direction, her tenure was characterized by a sense of stagnation. Board members grew increasingly disillusioned as they observed a lack of meaningful progress or positive changes under her leadership. Evidently, the same goals and strategies from the previous administration persisted without adaptation or evolution.

Realizing the gravity of the situation, Jamie promised to enact changes to address the company's stagnation. However, these pledges remained unfulfilled, making the board skeptical of her ability to transform meaningfully.

As the company entered its third year under Jamie's leadership, it became apparent that decisive action was necessary. In a difficult decision, Jamie was relieved of her position as CEO, prompting the commencement of a new search for leadership capable of guiding the company toward a more promising future.

At the opposite end of the spectrum lies the destructive CEO. This type of leader fails to improve their organization and actively undermines its success through reckless decision-making, toxic behavior, and a disregard for ethical standards. Their leadership style is marked by egocentrism, impulsivity, and a propensity for creating chaos and dysfunction.

To transition from being an ineffective or destructive CEO to a successful one requires a concerted effort to address internal and external barriers. This involves engaging in workshops, training programs, and individual counseling to gain insights into one's strengths, weaknesses, and areas for growth. By shining a light on the murky depths of their psyche and confronting their inner demons, leaders can clear the metaphorical mirror and project a brighter, more impactful beam of light outward.

THE DESTRUCTIVE LEADER:

Mr. Fischer's tenure as CEO, beginning in 2015, paints a cautionary tale of the destructive impact of leadership gone awry. His initial decision to import his senior staff from a previous role set a troubling precedent, as they failed to integrate with the existing hospital culture.

Rather than fostering a climate of collaboration and trust, Mr. Fischer and his team propagated an atmosphere of fear and compliance. This toxic culture eroded morale among staff, who felt compelled to adhere to a rigid "do as I say" mentality rather than feeling empowered to contribute meaningfully.

The deterioration of organizational culture didn't go unnoticed. The board of directors grew increasingly concerned about the disconnect between the leadership and staff, as evidenced by canceled team meetings and declining levels of customer service reported by vendors.

As discontent simmered among long-time staff, the situation reached a breaking point. Resignations mounted, and labor relations became inundated with complaints of mistreatment and negativity propagated by Mr. Fischer and his cadre of senior staff.

Ultimately, the board of directors was forced to confront the reality of the situation. In a decisive move, they confronted Mr. Fischer with the damning evidence of his leadership failures. Faced with the prospect of resignation or termination, Mr. Fischer reluctantly stepped down, leaving behind a wake of damage that would take time and effort to repair.

The journey towards becoming a successful leader is not easy; it requires humility, self-awareness, and a willingness to embrace discomfort. It involves acknowledging past mistakes, learning from failures, and committing to ongoing personal and professional development. Only through this introspective journey can leaders unlock their full potential and inspire meaningful change within their organizations.

In conclusion, understanding the three types of CEOs or leaders—successful, non-effective, and destructive—is essential for aspiring leaders seeking to impact their organizations positively. By confronting internal and external barriers and cultivating self-awareness and resilience, leaders can transcend their limitations and lead with purpose, vision, and integrity.

Understanding the diverse spectrum of leadership styles is essential for fostering organizational growth and success. Alongside the successful, ineffective, and destructive leaders, there exists another archetype—the stagnant leader. This type of leader neither propels their organization forward nor actively impedes its progress. Instead, they remain mired in a state of personal stagnation, unable or unwilling to engage with the challenges and opportunities before them fully.

A lack of direction, motivation, and initiative characterizes stagnant leaders. They may possess the technical skills and knowledge required for their role but lack the vision and drive to inspire and empower their teams. While they may not actively harm their organization, their lack of leadership effectively results in a state of inertia, where progress is slow or non-existent.

Unlike the non-effective leader, who may exhibit similar traits but lack self-awareness or motivation to improve, stagnant leaders are often aware of their shortcomings. They may grapple with internal struggles or unresolved issues that hinder their ability to lead effectively. These leaders may be grappling with personal demons, navigating uncharted territory, or struggling to find their footing in a rapidly evolving landscape.

Stagnant leaders typically struggle to connect with others and foster meaningful relationships within their organizations. Their lack of engagement and enthusiasm can be contagious, resulting in low morale and diminished productivity among team members. Without a clear sense of purpose or direction, employees may feel adrift and unsure of how to contribute meaningfully to the organization's goals.

While stagnant leaders may not actively harm their organization in the same way as destructive leaders, their lack of leadership can still have significant consequences. Without strong direction and guidance from above, organizations may struggle to adapt to changing market conditions, innovate new products or services, or attract and retain top talent. In essence, the organization may find itself stuck in a state of limbo, unable to move forward or backward.

To overcome stagnation and become a successful leader, individuals must be willing to engage in introspection and self-reflection. They must confront their internal struggles and actively work to overcome them, whether through personal development initiatives, coaching, or therapy. Additionally, they must cultivate a sense of purpose and vision that inspires and motivates both themselves and those around them.

In conclusion, understanding the various types of leaders, including stagnant leaders, is essential for fostering a culture of growth and success within organizations. By recognizing the signs of stagnation and taking proactive steps to address them, individuals can unlock their full potential as leaders and drive meaningful change within their organizations.

Chapter 6: Unveiling the Crucial Insights: Transformative Lessons from Dr. Scot Conway

Allen Private's journey took an unexpected turn when he found himself at a seminar hosted by Dr. Scot Conway. Little did he know that this encounter would not only alter his perspective but also shed light on the critical factors that contributed to the downfall of his company. As Allen reflects on his experience listening to Conway, he unveils a profound realization – had he possessed Conway's insights earlier, his company might have thrived instead of faltering.

Conway's expertise lies in understanding the intricate dynamics of personalities within an organizational context. His program offers invaluable guidance on navigating the diverse array of personalities present in any workplace, a skill set that Allen now recognizes as indispensable for effective leadership and organizational success.

Listening to Conway's insights, Allen couldn't help but draw parallels to his own experiences. He vividly recalls moments when misunderstandings and conflicts arose due to a lack of awareness and appreciation for the unique personalities within his team. Had he been equipped with Conway's strategies for managing these differences, Allen believes that many of these challenges could have been preempted, ultimately steering his company towards a brighter future.

Although Allen acknowledges that hindsight is 20/20, he remains determined to share the wisdom gleaned from Conway's program with others. By distilling key lessons and insights, Allen aims to illuminate the path for fellow entrepreneurs and leaders, empowering them to navigate the complexities of human behavior with confidence and insight.

One of the fundamental principles highlighted by Conway is the importance of recognizing and leveraging the strengths inherent in different personality types. Rather than viewing diversity as a source of conflict, Conway advocates for embracing it as a catalyst for innovation and growth. Through practical strategies and real-world examples, Conway demonstrates how leaders can harness the collective potential of their team, fostering a culture of collaboration and mutual respect.

Furthermore, Conway emphasizes the role of effective communication in bridging the gap between disparate personalities. By honing active listening skills and fostering open dialogue, leaders can cultivate an environment where every voice is valued and heard. Allen recognizes the impact that improved communication could have had on his own company, where misunderstandings often led to inefficiencies and discord.

As Allen continues to reflect on the profound impact of Conway's program, he is filled with a sense of determination and optimism. While he may not be able to rewrite the past, Allen is committed to embracing the lessons learned and applying them to his future endeavors. Through sharing Conway's insights with others, Allen hopes to catalyze positive change within the business community, empowering leaders to unlock the full potential of their organizations.

In conclusion, Allen Private's journey serves as a testament to the transformative power of knowledge. By embracing the insights of thought leaders like Dr. Scot Conway, individuals and organizations alike can overcome obstacles, foster collaboration, and chart a course towards enduring success.

Title: Embracing the OHANA Philosophy: A Blueprint for Organizational Excellence

In the bustling realm of business, success often hinges not just on profits and productivity, but on the intangible bonds that unite individuals within an organization. At the heart of this ethos lies OHANA – a concept that transcends mere affiliation, encapsulating the profound interconnectedness and shared purpose that define a cohesive community.

OHANA, derived from the Hawaiian word for family, serves as a guiding light for organizations seeking to foster a culture of camaraderie, collaboration, and compassion.

Allen realized how often he treated his employees like cogs in his machine. Customers were wallets waiting to be opened. Conway said "Business may be business, but business people are still people; Treat them like people."

Allen realized how much he hated being treated like a machine. Angry customers seemed to say anything they wanted to try to get their way, and Allen didn't like it when they did that. Of course, as the owner, he was called in for the worst of them. Employees often treated him like a wallet waiting to be opened and didn't seem to care at all.

But that was all fair. He realized he didn't treat them like people. Of course they did the same in return. He didn't like it, but he could hardly expect better from others than he was delivering himself. Already the gears were turning in his head.

That "family" idea, though. He was always told to NEVER treat people as "family." They'll take advantage of you. If Conway was right, though, there was a way to make that all work. There was a way everyone would be fair with everyone else. But how could this work?

While OHANA technically stands for Oasis, Harmony, Assertiveness, Nobility, and Aloha, its significance extends far beyond the sum of its parts. Let us delve into each element of the OHANA philosophy, unveiling the profound principles that underpin its ethos:

O - Oasis: Be a Refreshing Refuge

In the midst of life's chaos and challenges, the OHANA Oasis serves as a sanctuary of solace and support. It embodies the commitment to create a nurturing environment where individuals can thrive, free from the burdens of the mundane and the pressures of the outside world. By fostering a culture of empathy and understanding, organizations can transform their workplaces into havens of inspiration and rejuvenation.

H - Harmony: Embrace Infinite Diversity in Infinite Combinations

True harmony arises from the symphony of diverse voices, each contributing its unique melody to the collective chorus. The OHANA Harmony celebrates this diversity, recognizing that greatness emerges not from uniformity, but from the fusion of disparate perspectives and experiences. By embracing inclusivity and valuing the richness of human variation, organizations can unlock boundless creativity and innovation.

A - Assertiveness: Moving Forward on Purpose with Respect for Others

Assertiveness lies at the core of the OHANA ethos, guiding individuals to navigate life with intentionality and integrity. It entails the courage to pursue one's goals with clarity and conviction, while also honoring the dignity and autonomy of others. By fostering assertive communication and decision-making, organizations empower their members to realize their full potential and contribute meaningfully to collective success.

N - Nobility: Be Our Highest and Best Selves

Nobility transcends mere material wealth or status, encompassing the pursuit of excellence and virtue in all endeavors. The OHANA Nobility beckons individuals to embody the qualities of honor, integrity, and service, striving to elevate themselves and others to loftier heights of achievement. By embracing the ideals of chivalry and righteousness, organizations cultivate a culture of ethical leadership and noble conduct.

A - Aloha: Love in All Its Many Meanings and Manifestations

At the heart of the OHANA philosophy lies the spirit of Aloha – a profound expression of love, compassion, and goodwill towards others. Beyond mere sentimentality, Aloha embodies a deep-seated desire for the well-being and happiness of all beings, transcending barriers of culture, creed, and circumstance. By infusing every interaction with the warmth and generosity of Aloha, organizations foster a sense of belonging and connectedness that transcends boundaries.

In essence, OHANA represents more than just an acronym – it embodies a way of being, a philosophy of interconnectedness and mutual respect that transcends the confines of the workplace. By embracing the principles of Oasis, Harmony, Assertiveness, Nobility, and Aloha, organizations can cultivate a culture of excellence, resilience, and compassion, paving the way for enduring success and fulfillment for all.

All that sounded good. It seemed like something someone could choose to do... but how did you get it?

"I understand you're upset, and I'm happy to listen. I try to practice something called Ohana, and that includes being an Oasis. That means I want to be a safe person for you to talk to. If you'd care to join me in trying to do that, we can focus on the problem and figure out how to get you what you want."

Would that actually work? Allen's mind jumped immediately to a few people he was sure it would definitely not work with. But what if it worked even half the time? That would be better. Just as he had the "better" thought, Conway said something important.

"Better is good. Better is winning. I like winning."

Hmmm... "better is winning." Yes, Allen though, it would definitely be better. Better did could pretty good. He was thinking about the "better" idea and nearly missed the next part.

Unveiling the Power of Ohana: Exploring the Ohana Five By Five

Ohana, meaning family, encompasses a set of ideals that extend far beyond mere kinship. Within the framework of Ohana, we find five core principles: Oasis, Harmony, Assertiveness, Nobility, and Aloha. These pillars serve as the foundation upon which we build strong, positive relationships and foster a culture of excellence. Delving deeper into each ideal, we uncover a wealth of insights and practices that enrich our lives and interactions.

Oasis - Creating a Refreshing Refuge: An Oasis represents a sanctuary amidst life's challenges. Within this sanctuary, we strive to make every interaction better by our presence. It's about offering solace and respite from the mundane and the chaotic. By embodying the spirit of Oasis, we become beacons of calm and positivity in the lives of others.

Harmony - Embracing Diversity for Greatness: Harmony celebrates the beauty of diversity and the power of collaboration. Just as a symphony orchestra blends various instruments and melodies to create exquisite music, so too do we embrace the infinite combinations of personalities and perspectives. In fostering harmony, we recognize that unity does not require uniformity but rather a mutual respect for differences.

Assertiveness - Moving Forward with Purpose and Respect: Assertiveness empowers us to navigate life with intention and integrity. It's about confidently expressing our needs and boundaries while respecting those of others. Whether in personal relationships or professional settings, assertiveness enables us to move forward purposefully, guided by a profound respect for ourselves and others.

Nobility - Striving for Our Highest Selves: Nobility beckons us to aspire to our highest and best selves. Drawing inspiration from the ideals of chivalry and honor, we embody virtues such as courage, integrity, and compassion. By cultivating nobility within ourselves, we elevate not only our own lives but also the lives of those around us.

Aloha - Love in All Its Manifestations: Aloha encapsulates the boundless spirit of love and compassion. It's about wanting the best for others, striving to be our best selves, and sharing in the joy of transcendental love. Whether expressed through greetings, farewells, or acts of kindness, Aloha permeates every interaction with warmth and sincerity.

Building upon these foundational principles, we unveil the Ohana Five By Five – a comprehensive framework consisting of twenty-five precise expressions of Ohana. This intricate tapestry of ideas is designed to be easily read, clearly understood, and immensely impactful when applied.

However, implementing the Ohana Five By Five is not an

instantaneous process. It requires intentional effort and gradual progression. Just as one would build a structure brick by brick, so too must we cultivate the Ohana ideals incrementally, starting with the basics and gradually incorporating additional elements.

To apply the Ohana Five By Five in real life, one must approach it with deliberation and mindfulness. Begin by familiarizing yourself with each concept and identify which ideas resonate most deeply with your current circumstances. Then, commit to implementing those ideas into your daily interactions and endeavors.

In essence, the Ohana Five By Five serves as a blueprint for building strong, nurturing relationships and fostering a culture of excellence and compassion. By embracing these ideals and putting them into practice, we pave the way for a future defined by unity, harmony, and boundless love.

Allen realized there was a lot here. His first idea was that he would just take this into his life and start doing it all immediately. Instead, he realized what Conway was talking about: Start small, add one thing at a time.

Sure, some of the stuff he already did. Allen checked off the things he thought he was doing okay. Could it be improved? Of course. It would do for now. He would make it better later. He saw that he had other things that would need work.

He wrote his notes quickly. Allen knew that on many of these, he'd need to give it more thoughts to come up with an idea or two about how to do it better. He'd start with these notes.

Unveiling the Power of Ohana: The Ohana Five By Five

In the intricate tapestry of human relationships, the concept of Ohana transcends mere familiarity; it embodies the essence of familial bonds, unity, and unconditional support. As we delve into the Ohana Five By Five, we embark on a journey to explore the nuanced expressions of this profound ideal, each encapsulating a pillar of strength and wisdom essential for building thriving relationships and fostering personal growth.

OASIS: Be a Refreshing Refuge At the heart of Ohana lies the notion of creating a sanctuary, a safe haven where individuals can find solace and renewal. The Ohana Five By Five for Oasis illuminates this principle, offering practical insights into cultivating an environment of warmth and hospitality:

Leave No Trace; Better Than You Found It: Strive to leave every interaction, every space, and every relationship better than you found it. Leave a positive imprint wherever you go.

Be a Safe Person; Create a Safe Place: Foster an atmosphere of trust and security where individuals feel comfortable expressing themselves authentically without fear of judgment or ridicule.

Give to Givers Who Give: Recognize and reciprocate the generosity of those who give freely of themselves, nurturing a culture of gratitude and abundance.

Win/Win or No Deal: Seek mutually beneficial solutions in all endeavors, refusing to compromise integrity or values for short-term gains.

Resolve (My, Your, Our), Concede (Trade Wins), Compromise: Approach conflicts with humility and a willingness to find common ground, prioritizing harmony and cooperation over ego-driven agendas.

HARMONY: Embrace Infinite Diversity in Infinite Combinations Aimed at Greatness Harmony arises from the acceptance and celebration of diversity, recognizing that strength lies in embracing the unique contributions of each individual. The Ohana Five By Five for Harmony advocates for inclusivity and collaboration:

Just Be Polite: Cultivate a culture of courtesy and respect, valuing the perspectives and experiences of others.

More For, Less Against. Focus on What You Do Want: Direct energy towards constructive dialogue and solution-oriented thinking, rather than dwelling on grievances or differences.

Facet Truths: Bring Truth Appropriate to the Relationship: Practice honesty tempered with empathy, tailoring communication to suit the needs and sensitivities of each relationship.

Differences are Issues to Navigate, Not Causes for Condemnation: Embrace diversity as an opportunity for growth and learning, reframing differences as catalysts for innovation.

Bad Things are Problems to Solve, Not Causes for Condemnation: Approach challenges with a mindset of resilience and problem-solving, viewing setbacks as temporary obstacles on the path to success.

ASSERTIVENESS: Moving Forward on Purpose with Respect for Others Assertiveness entails the courage to pursue one's goals while honoring the autonomy and dignity of others. The Ohana Five By Five for Assertiveness advocates for clear communication and principled action:

I Have a Point; You May Also Have a Point: Acknowledge the validity of differing perspectives, fostering constructive dialogue and mutual understanding.

More Yes/And, Less No/But: Cultivate a mindset of collaboration and creativity, seeking opportunities for synergy and collective achievement.

Define Your Win: Values, Goals, and Roles: Clarify personal and collective objectives, aligning actions with overarching values and aspirations.

Compelling Future: Choose. Plan. Check In: Set ambitious yet achievable goals, charting a course for progress and growth while remaining adaptable to changing circumstances.

Ecology Check: Consider the broader impact of actions and decisions on oneself, others, and the environment, striving for balance and sustainability in all endeavors.

NOBILITY: Royal Knight: Be our highest and best selves Nobility calls upon individuals to embody virtues of integrity, compassion, and honor, aspiring to exemplify the noblest qualities of humanity. The Ohana Five By Five for Nobility promotes ethical leadership and personal excellence:

Language Of Emotions: Cultivate emotional intelligence and empathy, fostering deeper connections and understanding with others.

Be a Light, Not a Judge: Lead by example, inspiring others through deeds of kindness, generosity, and moral courage.

Self-Leadership: Take ownership of one's thoughts, emotions, and actions, exercising self-discipline and self-awareness in pursuit of personal growth.

360 Degree Leadership: 4P360: Lead from all directions, empowering and supporting others to reach their full potential.

Living By a Code: Adhere to a set of guiding principles and values, anchoring decisions and behaviors in integrity and moral fortitude.

ALOHA: Love At the core of Ohana lies love in its myriad forms – love that uplifts, nurtures, and transcends boundaries. The Ohana Five By Five for Aloha celebrates the transformative power of love:

Love Stack: Agape, Phileo, Eros: Embrace love in its various dimensions, from selfless compassion to passionate devotion, fostering deeper connections and intimacy.

Love Is & Love Is Not: A Self-Check: Reflect on the true essence of love, distinguishing between genuine affection and mere sentimentality.

Phileo Bank Account: Positive On Purpose: Invest in relationships with care and intentionality, depositing acts of kindness and support to cultivate enduring bonds.

Love, Joy, Peace; God, People, Self: Cultivate a spirit of love, joy, and peace in all interactions, radiating positivity and goodwill towards oneself and others.

100 Ways to Win: YORI: Explore diverse expressions of love, finding joy and fulfillment in acts of service, affirmation, and companionship.

In summary, the Ohana Five By Five serves as a blueprint for cultivating meaningful relationships, fostering personal growth, and creating a culture of positivity and abundance. By embracing the principles of Oasis, Harmony, Assertiveness, Nobility, and Aloha, individuals can navigate the complexities of human interaction with grace, compassion, and integrity. As we apply these principles in our daily lives, let us remember that change is a journey, not a destination – start small, be intentional, and let the ripple effects of Ohana transform our world one interaction at a time.

HERO, VILLAIN, AND VICTIM: Understanding Ohana 101

In the intricate dynamics of human relationships, the roles of Hero, Villain, and Victim often play a defining role in shaping our interactions and outcomes. This simple yet profound model, known as Ohana 101, provides a framework for understanding how individuals can navigate challenges and conflicts with grace and wisdom.

Hero – One who makes it better. The Hero embodies the essence of positive change and improvement. They are proactive in seeking solutions and creating a better environment for themselves and others.

Villain – One who makes it worse. The Villain represents behaviors or actions that contribute to negative outcomes or conflicts. It's important to note that the Villain is not necessarily a person but can also be a problem or challenge that needs to be addressed.

Victim – One for whom it is made worse. The Victim is the one who experiences the negative impact of a situation or behavior. They are often in a vulnerable position and may need support or assistance to overcome the challenges they face.

GUARANTEED LACK OF PERFECTION

Central to the understanding of Ohana 101 is the recognition of our inherent imperfections as human beings. No one is perfect, and we are all prone to making mistakes or facing challenges. This Guaranteed Lack of Perfection underscores the importance of compassion, understanding, and forgiveness in our interactions with others.

Handling People Problems When faced with People Problems, individuals often respond in two common ways:

Avoidance: Some may choose to avoid addressing the issue, either out of fear of confrontation or a belief that the problem will resolve itself. This passive approach can lead to unresolved conflicts and ongoing challenges.

Confrontation: Others may confront the issue head-on, but in a harsh or accusatory manner. This approach can escalate tensions and lead to further misunderstandings.

The Hero Frame The key to effective conflict resolution lies in adopting the Hero Frame. Rather than viewing others as Villains or Victims, we should see them as potential Heroes – individuals who can contribute positively to resolving the problem.

Recruiting Heroes In the Hero Frame, the focus shifts from assigning blame to recruiting allies. By externalizing the problem as the Villain, individuals can work together as a team of Heroes to address the issue constructively.

Avoiding Loss A critical aspect of the Hero Frame is to avoid arguing for a premise where winning means losing what truly matters. Instead of labeling others as Villains, focus on their behavior and the desired outcome. This approach helps prevent unnecessary conflict and fosters a more collaborative environment.

Building Ohana In essence, Ohana 101 teaches us to be

compassionate, understanding, and proactive in our interactions with others. By embracing the roles of Hero and recruiting others to join us, we can create a supportive and empowering environment where everyone has the opportunity to thrive.

In conclusion, Ohana 101 serves as a guiding principle for building positive relationships and resolving conflicts with grace and empathy. By embracing the Hero Frame and recruiting others to join us, we can create a culture of support, understanding, and growth – a true embodiment of Ohana.

Allen saw that he had a lot of work to do. If he just worked on one part of this each week, it would take most of a year. Reflecting back on everything that didn't improve and the handful of things that went backwards in this last year, being this much better one year from now was exciting!

Ohana.

What a great concept!

Chapter 7: The Seven Principles of Building a Strong Management Team and Demonstrating Leadership Skills

In Allan Private's journey toward success, he realized that realizing the full potential of his company hinged on having a strong management team in place—both at the middle and senior levels. You probably already know that true success requires more than just having good managers; it's about transforming how your company operates from within. Allan identified seven key principles that easily build a robust management team while naturally demonstrating leadership that others follow. These principles are designed to expand beyond the usual methods, tapping into a deeper level of engagement and purpose within every team member.

Principle 1: Teach Your Team Something of Value and Instill a Sense of Purpose

Allan discovered that one of the most powerful ways to build a strong management team is by ensuring that every team member understands the value behind the company's mission. It wasn't enough to tell them what to do—they needed to know why it mattered. Maybe you haven't yet realized how much people are driven by purpose, but Allan found that when employees see how their personal values align with the company's mission, they experience a sense of belonging that ignites their commitment.

I'm curious—can you imagine what would happen if your team's personal values aligned perfectly with the goals of the organization? Allan saw it firsthand when employees felt that connection between their values and the company's mission; they became more motivated, engaged, and dedicated to contributing to the company's overall success.

Allan implemented a series of workshops designed to help employees identify their personal values to create this alignment. These workshops helped everyone understand how their individual values could seamlessly integrate with the company's mission. Naturally, when people saw how their personal goals aligned with the larger company's purpose, they became aware of their deeper role within the organization. After all, when values are aligned, employees feel connected, purposeful, and eager to contribute.

Transformational Moment: When Values Align with Mission

You probably already know that a disconnect between employees and the company mission can stifle progress. But here's what happened when Allan addressed that gap. One day, during a workshop, a team member who had struggled to fully grasp the company's mission had a breakthrough. Three of her top five personal values aligned perfectly with the company's mission! I wonder if you can imagine the shift that occurred when she realized this. It was as if the pieces of a puzzle suddenly fell into place.

After that eye-opening moment, Allan held a company-wide workshop where employees could discover their top ten personal values. The result? The team felt a deeper connection to the company's purpose, unlocking a newfound sense of unity and motivation. Now, the team moved forward with greater clarity and focus, naturally working together toward a shared goal. It was a complete game-changer for their dynamics and productivity.

By implementing this principle, Allan created a foundation where each management team member understood their role and felt empowered to lead with purpose. Maybe you will notice the same shift in your organization when personal and organizational values align—because when people are connected to the "why," they are unstoppable. Can you imagine the exponential growth that comes from a team working in harmony toward a shared vision?

With this first principle firmly in place, Allan was ready to expand beyond basic leadership techniques and implement the next steps to build a management team that would lead and inspire.

Principle 2: Find One Activity to Do with Your Team

In the not-so-distant future, Allan Private began noticing a troubling pattern within his company. His employees weren't interacting or building rapport effectively. The atmosphere felt tense, with conversations often escalating into yelling matches and very little active listening. Allan realized that this hostile environment was naturally eroding team cohesion, and as a result, productivity was suffering.

I'm wondering if you've ever experienced a similar situation in your team where the lack of connection holds everyone back. Maybe you haven't yet considered how much rapport matters, but after hearing this, you'll see its unlimited potential to transform your team.

A mentor explained to Allan that fear might temporarily push a team to perform, but it's not sustainable. The most successful companies, you probably already know, are built on strong, positive interactions. Allan became aware that if he could foster a sense of genuine teamwork, his company's productivity could easily increase by over 70%.

Can you imagine the power of that shift?

The solution was simple: Allan needed to find one activity to share with his team. Something fun, something that brought people together. Something that would build rapport and trust. Naturally, these shared experiences would break down barriers and expand beyond workplace formality, creating a stronger bond.

I'm curious: could you find one activity to share with your team? It could be something simple yet meaningful, designed to build stronger relationships. Allan tried different activities and saw firsthand the magic of connection unfold:

- Playing Golf: A round of golf provided a relaxed, open setting for conversation. Maybe you will find that out on the golf course; people open up in ways they don't in the office.
- Attending a Sporting Event: Sharing the thrill of a live game created lasting memories and camaraderie among his team.

You probably already know how energizing and unifying the excitement of sports can be.
- Creating a Book Club: Discussing books opened up deeper conversations. Through this, Allan's team discovered new perspectives and built emotional connections.
- Going to Church Together: For those who shared similar faiths, attending a service together strengthened their bond through shared values and beliefs.

After engaging in these activities, Allan soon realized that his team's productivity began to soar. The personal connections they built with each other naturally translated into mutual trust and respect, fostering a harmonious and highly effective environment. Maybe you haven't tried this with your team, but imagine the impact of finding that special activity that resonates with everyone.

By integrating such activities into his routine, Allan demonstrated genuine care for his team members, showing them that he valued their work and who they were as individuals. This small shift in approach created a foundation of rapport and teamwork that drove the company's success to new heights.

Building a Family, Not Just a Team: Allan's Secret to Success

Allan Private knew that connection was key. So, he began a monthly tradition—bowling sessions with his staff. It was a stroke of genius. As the team laced up their shoes and let the pins fly, Allan watched as:

- Competitive spirits ignited
- Leadership skills naturally shone
- Laughter and camaraderie flowed as freely as the food

But the most powerful change? They stopped being just colleagues. They became a family. A family that respected, supported, and genuinely cared for one another. Allan created an authentic, inclusive, and driven workplace culture by investing in his team's personal connections. His team's newfound bond naturally led to higher collaboration, trust, and productivity.

Now, perhaps you're realizing that by finding just one activity to do with your team, you can create that same environment—one where your team doesn't just work together but thrives together. When you stop viewing your team as just employees and start building a family, success follows easily.

Principle 3: Do Something with Your Managers, Nothing Materialistic

Once at the helm of a Fortune 100 company, Allan Private believed he was delivering outstanding service to his employees. Yet, over time, he realized he had barely understood the six fundamental needs that drive people. Maybe you already know that feeling—where something seems off, but you can't quite put your finger on it. Allan reflected on his leadership, admitting, "Back then, it was all about me. If they didn't like it, they could leave."

This moment of awareness was Allan's turning point. He understood that connecting with employees on a deeper level requires more than transactional interactions. Can you imagine what happens when you tap into your employees' core needs? Allan discovered that he had to expand beyond material incentives to foster meaningful relationships and create a thriving company culture.

Now, you might be wondering, I know you like me, how do you do that? Allan found the key: focus on nothing materialistic—instead, connect through shared experiences, addressing the six core human needs: security, variety, connection, significance, contribution, and growth. You probably already know how powerful it is when people feel understood at their core.

Allan realized that after identifying the top two needs of each employee, he could tailor his interactions to foster genuine connections. By naturally understanding these needs, he created stronger bonds with his team.

Creative Connections That Go Beyond the Material

During a Palm Desert, CA seminar, Allan emphasized the importance of managers creating connections with their teams that expand beyond material rewards. One of the biggest shifts he saw was when managers started getting creative with building rapport—through shared experiences and activities that brought the team closer together. I'm curious if you've ever considered how simple actions could profoundly impact your team.

For example, some managers shared their success stories:

- One manager connected with her team by listening to house music together. Music became a shared language, creating a rhythm that easily built rapport.
- Another manager and their team hit the gym regularly, blending fitness with casual conversation—a perfect setting for open dialogue.
- Yet another manager joined a dance class with her employees, tapping into a fun, engaging way to bond.

Can you imagine how simple, non-material activities like these naturally create a connection? These small, personal experiences transform relationships, fostering deeper trust and respect.

Creative Ways to Connect with Your Team

Allan believed that after realizing the power of personal connection, you no longer need to rely on bonuses or material rewards to engage your employees. In fact, it's the non-materialistic interactions that create lasting bonds. Maybe you haven't tried these strategies, but they easily bring out the best in your team. Here are some creative, cost-effective ways to build rapport:

1. Host Weekly Brainstorming Sessions: Encourage open dialogue where ideas flow naturally.
2. Organize Group Walks or Jogging Sessions: Blend health and casual conversation into team-building.
3. Create a Book Club: Engage minds and discover new perspectives through shared reading.

4. Arrange Potluck Lunches: Share homemade meals, creating a relaxed and warm environment.
5. Implement Peer Recognition Programs: Let employees recognize each other's efforts in real time.
6. Conduct Informal Coffee Chats: No agenda—just genuine conversations.
7. Facilitate Hobby Groups: Whether gardening, photography, or crafts, common interests create strong bonds.
8. Volunteer Together: Join forces in giving back to the community, fostering a sense of purpose.
9. Set Up a Mentorship Program: Create opportunities for learning and growth by pairing employees.
10. Celebrate Personal Milestones: Acknowledge birthdays, anniversaries, and life's special moments.

I'm wondering if you're beginning to notice how easily these activities can transform the workplace into something more. In this community, employees feel valued for who they are, not just what they do. When managers naturally take an interest in their employees' personal lives, it creates a culture where people feel appreciated and connected, leading to higher morale and performance.

Building a Positive Culture, Not Just a Workforce

Allan learned you must foster real connections to build a successful management team. It's not about rewards or incentives; it's about shared experiences that naturally bring people together. Through simple activities, managers can create a foundation of trust, respect, and camaraderie that drives the team forward.

Now, maybe you're realizing that by engaging in these activities, you're not just fostering connections—you're helping your team tap into their "seed of greatness," unlocking their full potential. When people feel truly connected, success becomes unlimited.

Principle 4: Give Your Employees What They Desire

Allan Private naturally realized that the key to a thriving company isn't just in what he wanted but in understanding and fulfilling the true desires of his employees. Have you ever noticed how powerful it can be when you align your team's personal goals with the company's growth? You probably already know that when employees feel supported in achieving their aspirations, their passion and dedication increase, leading to unlimited success.

Allan discovered that by focusing on what his team members truly wanted—what they naturally desired—he could train and develop them more effectively. Maybe you haven't considered how much impact you could have by doing the same. When employees see that their personal goals align with the company's mission, they become aware of their role in driving their success and the company's. Understanding Employee Desires

To truly support your employees, you must ask the right questions and naturally listen to their answers. This is where individualized action plans come into play—tailoring the company's development strategy to meet organizational and personal goals.

Here's how Allan approached it:

- Conduct Individual Consultations: Allan held one-on-one meetings with his employees to discuss their career goals and personal aspirations. I wonder if you've ever noticed the power of these conversations—when employees feel heard, they become more engaged.
- Survey for Feedback: Allan also used anonymous surveys to gather collective insights. This helped him easily understand the desires and aspirations his team might not feel comfortable sharing face-to-face.
- Create Personalized Development Plans: Maybe you will see how crucial this step is. Based on the feedback, Allan developed individualized action plans that outlined clear steps for each employee to achieve their goals within the company. After all, when people feel their growth is part of the plan, they invest more of themselves into the work.

Creating an In-House University

To expand beyond traditional training methods, Allan introduced a groundbreaking concept to nurture his team's talent—an in-house university. Can you imagine what it would be like to offer your employees continuous learning opportunities that align perfectly with their goals and the company's objectives?

Here's how Allan did it:

- Leverage Internal Expertise: Allan tapped into the experience of senior managers and professionals within the company, turning them into instructors and mentors. You probably already know how much value this brings—real-world, practical knowledge passed on within the company.
- Develop a Structured Curriculum: Allan's curriculum wasn't just about technical skills. It included leadership training, personal growth, and areas of development that employees themselves desired. This made the learning process align with personal and company growth.
- Utilize Online Learning Platforms: Allan implemented online courses and workshops using platforms like Coursera and custom learning systems for added flexibility. Employees could easily access these resources, further empowering them to take control of their development.
- Regular Assessments and Feedback: I'm curious: do you have a system in place that regularly tracks progress? Allan conducted frequent assessments and provided feedback to ensure the training remained relevant and impactful, keeping the momentum going.

Fostering Passion and Excitement

When employees feel that their personal goals are being supported, their enthusiasm for the company's mission grows naturally. They become more passionate and excited about their work because they see a clear connection between their personal development and the company's success.

- Empowerment Through Learning: Allan's employees felt empowered and valued by offering these opportunities. This easily translated into higher motivation and job satisfaction. I'm wondering if you can imagine the transformation when your employees feel truly invested.
- Recognition and Rewards: Acknowledging achievements was critical. Allan celebrated milestones and recognized efforts publicly, reinforcing the importance of their growth. After all, when employees feel their progress matters, they push harder toward the next milestone.
- Enhanced Job Satisfaction: Allan's approach created a culture where employees were more satisfied with their roles, resulting in reduced turnover and increased loyalty. Maybe you haven't yet experienced this level of engagement in your team, but once you do, you'll wonder why you didn't start sooner.

Practical Steps to Implement

You probably already know how important it is to act on these insights. Here's what Allan suggests:

1. Ask and Listen: Regularly check in with employees through surveys, meetings, and informal conversations to understand their desires. Now, you might notice how much employees appreciate being asked about their aspirations.
2. Plan and Act: Develop a detailed action plan based on the feedback, outlining how you will support each employee's goals. Maybe you will find that the more aligned your plan is with their goals, the more successful your team becomes.
3. Build and Sustain: Establish your in-house university with a robust curriculum, leveraging internal and external resources. This will help you expand beyond basic training and foster continuous growth.
4. Evaluate and Improve: Continuously assess the effectiveness of your programs and make necessary adjustments to keep them relevant and impactful.

A Transformative Moment: Allan Private's Journey to Building a High-Performing Team

Allan vividly recalls when his mentor, Dr. John Oda, shared a transformative story about a company that created an in-house university. The twist? They hired only from within, rewarding dedication and hard work. This concept deeply resonated with Allan, inspiring him to implement the same model in his company.

Allan introduced training programs focused on leadership, management, and personal growth. Naturally, the results were profound. His employees realized that with effort, they could achieve unlimited success. The company's culture shifted toward growth, internal promotion, and shared ambition. His team became a high-performing, cohesive unit driven by a clear sense of purpose.

Now, maybe you're realizing that by giving your employees what they desire, you create a culture that thrives—where growth is a shared experience, and success is easily within reach for everyone. Because when personal and organizational goals align, there are no limits to what can be achieved.

Principle 5: Engage Your Employees in Conversation

Allan Private discovered that one of the greatest downfalls in his business was failing to engage in meaningful conversations with his key people. He realized that maybe you haven't noticed how easily communication can be overlooked, especially when focused on achieving results. Allan once relied on shortcuts, thinking they would drive success. However, he soon became aware he was missing a crucial element in fostering team growth and connection by skipping genuine engagement. I'm curious: have you ever experienced this in your leadership journey?

Allan knew he needed to change. He started by implementing weekly check-ins to see how his employees were doing and identify areas for improvement. You probably already know that regular engagement creates a culture of trust and openness. Allan encouraged his team to adopt the CANI—Constant and Never-Ending Improvement principle. By aiming for just a 1% improvement daily in every area, his team began to naturally grow and adapt, creating a more flexible and resilient work environment.

Can you imagine the impact of making this shift with your team? Maybe you will find that when you start having these conversations, the entire energy of your workplace transforms.

Starting the Conversation

To easily engage your employees in meaningful conversation, asking the right questions is essential. After all, when you dig a little deeper, you unlock opportunities for growth and connection. Here are a few key questions Allan used to begin these conversations:

- How are you feeling today?
  If your employee says "okay," don't stop there. I'm wondering if you've ever noticed how often people give surface answers. Ask them what needs to happen for them to feel even better. This opens the door to discovering their true state of mind, what's going on in their job, and what challenges they might face. You probably already know that coaching them through these challenges strengthens your relationship and helps them thrive.

- What's going on at work?
  Understanding the work environment is crucial. Who are they spending their time with? Who is influencing their decisions or performance? Maybe you haven't considered how much the people around your employees shape their mindset and outcomes. This question reveals dynamics that might need your attention, especially if outside influences, like friends or family, steer them in the wrong direction.

- What are your hobbies?
  Learn what they love outside of work. Whether it's sports, music, or another passion, knowing their interests helps you connect personally. I'm curious: have you ever noticed how these personal insights open doors for bonding? They can also create meaningful opportunities to spend time together or give you topics to discuss and build rapport.

- How are you getting along with everyone, and who is causing you problems?
  This question helps you address potential conflicts early. By asking open-ended questions, you give your employees space to share any issues or tensions they might be experiencing. Naturally, this allows you to offer support and solutions before problems escalate.

The Art of Engagement

When you engage in these conversations, give your employees your full attention. You probably already know how powerful it is when someone feels truly heard. That means no distractions—no phones, no computers, no television. Make eye contact and practice active listening, showing you genuinely value their input. Maybe you will find that by focusing on connecting rather than lecturing, the conversations will flow more easily, building stronger trust.
Use open-ended questions to keep the dialogue going. This creates space for deeper insights and makes your employees feel valued. I know you, like me, understand the importance of going beyond surface-level chats and getting to the heart of what matters to your team members.

Practical Tips for Engagement

Here are a few practical tips to help you build the habit of meaningful conversations with your team:

- Role-Playing: Practice these conversational tools with role-playing exercises. This makes managers more comfortable asking open-ended questions and actively listening. After all,

the more you practice, the easier it becomes to engage your employees in deeper dialogue.
- Make It Fun: Turn these engagements into a game. I wonder if you've noticed how lighthearted approaches can easily make serious topics less intimidating. Keeping the atmosphere fun helps everyone feel more relaxed and open to conversation.
- Consistency: Regularly schedule these conversations to build a habit of open communication and trust. Maybe you haven't yet built this routine, but after you do, you'll see how consistency strengthens bonds over time.

Benefits of Meaningful Conversations

Engaging your employees in real conversations fosters a sense of belonging, support, and trust. It shows them that you care not only about their work but also their well-being and professional growth. This approach allows you to identify and resolve potential issues early while also boosting morale and productivity. Can you imagine the impact of creating a culture where every employee feels heard and valued?

Allan Private's shift to regular, meaningful conversations led to a stronger, more connected workplace. His team felt supported, understood, and motivated to improve each day. By embracing this principle and engaging in genuine conversations with your employees, you can naturally build a foundation of trust, support, and success. Because when people feel heard, they invest more of themselves in their work, and that's when unlimited growth happens.

Principle 6: Tell Your Employees You Are Proud of Them and Respect What They Do

Allan Private came to a powerful realization: showing genuine pride and respect for his employees' work could easily boost morale, performance, and job satisfaction. I'm curious: have you noticed how a simple acknowledgment can transform an employee's mindset? Maybe you haven't fully embraced how far a little recognition can go, but after hearing this, you'll see how much it can naturally elevate your team's performance.

You probably already know that everyone craves acknowledgment—whether it's a kind word, a heartfelt compliment, or a public expression of pride. Allan discovered that telling his employees he was proud of them made them feel valued and inspired them to give their very best. Can you imagine how something as simple as expressing respect can create unlimited motivation across your team?

Ways to Show Appreciation

Allan began to recognize that there are many ways to express appreciation, and they don't always have to be grand gestures. Sometimes, it's the smallest things that have the biggest impact. Here are some ways Allan showed his team just how much he valued their efforts:

- Handwritten Notes: Allan took time to write personalized, handwritten notes to his employees. He would express genuine gratitude and specifically acknowledge their hard work. I'm wondering if you've ever experienced how something as personal as a handwritten note can naturally make someone feel seen and appreciated.
- Public Praise: Allan would highlight achievements in team meetings or company-wide announcements and give genuine thanks. You probably already know how motivating public recognition can be. It reinforces the positive behavior not only for the individual being praised but also for the entire team.
- Personalized Statements: Allan understood that each person has different ways they like to be appreciated—some are visual, some auditory, and others kinesthetic (VAK). Can you imagine how powerful it is to tailor your praise to what moves them most? (For more on this, see Chapter 4 on Rapport Skills.)

Understanding What Moves Your Employees

It's important to go beyond surface-level recognition and understand what motivates each employee. I'm curious: have you taken the time to notice what makes your team tick? For example, Allan had a coaching client who shared that one of her employees valued verbal praise more than a bonus. Maybe you will find that once you understand these deeper drivers, your recognition will feel more natural and impactful.

Practical Steps for Expressing Genuine Gratitude

1. Identify Motivators: Know what drives each of your employees. Have one-on-one conversations, send surveys, or casually chat about their environment and motivations. You probably already know that understanding what moves them can easily transform how you show appreciation.

2. Express Genuine Gratitude: Be specific and heartfelt when you praise. Saying something simple like, "I'm so proud of you" or "You're excellent at accounting" can make a huge difference. I'm wondering if you've noticed how much more meaningful specific compliments feel compared to general statements.

3. Public Recognition: Thank your employees in front of their peers. After all, public praise boosts the individual's morale and sets a positive example for the rest of the team. It fosters a culture of appreciation that naturally motivates everyone to strive for excellence.

Benefits of Showing Appreciation

When you take the time to tell your employees you are proud of them and respect what they do, the benefits naturally ripple throughout your organization:

- Increased Motivation: Employees who feel appreciated are likelier to put in extra effort and strive for excellence. Maybe you haven't yet realized how much a simple "thank you" can inspire greatness.

- Improved Performance: Recognizing achievements boosts confidence and encourages employees to maintain high performance. Now, you might notice how performance improves when people feel truly valued.

- Enhanced Team Morale: Public praise fosters a positive work environment and strengthens team cohesion. You probably already know how much morale impacts productivity—and appreciation is a surefire way to boost it.

Implementation Tips

1. Consistency: Regularly recognize and appreciate your employees to create a culture of appreciation. Naturally, making this a habit ensures that no one's efforts go unnoticed.

2. Personalization: Tailor your recognition to each employee's preferences and motivational triggers. I wonder if you'll find that some employees prefer quiet acknowledgment while others thrive on public praise.

3. Visibility: Make sure your expressions of gratitude are visible to the entire team. This easily reinforces a culture of recognition and respect, creating a supportive and motivating environment.

A Lesson in Appreciation: Allan Private's Wake-Up Call

Allan Private recalls a pivotal moment when he learned the true power of recognition. He had given a raise to an employee, assuming the financial reward would speak for itself. However, during the employee's annual review, he was surprised to hear that they felt uncertain about their performance. The issue? Allan had never explicitly praised their work. Can you imagine the impact of that realization?

This experience was a wake-up call for Allan. He realized that while tangible rewards like raises are important, people naturally crave acknowledgment. Everyone wants to be seen, heard, and appreciated for their efforts. Allan also understood that many people's self-perception is deeply shaped by past feedback and childhood experiences—this can influence how they internalize success and failure.

From that day on, Allan made it a point to regularly express genuine appreciation and praise his employees in front of their peers. He fostered a culture of loyalty, respect, and trust. Maybe you will start to see how a simple 'thank you' or word of acknowledgment can motivate your team and reinforce positive behavior.

After all, building strong relationships and creating a supportive work environment starts with letting people know you truly value them. By showing your employees that you are proud of them and respect what they do, you'll naturally inspire them to perform at their best, helping your organization reach new heights of success.

Principle 7: Have an Attitude of Gratitude

Creating a culture of gratitude in your business is naturally one of the most powerful ways to foster a positive, productive work environment. Allan Private discovered that by focusing on what he was grateful for in his employees, he could easily shift the overall atmosphere of the workplace and expand beyond the usual frustrations that often plague leaders. I'm curious: have you noticed how gratitude can transform your mindset and those around you?

You probably already know that many business owners fall into the trap of constantly complaining about their employees—whether it's about missed sales targets, lateness, or failure to meet expectations. Maybe you haven't realized that this negative focus only perpetuates dissatisfaction, disengagement, and low morale. Can you imagine how much energy this takes away from the growth potential?
Allan, however, learned that by adopting an attitude of gratitude, he could transform not just himself but the entire company. He noticed a profound shift when he focused on being thankful for his employees and naturally recognizing their efforts. The environment became more positive and more supportive, and, as a result, performance improved. After all, when people feel appreciated, they thrive.

The Importance of Gratitude

Allan realized that constantly focusing on the negatives was a pattern holding him back. I'm wondering if you've ever caught yourself doing the same—lamenting over what's not working instead of celebrating what is. But Allan discovered that by switching his focus to gratitude, his employees felt more motivated, engaged, and aligned with the company's goals.

Maybe you will start to see how this simple shift in mindset can have unlimited benefits.

Practicing Daily Gratitude

Allan began to make gratitude a daily habit. Here's how you can do the same:

- Identify Positives: For each employee, find three things to be grateful for. It could be their punctuality, dedication, or positive attitude. You probably already know how important these little things are, and now you can consciously notice and appreciate them daily.

- Daily Focus: Focus on these positives each day. After all, when you train yourself to look for the good, you reinforce positive behaviors and help build a culture of gratitude and recognition.

Changing the Narrative

It's easy for business owners to get caught up in the negatives—low sales, staffing issues, financial struggles. Can you imagine how much lighter things would feel if you shifted focus? Allan teaches that after focusing on the positives, you can change the entire dynamic of your business.
Be thankful that your employees are showing up, making calls, and putting in effort. This mindset shift can significantly change how you lead, how your employees respond, and the overall energy within your company. I'm curious: how would things change for you if you embraced this way of thinking?

Steps to Implement Gratitude

- Reflect on Positives: Spend just a few minutes each day reflecting on what you appreciate about your employees. Maybe you haven't yet started this practice, but now is the time to begin.
- Express Gratitude: Verbalize your gratitude regularly. Let your team know you value their contributions, whether big or small. Saying it out loud reinforces it not just for them but for you.
- Gratitude List: Create a list of ten things you are grateful for about your employees or business. This practice can easily shift your mindset toward a more positive outlook and be a powerful motivational tool for you.

Benefits of Gratitude

Gratitude doesn't just feel good—it has unlimited benefits:

- Improved Morale: Employees who feel appreciated are naturally more motivated, engaged, and invested in their work.
- Positive Work Environment: A culture of gratitude fosters a supportive, harmonious workplace where everyone feels valued.
- Enhanced Performance: When gratitude flows, so does productivity. Employees who feel appreciated tend to work harder, increasing their job satisfaction.

Action Plan

1. Make a List: Write down ten things you are grateful for about your employees or business. This small action will help you start the day with a positive mindset.
2. Daily Practice: Integrate this gratitude practice into your daily routine. Don't wait—start today and watch how it naturally transforms your business environment.

A Lesson in Gratitude: Allan Private's Wake-Up Call

Allan Private experienced a transformative moment when he realized the true power of gratitude. He used to assume that giving employees a raise or a promotion was enough. However, during one annual review, he was surprised that one of his employees still felt unappreciated. The reason? Allan hadn't said, "I'm proud of you," or "I'm grateful for your hard work."

This eye-opening experience taught Allan a valuable lesson—everyone craves acknowledgment. You probably already know that we're wired to want validation, and a simple 'thank you' can easily go further than a financial reward ever could. Allan discovered that a culture of gratitude not only improved employee morale but also created loyalty and trust.

From that moment on, Allan made gratitude a priority. He began regularly expressing his appreciation and actively acknowledging his team's efforts. By doing so, he built a workplace culture of loyalty, respect, and positivity, where employees felt valued and inspired to give their best every day.

Now, I'm curious: are you ready to adopt an attitude of gratitude and experience how it can easily transform your business? Maybe you haven't yet fully embraced the power of gratitude, but after you do, you'll see how this principle creates unlimited potential for your team's success.

Chapter 8: Mental Health

In exploring the journey of Allan Private, it becomes evident that his struggles with mental health during his teenage years shaped every corner of his life. I'm curious: have you ever noticed how the patterns we experience in our youth can naturally follow us into adulthood? You probably already know that unresolved challenges often find new ways to manifest, creating obstacles later in life. For Allan, the connection between his mental health and his eventual downfall was undeniable.

Delving into "Connecting with Your Teen" by Dr. John Oda provides a profound understanding of Allan's life trajectory, offering a glimpse into the challenges that defined his early years. As a teenager, Allan faced multifaceted struggles—academic pressures, familial conflicts, and personal battles with addiction. Can you imagine the weight of trying to navigate all that while being drawn into the nightlife scene, including rave parties? Allan's journey took a tragic turn when he was involved in a fatal accident, resulting in the loss of another life. Now, maybe you will start to realize how these unaddressed mental health issues became the underlying force that eventually unraveled Allan's success. Despite building a billion-dollar empire, the traumas and unresolved pain from his adolescence lingered like shadows, ready to resurface. His meteoric rise came crashing down because the psychological burdens he carried hadn't been addressed.

The Role of Mental Health in Allan's Downfall

Reflecting on Allan's story, it becomes clear that mental health cannot be separated from success or well-being. I'm wondering if you've ever seen this in your own life or others—how unresolved issues from the past can naturally reappear in destructive ways, even after achieving outward success. Allan's inability to confront the mental health struggles from his teenage years was pivotal to his downfall. He lost everything he had worked for because the inner turmoil he had avoided easily found its way into his decision-making and behaviors as an adult.

The story of Allan Private is a poignant reminder that mental health must be prioritized—especially during adolescence. What we often ignore during these formative years doesn't just disappear; it evolves, manifesting in different forms as we grow. Maybe you haven't yet considered how crucial early intervention is for young people, but after hearing Allan's story, it becomes clear that support during these years can change everything.

The Importance of Early Intervention

As seen through Allan's journey, addressing mental health early on is critical. You probably already know that teenagers face their own set of unique challenges—emotional volatility, identity crises, peer pressure—and without proper support, these struggles can easily escalate. Allan's life could have taken a different path if he had received the help he needed early on.

Can you imagine how much resilience young people can develop when they are given the tools to face their demons head-on? By fostering environments that encourage open communication, empathy, and access to mental health resources, we can naturally empower individuals like Allan to confront their struggles before they spiral out of control. Maybe you will notice how early intervention sets the stage for growth and healing rather than a lifetime of avoiding the pain.
Understanding Mental Health's Impact on Every Aspect of Life

In my years of experience, I've seen a recurring pattern: the tendency to avoid mental health issues, hoping they will fade away on their own. But ignoring mental health is like ignoring a malignant tumor. I'm wondering if you've ever thought about how dangerous that can be—letting things fester until they spread into every facet of your life. That's exactly what happened to Allan. His failure to address his mental health early on became the invisible hand guiding his future downfall.

The insidious nature of mental health challenges is that they don't just disappear. They infiltrate decisions, relationships, and even success itself. You probably already know how important it is to break this pattern. By addressing mental health at its root, we expand beyond the surface and create a foundation for a healthier, more resilient life.

A Cautionary Tale with a Transformative Message

Allan's journey serves as a cautionary tale, but it also offers hope. His story reminds us that mental health is deeply intertwined with well-being and success. It's a message that echoes the importance of intervention, support, and healing during the formative teenage years. Now, more than ever, it's essential to prioritize these aspects—not just for success but for life itself.

Connecting with Your Teen reveals that Allan's transformation was not just about external success but internal healing. You probably already know that true fulfillment comes from addressing what's inside, not just what's seen on the outside. Through understanding, compassion, and proactive support, we can help others like Allan navigate their own turbulent journeys and easily emerge stronger, wiser, and more resilient. Because when we prioritize mental health, we build a future where success is not just something we achieve—but something we sustain.

I'm curious if you can imagine how easily and naturally Allan Private's journey unfolds as he reflects on his past. You probably already know that success often masks deeper struggles, and Allan, despite his remarkable achievements, failed to recognize the patterns that limited him. Maybe you haven't yet realized how unresolved issues, like Allan's teenage battles with mental health, can expand beyond our awareness and begin to unravel all that we've built—until it's too late.

You'll notice how Allan's avoidance of his inner battles didn't just impact his mental well-being but also corroded the relationships he cherished most, from his family to his colleagues. Can you imagine what could have happened if Allan had confronted those issues early on? After all, just as early intervention can halt the spread of a disease, timely support for mental health can stop the erosion of success and expand beyond what we think is possible.

Now, stop for a moment and consider how, had Allan been more aware, he could have preserved his company, reputation, and relationships. Maybe you will notice that his avoidance became a pattern that echoed throughout his life, silently driving the behaviors that ultimately led to his downfall. It's as if those same patterns of disrespect from his youth naturally resurfaced in his leadership, causing a breakdown in trust and cooperation.

Allan now realizes that his leadership style reflected those unresolved struggles. Because when we ignore the past, it tends to shape the future in ways we never intended. Now, he sees that his company's collapse was not just a business failure but a personal one, rooted in the behaviors that limited him as a teenager.

Dr. John Oda would probably tell you that true strength lies in confronting these inner struggles head-on, allowing you to expand beyond your limitations. Maybe you already know this, but Allan's story is a powerful reminder that now, more than ever, mental health should be as much of a priority as physical health. When you begin to make those connections in your own life, you'll see how tackling these issues now will create a ripple effect of unlimited potential, personally and professionally.

Allan's cautionary tale is a call to action: notice the patterns, stop avoiding them, and expand beyond the limiting beliefs that may still be holding you back.

Now, Allan Private, armed with newfound awareness and a deep sense of humility, steps into his future with purpose. Can you imagine the weight lifted from him as he naturally breaks free from the shackles of his past? He realizes he's been handed a rare opportunity—a second chance, and with it, the ability to rewrite his story. Maybe you haven't realized how powerful it is to recognize this moment, but Allan does. He knows this is the time to rebuild trust, foster respect, and instill integrity and accountability into every fiber of his organization.

Now, Allan is fully aware that true leadership is not about wielding power but about empowering others to expand beyond their limitations. He's committed to replacing those toxic patterns of the past with values of empathy, transparency, and responsibility. Because he knows that his strength lies in inspiring those around him to rise to their fullest potential—maybe you will start noticing this kind of shift, too.

Allan is on a mission, driven by the conviction that no one should suffer from the same missteps he made. You see, he naturally understands his choices' profound impact—not just on his own life but on those around him. And now, with this understanding, he's rewriting the narrative—a story of resilience, growth, and redemption.

Stop for a moment and imagine Allan's pain transforming into purpose, his failures into lessons, and his past fueling positive change. He's stepping into this new journey, and his renewed hope and determination are palpable as he looks toward the future. You probably already know that true strength lies in confronting our inner struggles. Allan is doing just that—leading by example and showing others how to embrace their humanity and forge a brighter path.

When we look at Allan's journey, from the collapse of his business to the remarkable success of his enterprise in 2054, it's clear that maybe you haven't yet noticed the magic of learning from past mistakes, but Allan has. He knows that confronting uncomfortable truths is the gateway to unlimited growth. His failure wasn't just about toxic workplace behaviors or unaddressed mental health concerns. It was the reflection of a leader avoiding the necessary hard conversations. But now, with a focus on transparency, accountability, and mental well-being, Allan has created a culture of trust and innovation.
Imagine what it feels like to be part of such an environment. An organization that thrives not because it avoids problems but because it naturally tackles them head-on. Allan has realized that by setting the tone as CEO, he has the power to shape an entire organization — one built on a foundation of respect, trust, and integrity. And perhaps, now, you're beginning to notice how this same power exists within you.

Now, in the CEO Mindset chapter of his remarkable journey, Allan dives deep into the transformative power of leadership. He guides readers to notice the profound impact a leader's mindset has on shaping organizational success. Can you imagine what becomes possible when cultivating a growth mindset, fostering resilience, and leading authentically? Maybe you haven't realized how powerful this can be, but Allan has lived it. Through introspective exercises and practical insights, he shares the pivotal lessons he learned—lessons that could easily transform how you lead.

Allan introduces you to the Ohana Way, a philosophy that will naturally resonate with anyone who understands the value of human connection. Maybe you're beginning to realize that true leadership involves seeing your organization as a family—where every member is valued, supported, and uplifted. Because when you create a culture of inclusion, collaboration, and mutual respect, you naturally unlock the full potential of your team. Allan's belief in diversity and fostering belonging expands beyond just a feel-good concept; it becomes the engine for innovation and sustainable growth.

But that's not all. Allan takes you deeper into the psychological framework underpinning human behavior—Metaprograms. Can you imagine understanding how people move toward or away from goals or how they react versus being proactive? Maybe you haven't noticed that these insights into human psychology can revolutionize your leadership approach. By identifying these patterns, Allan reveals how understanding human behavior enhances your strategies and the interpersonal dynamics within your organization.

Through self-reflection, continuous learning, and an unwavering commitment to growth, Allan didn't just save his company—he transformed it. Stop and think about this moment: from the brink of collapse to a thriving enterprise valued at sextillions in under 30 years. It sounds unbelievable, but anything is possible with courage, resilience, and the ability to confront our shortcomings.

And here's where it gets even more profound: Addressing mental health issues became Allan's greatest breakthrough. After countless conversations with top CEOs, Allan realized that the silent destroyer of companies often lies in the neglect of mental health, especially within leadership. Can you imagine the impact on an organization when its leaders overlook their well-being? By bringing these issues to light, Allan elevated his leadership and created an environment where everyone could thrive—personally and professionally.

Maybe you haven't realized that the biggest breakthroughs often come from within. Allan's journey is a powerful reminder that you can achieve unlimited success when you prioritize growth, mental health, and the human side of leadership.

Consider the implications: How can any leader truly inspire, guide, or elevate a team if they are silently grappling with unaddressed mental health challenges? Now, think about this—leadership is built on navigating complexities, motivating others, and creating a supportive space for growth and innovation. But when leaders carry the weight of their unresolved struggles, how can they fulfill these critical responsibilities?

The reality is stark, and maybe you're beginning to notice: unresolved mental health issues within leadership don't just affect the individual—they ripple outward, impairing decision-making, undermining communication, and eroding team morale. Because when leaders are struggling internally, the consequences seep into the organization's fabric, sowing discord, dysfunction, and disconnection.

I've seen it happen time and again. Leaders who fail to confront their own mental health challenges often, without realizing it, set the tone for a culture of silence—a culture where mental health issues are swept under the rug, where employees hesitate to seek help, and where stigma reigns. Maybe you've already noticed this in your own experience, where the unspoken message is clear: mental health is not something we talk about here.

Stop and think about the profound shift when leaders prioritize their mental well-being. They set a new precedent when they step forward openly, acknowledging their struggles and seeking help when needed. They create a space where vulnerability, support, and resilience are celebrated, not hidden. This is the essence of true leadership—leading by example, showing others that it's okay to confront their challenges and emerge stronger for it.

And here's the key: addressing mental health within leadership isn't just about personal well-being—it's a strategic imperative. Leaders who invest in their mental health create the foundation for a resilient, high-performing team. Imagine what's possible when a leader is mentally clear, emotionally grounded, and fully present. Maybe you're beginning to realize that this kind of leadership cultivates a culture of trust, innovation, and openness, empowering the entire organization to navigate challenges with clarity and courage.

In today's high-pressure business world, mental health is not just important—it's everything. As leaders, we must step forward and create an environment of psychological safety where everyone feels valued and supported. After all, only when we prioritize our mental health can we truly unlock the full potential of our teams, leading them to sustainable success, not just for today but for the long term. Maybe you haven't yet realized, but this is where real, lasting transformation begins.

Now, imagine stepping into a world where success is not only achievable but inevitable—naturally and systematically. I was immediately intrigued when I first encountered Dr. John Oda and his groundbreaking work in Neuro-Linguistic Programming (NLP). As a master trainer who studied under the legendary Dr. William Horton and Joseph McClendon III, Oda didn't just follow the traditional NLP path; he pioneered a new frontier: Neuro Business Conditioning (NBC). This revolutionary approach, crafted specifically for the business world, redefined how we create success in businesses across the globe.

Maybe you realize that NBC represents a powerful pivot driven by Oda's vast experience as a Master Business Coach and Vice President of Consulting for Business Breakthroughs International, a company co-founded by Chet Holmes and Tony Robbins. His expertise has been honed by guiding entrepreneurs, CEOs, and business leaders from over 46 countries through "Business Mastery." Alongside industry giants like Jay Abraham, Gary Vaynerchuk, and Frank Kern, Oda shared his strategic brilliance, crafting business success stories alongside the world's greatest.

What sets Oda apart? His ability to notice what others miss— recognizing the unique challenges within the corporate world and modeling the strategies of the most successful individuals. This is the genesis of Neuro Business Conditioning. Why reinvent the wheel when you can take the best practices from legends like Anthony Robbins, Stephen Covey, Dan Kennedy, and Les Brown and expand beyond them to create something even more effective?

What makes Oda's Neuro Business Conditioning so transformative are three key pillars: Mental Health, Executive Business Coaching, and Monetization. With 38 years in mental health and over two decades working with teenagers on behavior issues, Oda brings a unique depth of insight. His ability to understand human behavior, unlock hidden potential, and facilitate profound mindset shifts gives him unparalleled power to help individuals and organizations evolve.

As an Executive Business Coach, Oda's results speak for themselves. For nearly three decades, he's helped clients double their businesses and profits—and that's not just an occasional win but a pattern of consistent, repeatable success. Maybe you haven't yet realized how much your business could thrive under this strategic guidance. Still, the truth is, after experiencing NBC, you'll naturally notice how these shifts drive unlimited growth potential.

But it doesn't stop there. Monetization is the final piece of the puzzle. Dr. Oda's genius lies in transforming personal and professional development into tangible financial gains. By optimizing performance through NLP principles, leaders don't just improve themselves—they translate that growth into real-world results that elevate their businesses. In today's hyper-competitive marketplace, this is the edge that separates success from mediocrity.

Stop and think for a moment about the possibilities. Now, with Dr. John Oda's Neuro Business Conditioning, there's a way to seamlessly combine the power of mental health mastery, strategic business coaching, and revenue generation into a single, cohesive system that works for anyone willing to embrace it.

Oda's journey from NLP to NBC is the natural evolution of a master dedicated to transforming lives. His desire to make a meaningful, lasting impact has led him to create a framework that drives professional success and personal fulfillment. Maybe you're starting to see the real potential of Neuro Business Conditioning, but now is the time to embrace it. This is more than just a strategy—it's a revolution in how we approach business, leadership, and success in every aspect of life.

Now, with Neuro Business Conditioning (NBC), Dr. John Oda is offering more than just a method—delivering a revolution in how we create success. Imagine unlocking your full potential, transcending limitations, and achieving unprecedented success—naturally and efficiently. Maybe you haven't yet realized, but with NBC, you are about to embark on a journey of self-discovery, growth, and transformation that could reshape your business and your entire life.

At the core of NBC, Oda introduces us to a neuroscience-based approach that demystifies the complexities of human behavior. Now, he's made these concepts easily accessible, distilling the intricate workings of the nervous system into practical, actionable strategies for businesses. Because when you understand how the brain processes information and drives behavior, you can effect change from the inside out, creating profound shifts with ease and efficiency. Can you imagine the power of understanding your mind—and using that insight to create limitless success?

The "Business" side of NBC is deeply rooted in Oda's partnerships with some of the most influential minds in the industry. Maybe you've already heard of Chet Holmes, the marketing genius behind The Ultimate Sales Machine, and Anthony Robbins, whose influence needs no introduction. These legends didn't just mentor Oda—they shaped his approach to business transformation. Through NBC, Oda integrates the wisdom he's gained from collaborating with titans like Robbins and organizations such as Business Breakthrough International (BBI), creating a powerful system that naturally delivers results.

Dr. Oda's ability to model success from these luminaries sets him apart. He's bringing their best practices into his executive coaching, not by reinventing the wheel, but by leveraging a proven system. Through decades of experience and strategic partnerships, Oda has refined his craft to help organizations unlock their full potential. His methods don't just scratch the surface—they dive deep, providing leaders with the tools to drive real, tangible results in their businesses. As you delve deeper into NBC, you'll notice that Oda's approach isn't just about business. It's about transforming every aspect of your life. Maybe you haven't yet realized how far-reaching these principles can be, but the truth is, after applying NBC, you'll see changes in your mindset, performance, and the overall trajectory of your success.

Now is the time to embrace Neuro Business Conditioning—a neuroscience-based system refined by industry giants and designed to unlock your ultimate potential. Maybe you're curious to see just how transformative this could be for you. Still, as you begin this journey, you'll discover that anything is possible when you understand the science of success and apply it to both your business and your life. Stop and think for a moment: if the greatest minds in business have shaped and embraced these strategies, what could be possible for you?

Now, I'm curious—can you imagine a shortcut to success that bypasses years of trial and error? Maybe you haven't yet realized, but Dr. John Oda's Neuro Business Conditioning (NBC) offers just that—a direct path to unlocking unlimited potential by harnessing the collective wisdom of industry titans like Chet Holmes and others. In Oda's view, this knowledge, refined over decades, is worth more than a billion in learning. You probably already know that success leaves clues, and with NBC, Oda distills these clues into a system that naturally accelerates personal and professional growth.

Oda's NBC is a convergence of neuroscience, business acumen, and performance psychology designed to expand beyond traditional approaches and create rapid, sustainable change. Maybe you're beginning to notice that Oda's approach is different. Because at the core of NBC is the concept of conditioning, where change is inevitable once the right leverage is applied. I know you like the sound of that—strategically unlocking the brain's latent potential and transforming behaviors, beliefs, and outcomes in ways that feel effortless.

In practical terms, Oda's NBC taps into the brain's adaptability. Now, by systematically reprogramming neural pathways, he aligns your brain with your highest aspirations, facilitating change that happens easily and naturally. After all, the brain is wired to respond to external stimuli, and Oda uses that to his client's advantage. Maybe you haven't yet experienced how quickly this process works, but with NBC, you'll notice rapid, measurable improvements in a fraction of the time traditional approaches take.

Central to this transformation is leverage—a tool Oda wields with precision. By identifying key leverage points and applying targeted pressure, he empowers clients to break free from limiting beliefs and patterns that hold them back. Now, stop and think: what would it feel like to experience growth and innovation for yourself and your entire organization? I'm wondering if you can see how these strategies create a ripple effect, driving collaboration and continuous improvement across every level of your business.

NBC operates on urgency and momentum. Whether through accountability, performance incentives, or carefully crafted interventions, Oda creates a sense of urgency that propels clients toward their goals with unprecedented speed. Maybe you will realize how NBC's strategic pressure points act as the catalysts for personal and organizational breakthroughs. Because when you rewire the brain for success, everything else falls into place.

In today's fast-paced business world, adapting quickly is key. NBC doesn't just focus on individual change but recognizes the interplay between personal growth and organizational dynamics. Oda's framework creates a culture of innovation, ensuring every team member thrives and the organization moves forward with agility and strength.

Stop and notice what's happening here: Neuro Business Conditioning is more than a system—it's a paradigm shift. By leveraging neuroscience and strategic pressure, Oda empowers individuals and organizations to break free from inertia, unlock unlimited potential, and achieve results beyond anything previously thought possible. Now, as you embrace the principles of NBC, you'll embark on a journey of rapid transformation, sustained growth, and unparalleled success.

Study Questions for this chapter:

1. I'm curious: how often do you reflect on your mental health, and have you noticed how it might silently impact your business decisions?

2. Maybe you haven't yet realized, but what patterns of thought or behavior keep you from reaching your full potential mentally and professionally?

3. Can you imagine how much more productive and effective you could be if your mental well-being were prioritized with the same urgency as your business goals?

4. Now, stop and think: what would happen to your leadership if you naturally integrated mental health practices into your daily routine?

5. I'm wondering if you've already noticed how unresolved mental health issues within your leadership team could be holding back the entire organization—what would change if you addressed them?

6. You probably already know that mental health is a key performance factor, but how often do you consider it as the foundation for your business success?

7. Maybe you haven't yet experienced the profound shifts from aligning mental health with business strategy. What would happen if you did?

8. After all, what's the cost of neglecting mental health in your team—how much potential are you leaving untapped because those challenges remain hidden?

9. Stop for a moment and ask yourself, what's the one mental block you've been carrying that's limiting your ability to lead effectively, and how would your life change if you let it go?

10. Now, imagine a business culture where mental health and performance conditioning work together—how much more could you and your team achieve with this balance?

Quadrant Three: Systemize

- **Chapter 9: Next-Level Sales Mastery**
- **Chapter 10: The Sextillion Time Management System**
- **Chapter 11: The Octopus Method of Marketing**

Chapter 9: Next Level Sales Mastery—Neuro Business Conditioning

Do you know what really happens when a prospect says, "No, I'm not interested"? Most sales representatives take that as a definitive rejection. But here's the truth—it's not a hard "no"; it's just the beginning of the conversation. Maybe you haven't yet realized, but persistence is where deals are made. Let me show you why.

- 48% of salespeople give up after just one rejection.
- 20% will try only two times.
- 7% will give it a go three times.
- And only 5% of salespeople will push past four rejections.

Now, ask yourself—where do you or your sales team stand in this spectrum? Are you part of the 5% who push forward, or are you giving up too soon? I'm curious, do you have a sales team, or are you handling the sales in your business yourself? Are you the type of rock star who goes after the deal relentlessly, more than four times if necessary?

Maybe you haven't noticed, but the difference between a salesperson making $20,000 per month and someone making $5,000—selling the same product or service—often boils down to one thing: Systems. Time and again, I see companies where top performers have the tools, the mindset, and the training, while others are left to figure it out on their own.

Here's what's missing in most organizations:

- No weekly sales training or hot seating sessions to sharpen skill sets and develop confidence.
- No sales scripts to follow—making consistency nearly impossible.
- No structured sales process—leaving deals to chance.
- No follow-up system—so leads fall through the cracks after a single "no."

Maybe you already know this, but people who are provided with the right systems, trained in those systems, and rewarded for using them, will use them. And businesses that implement these systems consistently are the ones that win.
So stop and think—does your team have the training and the systems in place to succeed? Are you equipping your team with what they need to follow up persistently, handle objections effectively, and close deals consistently?

Maybe you haven't yet realized, but the difference between mediocrity and excellence isn't about luck—it's about having a repeatable system. The businesses that train, support, and hold their teams accountable will always outperform the rest. After all, success isn't just about selling—it's about mastering the process that gets you there.

Now, the question is: are you ready to put those systems in place and start winning.

Now, imagine what's possible when you master the art of influence—how effortlessly your business could take off. Maybe you haven't yet realized that these seven steps of influence, once mastered, can transform not only your business but your entire approach to sales. When Allan Private understood these seven steps, his business skyrocketed. You probably already know that influence is something we've all practiced since childhood. I'm curious, do you remember convincing your parents or teachers that you were a nice person? That's influence. But here's the key: the skills you learned as a child can be enhanced and transformed into a powerful tool for business success.

Next Level Sales Mastery—Neuro Business Conditioning, we're diving deep into how to easily take your influence skills to the next level. Because when you apply NBC, you're not just mastering conscious influence—you're tapping into the unconscious mind to create deep, meaningful connections with your clients. Stop and think about this for a moment: what if you could connect with your clients so profoundly that they naturally love your product and services?

Let's start with Step One: Mindset and Building Rapport. Maybe you haven't noticed, but the mindset is everything. Using NBC, you'll not only learn how to connect with your clients consciously but also tap into their unconscious minds to influence their decisions. Now, imagine having the confidence to overcome mental blocks, speak with authority, and become an effective leader. This is where you close your internal gaps and emerge as a rock star in your industry. After all, great salespeople have three core components:

1. Ego/Confidence (33%): Too much ego, and you come across as arrogant. But just the right amount gives you the confidence to close any deal.
2. Empathy (33%): Too much empathy, and you'll be a doormat. But when you balance it, you can notice your client's needs, listen to their story, and take appropriate action while staying focused on results.
3. Charisma (34%): Maybe you haven't yet realized that charisma is the secret sauce. You need to be able to lead people, just like the Pied Piper.

When you master the secret language of influence, everything changes. You'll learn how to match and mirror your client's behavior to gain rapport instantly. Can you imagine how powerful it is to match their words, tone, tempo, and body language to create a connection so close that doing business with you feels natural to them?

With Neuro Business Conditioning, influence isn't just a skill—it becomes second nature. Now, get ready to take your sales mastery to the next level.

Now, let's talk about one of the most powerful tools in the business world: rapport. Maybe you haven't yet realized, but building rapport is like creating a connection that goes beyond words—it's an unspoken bond, an energy where trust, openness, and comfort flow naturally. I'm curious, can you imagine the impact of having your clients feel so comfortable with you that they naturally open up, trust you, and even enjoy working with you?

Rapport is like a beautiful dance, where everyone is moving in sync, on the same beat. You probably already know that when rapport is strong, it creates a sense of trust, understanding, and connection that easily transforms business relationships. Think of rapport as the glue that makes everything stick.

Take this example: Two employers—both with the same education, same background, and two salespeople. Janice and her employee constantly argue and never seem to get along. Karen, on the other hand, has an amazing connection with her employee. They communicate openly, trust each other, and are always on the same page. What's the difference? Rapport. Karen has mastered the art of matching and mirroring her employee's communication patterns. She has built an authentic, trusting bond where both feel appreciated and understood. I'm wondering if you've already noticed how this simple skill could transform your own relationships.

Achieving Rapport is about being in sync. Have you ever met someone and felt like you've known them all your life? That instant connection, where you both seem to be on the same wavelength? That's rapport. Maybe you haven't yet noticed, but it's more than just words—it's about mirroring the unspoken language that people use every day. Non-verbal communication is a powerful tool. From body language to tone of voice, everything we do communicates. Now, let's break it down:

- Words (7%): Words matter, but they are just a small part of the bigger picture. When you focus on the words your client uses most often, you're entering their world, not your own.
- Tone, Tempo, and Tonality (38%): Have you ever noticed how a lullaby, like "Rock-a-bye Baby," naturally soothes a child? It's not just the words—it's the tone, tempo, and tonality that create a sense of comfort. When speaking with clients, pay attention to the pitch, volume, and rhythm of their speech, and match it. This creates an instant bond.
- Physiology (55%): Body language is everything—eye contact, hand movements, posture. Stop and think, how do you position yourself when communicating? Maybe you will notice that when you mirror the body language of your client—whether it's their breathing, their gestures, or even their weight shifting—you create a deep connection, even over the phone.

Now, here's the secret to mastering rapport: match and mirror. When you're on a call, match their voice volume, pace, and tone, while maintaining a positive physiology—put a smile on your face, even if they can't see it. This will naturally enhance your connection, making them feel more comfortable. After all, people do business with those they feel connected to, and rapport makes that connection stronger.

Maybe you haven't yet realized how powerful these techniques are, but once you master them, you'll experience how effortlessly you can build relationships, influence decisions, and create a sense of trust that's unshakable.

Now, imagine what it would be like to truly bond with your clients. Can you imagine the power of being completely aligned with their mindset, having mutual respect, and appreciating each other's point of view? Maybe you haven't yet realized, but these techniques can transform a salesperson's approach—allowing them to connect on a deeper level, naturally building trust, and influencing decisions with ease. I'm curious, how powerful would these skills be in your own business if you mastered them?

As a salesperson, you already have the ability to tap into these powerful techniques. With practice, you'll learn how to establish rapport with almost anyone, creating an atmosphere where communication flows easily and your clients feel naturally connected to you. Now, think about this: What would happen if you didn't build that connection with your client and someone else—maybe a competitor—does? Maybe you already know how critical it is to be the one who earns that trust.

My goal here is simple: to give you the knowledge and tools to build unbreakable rapport with your clients. After all, rapport is the foundation of:

- Trust
- Confidence
- Cooperation

When these three elements are in place, your client will naturally respond openly, feeling a sense of safety and connection that makes doing business with you the easiest choice. I'm wondering if you've noticed how much easier sales become when your clients trust you implicitly?

One of the key benefits of rapport is creating a feeling of sameness—the sense that you and your client are moving through time together. You don't need to share identical worldviews. Rapport is simply about creating a space where your client feels understood and appreciated. Maybe you will realize that once your client feels this connection, they'll start to adopt your values naturally. Psychologists used to call this the development of the superego, where people unconsciously adopt the values of those they trust.

Stop and think about the kind of bond you can create with your client when they know they can turn to you for support, that you genuinely understand their needs, and that you're there for them—not just as a salesperson, but as a partner in their success.

When studying how to build rapport, it all starts with listening. Really listening to your client—asking for clarification when needed and matching your words to theirs. Notice when your client uses words like "outstanding." When you respond, use that same word, and watch how easily they begin to feel connected to you. These subtle techniques create an unconscious bond that is incredibly powerful.

Pay close attention to not just what your client says, but how they say it. Observe their behaviors in every situation—whether they're interacting with co-workers, at social gatherings, or in business meetings. When you understand their world, their body language, and their attitudes, you can naturally establish rapport in a way that feels effortless.

When you are truly tuned in to your client—when you understand them deeply—you unlock the greatest opportunity for connection. It's not just about words. It requires a heart full of compassion and understanding. Maybe you will start to notice that when people are in rapport, their communication becomes a beautiful dance. Their words and movements flow together, and they unconsciously mirror each other's rhythms.

Now, imagine mastering these skills. Imagine your conversations flowing with ease, your clients feeling deeply understood, and the level of trust you build through these small but significant techniques. This is the power of rapport—it's the foundation for long-term success and extraordinary relationships with your clients.

Now, let's talk about one of the most subtle yet powerful techniques you can use to create connection—mirroring. Maybe you haven't yet realized, but mirroring happens all around us, every day, and it's one of the easiest ways to build rapport without even thinking about it. I'm curious, have you ever noticed how two people who are deeply connected tend to adopt the same posture, mannerisms, and even tone of voice? This is mirroring in action—where one person becomes a reflection of the other, creating an unconscious bond.

When people are in deep rapport, mirroring occurs naturally and effortlessly. You probably already know that as a parent, you've seen this when your teen is with their best friend. They mirror each other so seamlessly that they move and speak in sync. They laugh at the same jokes, adopt the same body language, and seem like they've known each other forever. Now, imagine having that same effortless connection with your clients or even your own teen. How powerful would that be?

Mirroring is about creating a reflection. If someone crosses their right leg over their left, and you do the same, you're offering them an unconscious signal that says, "I understand you. We are in sync." This psychological synchronization creates a sense of comfort and connection that allows communication to flow easily. Stop and think about how difficult it feels to connect with someone whose body language is completely different from yours. If your teen's arms are crossed and yours are open, there's a disconnect. Their body language is saying, "I'm not ready to connect."

By mirroring their posture, you're offering them an unconscious reflection of themselves. Maybe you haven't noticed, but this simple technique can have a powerful impact. When you mirror your teen's—or anyone's—body language, you're sending them a signal that you understand them, and in return, they'll feel more connected to you. Now, imagine your teen beginning to feel like you truly "get" them, and because of that, they open up to you in ways they haven't before.

Mirroring can be used to reinforce positive behaviors as well. When teens see their parents reflecting their own behavior back at them, it creates a sense of understanding and connection. I'm wondering if you've noticed how powerful this can be—your teen begins to feel that you're on the same page, that you know where they're coming from, and that they can talk to you about anything.

Now, mirroring doesn't just apply to parenting—it's an invaluable tool in business, too. Whether you're connecting with a client, a colleague, or a team member, mirroring helps create an environment where people feel naturally comfortable and understood. After all, people like to do business with those they feel connected to.

So stop and notice how mirroring happens all around you. Maybe you haven't yet realized, but when people are in sync, they mirror each other effortlessly. With this simple technique, you can build rapport, create stronger connections, and deepen your relationships—both personally and professionally.

Now, let's dive into the subtle art of matching, one of the most powerful rapport-building techniques you can use to create deep, unconscious connections. Maybe you haven't yet realized, but matching occurs when your behavior mirrors your client's actions in a way that feels natural and seamless. I'm curious, have you noticed how effortless communication becomes when people feel like they're on the same wavelength? That's matching in action.

For example, if your client crosses their leg, you can do the same thing a few seconds later—but not in a way that feels obvious or like you're mimicking them. It's about creating a reflection that is similar enough to make them feel connected, yet subtle enough that it doesn't feel forced. You probably already know that this kind of rapport allows the conversation to flow more easily, making your client feel comfortable and understood.

Matching should feel effortless. When you're in sync with your client, everything flows naturally. For instance, if your client is tapping a pen, you might tap your foot in the same rhythmic way. The unconscious mind perceives this as a reflection of their own actions, creating a sense of connection that transcends words. Can you imagine how powerful this can be, not just in business but in everyday relationships?

Let me give you an example. I had a client who would constantly tap his pen to the beat of a song during our meetings. I repeatedly asked him to stop, explaining that we needed to focus. He would agree, but then within moments, he'd start tapping again. The next day, I decided to approach it differently. Instead of asking him to stop, I matched his behavior by tapping my foot to the same beat. And then something incredible happened—he stopped tapping, and we had one of the most productive sessions ever. I'm wondering if you've noticed how sometimes the simplest shifts can have the most profound impact?

Matching works because it taps into the unconscious mind. Your client feels like you're aligned with them, that you understand them at a deeper level. And after all, we all want to feel that connection, whether it's with a client, a colleague, or even a family member.

The key to matching is subtlety. Maybe you haven't yet noticed how much power there is in small actions like these, but when you match someone's movements, posture, or rhythm, you're building rapport in a way that feels natural and effortless. Stop and think about how much smoother your interactions can be when your client feels completely at ease with you.

Now, imagine using this technique in your business. You'll create stronger bonds, enhance communication, and open the door to more meaningful, productive relationships—just by matching the small, unconscious behaviors of the people you're interacting with. This is the power of matching, and once you master it, you'll see how it naturally transforms your ability to connect and influence others.

Now, let's talk about the results of creating rapport. When you successfully establish rapport, you're not just communicating with the conscious mind—you're tapping into the unconscious. Maybe you haven't yet realized how powerful this can be, but getting into the same mindset as your client or teen is where true connection happens. I'm curious, have you ever noticed how two best friends seem to mirror each other almost effortlessly? They move the same way, they talk the same way—it's as if they're in perfect sync. This is rapport at its highest level.

One of the simplest ways to create this kind of connection is by matching your client's physiology. You probably already know that matching someone's body language, breathing patterns, and voice tone creates an almost instant sense of comfort and familiarity. When you match these aspects of your client or teen, you're telling their unconscious mind, "We're the same." And now, the magic happens—communication flows easily, trust is built naturally, and your client or teen feels deeply understood.

Maybe you haven't noticed yet, but even something as simple as matching your teen's voice—whether it's their tone, tempo, or pitch—can have a profound impact. If their voice is low, bring yours down to match. If they're speaking quickly, notice their rhythm and match it. This creates a powerful connection that speaks directly to the unconscious, making them feel like you naturally understand where they're coming from. Stop and think about how much easier it becomes to communicate when you're both on the same wavelength.

But rapport goes beyond just voice and tone. Another key is matching their physiology—their breathing patterns, gestures, and movements. Now, imagine the bonding power that comes from matching someone's breathing pattern. I'm wondering if you've experienced that moment when you feel completely in sync with someone, where it seems like you're almost breathing together. This is no accident—it's an unconscious signal of trust and connection, and it's one of the most powerful ways to create rapport.

Here's an overview of how to create rapport:

- Physiology: Mirror your client's or teen's body position, breathing, voice, and hand movements. Matching their gestures and physical cues brings you into alignment with them, building rapport unconsciously.
- Movements: Pay attention to how they move. Matching their gestures creates a feeling of synchronization, helping them feel more connected to you.
- Strategies: Observe how they think and act. Matching their strategies for doing things—whether in problem-solving or their approach to activities—helps establish deeper rapport.
- Tone, Tempo, and Tonality: Match the rhythm of their words, the pitch of their voice, and the tempo of their speech. You'll notice that when your voice and theirs align, trust and comfort are created almost immediately.

When observing people who are in deep rapport, you'll often see them unconsciously matching each other in several key areas, including:

- Breathing
- Voice tone and tonality
- Posture, body movement, and gestures
- Language content and use of key words
- Visual, auditory, and feeling cues
- Beliefs and values

Now, think about what happens when you bring these elements into your interactions. Maybe you haven't yet experienced the full power of rapport, but once you start mirroring and matching, the results are undeniable. After all, rapport is the foundation of deep connection, trust, and influence—and it happens when you're in perfect sync, both consciously and unconsciously.

Now, let's dive into Step Two: Finding the Needs of the Client—a critical step in mastering influence. Maybe you haven't yet realized that understanding your client's top needs can bring you significantly closer to closing the deal. Allan mentioned that he learned these six human needs during one of my seminars, where I shared insights gained from working with titans of business for almost a decade. I'm curious, can you imagine how much more effective your sales process will be when you know exactly what drives your client?

Here's a key insight: 80% of people are driven by security and the desire to feel important. You probably already know that if you can uncover your client's top two needs, you're already 25% closer to closing the deal. And when you combine this with mindset and rapport, you're already 65% of the way there. Let's break down these six human needs and explore how to identify them in your clients:

1. Security-Driven

Everyone seeks security—whether it's financial stability, the assurance that their basic needs will be met, or the certainty that their business will thrive. Now, think about how much easier it is to connect with a client when you can show them that your product or service offers security. But security isn't just about positive reinforcement—it can also manifest in negative ways, like controlling everything, micromanaging, or turning to destructive behaviors like alcohol, drugs, or food.

I'm wondering if you've noticed how some clients may resist change because they fear losing control. The key is to position your offering as a safe, reliable solution that protects their sense of stability. After all, the more secure your clients feel, the closer they are to doing business with you.

2. Variety

Everyone craves variety, a sense of excitement, or a challenge that makes them feel fully alive. Maybe you haven't yet noticed, but people seek variety to avoid the monotony of everyday life. Think of adventure seekers or those who thrive on change and new experiences.

But just like with security, variety can be sought in negative ways—through mood swings, addiction, or destructive habits. Now, consider how your product or service introduces variety. Does it bring excitement, new opportunities, or a sense of adventure? If so, you're aligning with this need in a powerful way.

3. Importance

Many clients are driven by the need to feel important. You probably already know people who define their success by titles, achievements, and recognition—whether it's being a pastor, doctor, or senator. They want to be the best, earn more money, and be seen as an expert.

But there are negative ways of fulfilling this need too—tearing others down, creating unsolvable problems, or using their position to assert dominance. I'm curious, how does your product or service help your client feel important? When you align with their need to feel recognized and valued, you create an unshakable bond that brings you closer to closing the deal.

4. Connection/Love

Most people want love but will settle for connection. This need drives many of our decisions, whether it's in relationships, business, or social circles. Now, think about how your client seeks connection. Are they driven by the desire to belong, to feel understood, or to be part of a larger community?

Negative expressions of this need include joining negative groups, spreading rumors, or engaging in gossip—anything to feel included. Maybe you will realize that when you can help your client feel connected—whether through personal attention, community, or shared values—you're creating an emotional bond that goes beyond just business.

5. Expanding

As the saying goes, "When you're green, you grow; when you're ripe, you rot." Everyone needs to feel like they are growing and expanding, whether it's through learning new skills, writing a book, or creating a seminar. Stop and think—is your client constantly seeking opportunities to grow?

If they're not growing, they feel unfulfilled, unhappy. Your product or service should offer a way for them to expand their horizons, reach new levels of success, or challenge themselves. After all, growth leads to fulfillment, and fulfillment leads to loyalty.

6. Service

The highest form of fulfillment often comes from serving others. Maybe you haven't yet realized how much your client values giving back—whether it's through their business, personal efforts, or involvement in a nonprofit. Now, think about how your offering helps your client serve others or create impact. The more clients you serve, the more opportunities you create for yourself and for them, generating both personal fulfillment and financial success.

When you understand and align with these six human needs, you unlock a powerful way to connect with your client on a deeper level. Now, with mindset, rapport, and an understanding of these needs, you're already more than halfway to closing the deal. Can you imagine the results when you fully embrace these principles in every conversation? This is the path to influence, and it's how you take your business to the next level.

Step Three: Value—one of the most critical elements in the influence model. Maybe you haven't yet realized how essential it is to add value before you ever talk about price, but this step will change the way you approach every client interaction. I'm curious, how often have you seen people dive straight into pricing without first establishing rapport or truly understanding the client's needs? You probably already know that doing this leads to missed opportunities, because without adding value, price is meaningless.

In the influence model, it's all about creating value for your client. Stop and think for a moment—when was the last time you asked your client what truly matters to them? What has to happen for them to feel comfortable doing business with you? Maybe you haven't yet asked, but when you take the time to uncover what your client values most, you're already positioning yourself as a trusted partner.

The key to adding value is simple: find out what your client values by asking the right questions. Ask them, "What needs to happen for you to trust me or do business with me?" This question alone opens the door to a deeper conversation—one where your client tells you exactly what they need, what they prioritize, and what their pain points are. Now, instead of talking about price, you're talking about solutions that solve their problems and meet their needs.

Maybe you've noticed how often people jump straight to price before they've even built rapport. This is a major mistake. Price is only important after you've shown your client how your product or service adds real value to their life or business. Without understanding their values and needs, price becomes a roadblock instead of a bridge to closing the deal.

Now, think about this: What if, before ever mentioning cost, you took the time to fully understand what your client values? You've already built rapport, you've identified their needs, and you've shown them how your offering aligns with their values. I'm wondering if you can imagine how much more likely they'd be to do business with you, simply because you took the time to focus on what matters to them.

The bottom line is this—value comes first. When you understand what your client values most, you're not just selling a product or service; you're offering them a solution that fits perfectly into their world. After all, value creates trust, and trust is the foundation of every successful business relationship.

So stop and notice how often you're talking about price before establishing value. Maybe you haven't yet realized, but once you start focusing on what your client values most, the entire conversation changes. Now, instead of negotiating on price, you're negotiating on the value you provide—and that's where influence truly begins.

Step Four: Desire—where the real magic happens. Maybe you haven't yet realized how important it is to create a burning desire for your product or service, but desire is what drives action. I'm curious, have you ever seen a client so captivated by an offer that they can't wait to do business with you? That's what happens when you build desire, and it's what turns a conversation into a sale.

To create desire, you need to make your product or service so irresistible that your clients feel compelled to act. You probably already know that one of the most effective ways to do this is by adding social proof—testimonies from satisfied clients who've already benefited from what you offer. Can you imagine how powerful it is when a potential client sees people just like them achieving success because of you? It's a trigger that builds trust, and once trust is there, desire follows naturally.

Another way to build desire is through educational-based marketing. Maybe you haven't noticed, but when you position yourself as an expert—someone who educates and solves problems—you're no longer just offering a product; you're offering a solution. Now, think about this: What if you could create a narrative where your client sees the pain points in their life or business, and your service becomes the remedy they've been searching for?

I'm wondering if you've ever experienced how powerful it is to tap into a client's pain points. When people see the gap between where they are and where they want to be, desire kicks in. You're not just selling a product anymore—you're solving a problem, eliminating frustration, and delivering the solution they didn't even know they needed.

Here's the key: Desire is built on emotion. When you weave social proof into your conversation or marketing, you're showing clients that others have already succeeded with you. When you create educational content that highlights their pain points and offers your product as the solution, you're showing them exactly how you can help. After all, people don't just buy products—they buy outcomes, they buy feelings, they buy relief from their problems.

Now, imagine how much more powerful your sales process will be when you're not just offering a service but creating desire. Stop and think about how different the conversation becomes when your client wants to do business with you—when they see you as the one with the answers, the solutions, and the results.

So stop and notice—how are you building desire in your current sales process? Maybe you haven't yet realized, but by adding social proof, using educational-based marketing, and highlighting pain points, you can naturally create a sense of urgency and desire that makes clients excited to work with you. This is where influence happens, and it's how you turn prospects into loyal clients who can't wait to say "yes."

Step Five: Objections—the moment where many people start to feel uncomfortable, but maybe you haven't yet realized that objections are actually a good thing. I'm curious, have you ever thought of objections as a sign of interest? Because that's exactly what they are. You probably already know that when someone raises an objection, it means they're engaged, they're listening, and they're considering your offer. Now, what if instead of fearing objections, you got excited every time you heard one?

Here's the key: I believe most people don't practice their objections enough. They shy away from them or try to avoid them altogether. But in reality, objections are your opportunity to add more value, to clarify misunderstandings, and to move closer to closing the deal. Stop and think about this—if they weren't interested, they wouldn't raise objections. So, when you hear them, get excited because this means they're intrigued by what you have and what you're saying.

Maybe you haven't yet realized, but objections are not the end of the conversation—they're the gateway to deeper engagement. When a client brings up an objection, it's an invitation for you to provide more clarity, reassurance, and confidence in your product or service. After all, the client wants to trust you—they just need a little more certainty before they move forward. I'm wondering if you've noticed how powerful it is when you handle objections with enthusiasm and confidence.

Here's the secret: objections are stepping stones. They give you insight into what your client is really thinking, and they provide you with the chance to address their concerns head-on. Maybe you haven't yet practiced handling objections enough, but once you start getting comfortable with them, you'll see how they can actually accelerate the closing process.

Think about it this way—when you welcome objections and handle them with ease, you're building trust. You're showing your client that you're not afraid to face their concerns, and you're confident in the value you bring. Now, instead of avoiding objections, embrace them. Listen carefully, respond thoughtfully, and use them as a tool to strengthen your rapport and increase your influence.

So stop and notice—the next time a client raises an objection, what's your immediate reaction? Maybe you haven't yet realized how much of an opportunity this is to solidify your offer and move closer to a "yes." After all, objections aren't barriers—they're bridges to closing the deal. When you get excited about hearing them, you're already on the path to success. This is where mastery happens, and it's how you take control of the conversation and guide your client confidently toward a decision.

Step Six: The Close—but here's the truth: Maybe you haven't yet realized that when you've mastered the steps of influence, there's really no such thing as "closing." I'm curious, what if instead of focusing on "closing the deal," you could just confidently ask your client, "What credit card are you using?" Because when you've done everything right, that's exactly how simple it becomes.

In the process of mastering the secret language of influence, if you've built rapport, found their needs, added value, and handled objections, the natural next step is for the client to take action. You probably already know that when someone is ready to buy, you don't need to push them—they're already mentally committed. All you have to do is ask for the payment details, and the rest falls into place. Maybe you haven't yet noticed, but this shift in mindset turns the close from a high-pressure moment into an effortless transition.

Here's the key: There's no pressure when the client already sees the value. You don't need to force the conversation toward a close—the decision has already been made in their mind. The rapport, trust, and understanding you've built naturally lead them to say "yes." Now, instead of seeing the close as an obstacle, see it as a simple question: "Which credit card will you be using?"

I'm wondering if you've ever experienced that moment when the client is practically ready to hand you their payment details before you even ask. That's not coincidence—that's the result of mastering the influence process. When you do everything right, you don't have to "close" in the traditional sense. The client already trusts you, sees the value, and wants what you're offering.

After all, when you lead with confidence and authenticity, the client doesn't feel like they're being sold to—they feel like they're making a smart, informed decision. Stop and think about how powerful this is: when you shift from "closing" to simply asking for the next step, you remove all the pressure and make it feel natural.

So stop and notice—how does your closing process feel right now? Maybe you haven't yet realized that when you ask the right questions, build desire, and handle objections with ease, the close happens naturally. After all, it's not about closing a deal—it's about guiding your client toward the outcome they already want. And when you've done everything right, the only question left is, "What credit card are you using?" This is where mastery happens, and it's how you take the stress out of closing and turn it into the easiest part of the conversation.

Step Seven: The Follow-Up—where the real long-term magic happens. Maybe you haven't yet realized how crucial follow-up is, but it's the key to staying top of mind and keeping your clients engaged. I'm curious, have you ever thought about follow-up in the same way you think about dating? Because when you meet someone who interests you, you don't just stop at the first encounter—you keep the conversation going. You send messages, plan coffee or lunch dates, and find ways to build rapport. Business follow-up works in exactly the same way.

I like to call it TOMA—Top of Mind Awareness. You probably already know that the more you can stay in front of your clients, the more likely they are to think of you when they're ready to make a decision. Now, here's the trick: follow-up doesn't have to feel formal or forced. One day, you might send them an article about a subject that's relevant to their interests, the next day you could send a white paper, and the following week, you might even throw in a lighthearted joke or something that gets them smiling.

Maybe you haven't yet noticed, but the follow-up isn't just about keeping your product or service in front of them—it's about creating an ongoing relationship. Think of it like dating: You don't propose on the first date, right? You build a connection, create trust, and gradually strengthen the relationship. The same applies to your business. I'm wondering if you've thought of follow-up this way before—like a series of small, meaningful interactions that lead to something much bigger.

The follow-up is about rapport—keeping your client thinking about you, but in a way that feels natural and genuine. After all, when people feel connected to you, when they see that you're offering value even when you're not selling, they start to trust you more and more. And the more trust you build, the more likely they are to do business with you.

Here's the key: Consistency is everything. Now, think about how you can keep your client engaged over time. You want to send the right mix of content—something educational, something personal, something lighthearted—to keep the conversation alive. Maybe you haven't yet realized, but each touchpoint is a chance to deepen the relationship.

Stop and think for a moment: How do you follow up with your clients right now? Are you keeping them engaged with a variety of content and interactions, or are you only reaching out when you want to sell something? The follow-up is your chance to show that you care about the relationship, not just the transaction. After all, business, like dating, is about nurturing a connection over time.

So stop and notice—how are you following up right now? Maybe you haven't yet realized how much rapport you can build through consistent, meaningful follow-up. This is where the relationship is strengthened, and it's how you turn prospects into loyal clients who think of you every time they need a solution. When you master follow-up, you're not just doing business—you're building a network of clients who are excited to stay connected with you.

Study Questions for this chapter:

1. I'm curious, how often are you following up with your clients after the initial interaction? Are you staying top of mind consistently?

2. Maybe you haven't yet realized, but are you diversifying your follow-up methods, like sending articles, white papers, or something fun, to keep your clients engaged?

3. Can you imagine how your business would change if you treated follow-up like dating—building rapport with consistent, meaningful interactions?

4. I'm wondering if you've thought about how the mix of educational content and personal touches in your follow-ups might create a stronger bond with your clients?

5. You probably already know that consistency is key in building relationships. How consistent are you in reaching out to your clients after your initial meeting?

6. Stop and think—how personalized are your follow-ups? Do they feel like valuable, tailored interactions, or do they seem transactional and impersonal?

7. Maybe you haven't noticed, but how much time do you spend nurturing relationships with clients who aren't ready to buy yet? Are you laying the groundwork for future business?

8. After all, what kind of impact could you create if your follow-ups were seen not as sales tactics but as genuine efforts to stay connected and provide value?

9. Now, how can you add more creativity to your follow-up process? What kind of content—beyond business—would keep your clients engaged with you regularly?

10. I'm curious, are you taking advantage of follow-ups to strengthen relationships over time, or are you only following up when there's an immediate need for your product or service?

Chapter 10: The Sextillion Time Management

In this chapter, Allan reflects on Dr. John Oda's time management system, which unveiled a transformative approach to productivity. Maybe you haven't yet realized, but the secret to mastering time isn't just about discipline—it's about emulating greatness. Dr. Oda, inspired by his father, Odessa Oda, modeled his father's impeccable time management skills to create a system that elevated his ability to navigate multiple roles with precision and efficiency.

Now, think about this: Dr. Oda's time management wasn't just about scheduling or multitasking—it was about learning from the best and adapting those principles to his own life. You probably already know that success leaves clues, and Dr. Oda understood that if he wanted to achieve greatness, he needed to model the practices of someone who had mastered it. By observing his father's capacity to juggle demanding responsibilities, Dr. Oda developed his own unique system that has become a blueprint for productivity and success.

For Allan, this revelation was a game-changer. I'm curious, have you ever considered how much more effective you could be by modeling the habits of successful individuals? Maybe you haven't yet realized, but by looking at those who have already achieved what you're striving for, you gain access to strategies and insights that can propel you forward.

Dr. Oda's journey wasn't just about mastering his own time—it was about understanding how emulation creates transformation. His father, Odessa Oda, balanced two full-time jobs, raised a large family, and maintained strong social ties, all while pursuing personal growth. Stop and think for a moment—how many people do you know who can handle that level of responsibility with grace and efficiency?

Here's the key: Modeling greatness is more than just copying someone's behavior—it's about understanding their mindset and their principles and adapting them to your unique circumstances. Maybe you haven't noticed, but by following Dr. Oda's lead, Allan discovered that greatness isn't just inherited—it's learned, shaped, and perfected through practice. Now, with this mindset, Allan began applying these principles to his own life, drawing inspiration from visionary leaders like Dr. Oda and his father.

In essence, Dr. Oda's approach to time management reflects a deeper philosophy—one rooted in the power of emulation and the ability to blend the wisdom of the past with the possibilities of the future. After all, the most successful individuals don't just manage time; they master it by learning from those who've already walked the path to greatness. Now, what if you embraced the same philosophy? What if you modeled the time management skills of those who have already achieved the desired level of success? I'm wondering if you can imagine how much more efficient and focused you'd become simply by following the steps laid out by those who have already mastered the art of time. This is what Dr. Oda's system teaches us—time management isn't just about the clock; it's about modeling greatness and using it to unlock your full potential.

Dr. John Oda paints a vivid picture of his upbringing, illuminating the remarkable figure of his father. This man seamlessly balanced multiple roles and embodied the essence of time management. Maybe you haven't yet realized, but Dr. Oda's profound ability to master productivity stems directly from the lessons he learned while observing his father. As he reflects on his childhood, Dr. Oda marvels at his father's seemingly endless capacity to handle everything with ease—managing two full-time jobs, nurturing a loving relationship with his wife for 67 years, and maintaining strong family bonds, all while still finding time for moments of joy, like watching TV together or engaging in heartfelt conversations.

I'm curious: Have you ever wondered how someone can juggle so many responsibilities while still appearing calm and collected? Dr. Oda often gets asked the same question. How does he write books, lead multiple companies, stick to a rigorous fitness routine, and still make time for his family? His answer is simple yet profound: his father—the ultimate example of efficiency, discipline, and dedication.

Dr. Oda vividly recalls the daily rhythm of his father's life, a perfect balance between relentless hard work and meaningful family connection. You probably already know that early risers tend to have more control over their day, and Dr. Oda's father was no exception. He would wake before dawn to tend to the family garden, head to work for long hours and come home briefly to connect with his family before returning to his professional responsibilities, often working late into the night. Even weekends were dedicated to additional factory work, ensuring a steady income. Now, imagine the strength and dedication required to maintain that level of commitment for four decades.

Stop and think about this: Dr. Oda's father didn't just work hard to survive—he worked hard to provide his children with opportunities. His tireless efforts allowed Dr. Oda and his siblings to pursue quality education and brighter futures. Maybe you haven't yet realized, but that kind of unwavering dedication to one's family and work is a masterclass in time management itself. It's not just about fitting tasks into your day; it's about prioritizing the things that matter most and doing them with intention.

Dr. Oda often reflects on a pivotal conversation from his childhood, one that left a lasting impact on his life and success. As a curious young boy, he asked his father why they kept a family garden. His father's answer was simple yet profound: the garden wasn't just for their family; it was a way to provide for their less fortunate neighbors. The garden was an act of kindness, a way to share abundance and offer support to those in need. This powerful lesson of generosity, mixed with practicality, stayed with Dr. Oda throughout his life.

In his father's dedication to working 16-hour days, day after day, Dr. Oda found the blueprint for success. Through emulation, Dr. Oda has carried forward the principles of hard work, sacrifice, and focus on the greater good. Maybe you haven't noticed yet, but true time management isn't about squeezing more tasks into the day—it's about making the most meaningful impact with the time you have.

As Dr. Oda reflects on his father's life, he finds both solace and inspiration in the timeless lessons of resilience, perseverance, and unwavering commitment to excellence. After all, greatness doesn't happen by accident—it's the result of disciplined time management, a principle passed down from generation to generation, creating a legacy that Dr. Oda continues to live by.

I'm wondering if you can imagine how transformative your life could be by adopting these principles—not just managing time but mastering it in the way Dr. Oda learned from his father. This is the essence of time management, and it's what makes greatness possible

Moreover, Dr. John Oda's father imparted invaluable lessons on the importance of meticulous planning and persistence. Maybe you haven't yet realized, but the principles of success—whether in gardening or life—are built on these foundations. Dr. Oda's father taught him that timing and foresight are critical to achieving any goal, just like deciding when and what to plant in the family garden. I'm curious: have you considered how much success depends on these two elements?

Now, imagine applying those same lessons to your personal or professional life. You probably already know that success doesn't come without challenges—it requires a steadfast commitment to weathering adversity. Dr. Oda recalls how his father's persistence through difficult seasons mirrored the persistence needed to achieve long-term success in any endeavor. Maybe you haven't noticed yet, but perseverance is often the missing ingredient in many failed attempts.

As Dr. Oda reflects on his father's wisdom, he finds timeless lessons that transcend the simplicity of gardening. Planning, persistence, and generosity were not just values—they became guiding beacons in their own journey toward success. Stop and think about how these principles might apply to your own challenges. After all, true achievement often comes not only from overcoming obstacles but also from extending kindness and generosity along the way.

In the legacy of his father's profound wisdom, Dr. Oda found more than just inspiration—he discovered a blueprint for living. The simple act of working in the family garden became a metaphor for life, teaching him the power of planning, the necessity of persevering, and the importance of compassion. I'm wondering if you've ever thought about how these lessons can transform the way you approach your own goals and relationships.

As Dr. Oda fondly recalls his childhood, he reflects on how his father's teachings shaped his approach to time management. It wasn't until after his father's passing that Dr. Oda fully realized how much of his own system had been influenced by his father's wisdom. The significance of the family garden loomed large in his memories, serving as a constant reminder of the importance of timing, preparation, and resource allocation.

Growing up in the Midwest, where the seasons dictated the success of gardening, Dr. Oda learned early on that timing is everything. You can't plant just any crop at any time—it requires forethought and strategic planning. Maybe you haven't yet realized how critical this same lesson is in business and life. The necessity of planting certain crops at specific times was more than a lesson in gardening—it was a lesson in life. It's about knowing when to act, how to prepare, and being adaptable when conditions change.

Dr. Oda synthesized these life lessons from his father's example into a comprehensive time management system. He seamlessly integrated the concepts of planning, timing, and adaptability into a framework for efficiency and productivity. You probably already know that great time management doesn't just happen—it's crafted with care and intention. Maybe you will start to notice how much your own life could benefit from a similar approach.

Yet, Dr. Oda's time management system wasn't shaped solely by his father's teachings. His mother also played a crucial role, alongside the many mentors he encountered throughout his journey. By amalgamating these personal experiences, familial wisdom, and external insights, Dr. Oda crafted a holistic approach to both personal development and time management.

Now, what if you adopted the same mindset—combining the lessons from your own life with the wisdom of those who have mentored you? After all, greatness is rarely achieved alone. It comes from absorbing, integrating, and applying the knowledge gained from those who came before us.

In hindsight, Dr. John Oda recognizes the profound impact of his upbringing, acknowledging the invaluable lessons passed down by his parents. The family garden, in particular, became a microcosm of life's challenges and opportunities, offering tangible lessons in resilience, adaptability, and perseverance. In this space, Dr. Oda learned to cultivate not just vegetables but the core principles that would guide his path toward personal and professional fulfillment.

Dr. Oda's time management system, aptly named "The ODA Secret Place," is a reflection of this legacy. Inspired by the wisdom of Psalms 91, it is rooted in his mother's spiritual teachings and his father's steadfast example. Maybe you haven't yet realized, but the synthesis of these familial lessons, coupled with external mentorship, formed the foundation of a comprehensive approach to productivity and personal growth. I'm curious: have you ever considered how deeply our upbringing influences our daily habits and time management?

At the heart of "The ODA Secret Place" is a central theme: outcome. You probably already know that clarity around the desired end result is critical to success. Whether it's acquiring a new home, launching a business, or cultivating a garden, Dr. Oda emphasizes the importance of having a clear vision. His father embodied this principle in the family garden, where the outcome—the fresh vegetables that nourished the family—was the tangible reward for careful planning and consistent action.

Maybe you haven't noticed yet, but when you align your actions with a clear outcome, the process becomes more purposeful. Just like Dr. Oda's father took pleasure in the harvest, we, too, can find fulfillment in the fruits of our labor when we operate with intentionality. After all, when you have a clear goal, the journey toward it becomes more focused, and the challenges along the way seem more manageable.

"The ODA Secret Place" is more than just a system; it's an invitation to embark on a transformative journey of self-discovery and fulfillment. Dr. Oda believes that by embracing the power of intentionality and aligning actions with desired outcomes, individuals can unlock the secrets to personal and professional success. Guided by the enduring wisdom of Psalms 91, practitioners of this system learn to navigate life's challenges with clarity, purpose, and compassion.

One of the core elements of "The ODA Secret Place" is the "D," which represents the Daily Method of Operations (DMO), combined with the desire to serve others, underpinned by making a Decision. I'm wondering if you've ever considered how much success hinges on consistent, intentional action. Dr. Oda draws inspiration from his father's daily care of the family garden—watering, pest control, and fertilization. These simple, consistent efforts were essential to ensuring the vitality of the garden, just as the DMO is essential to the health of a business.

In business, the DMO involves making phone calls, conducting follow-ups, supervising staff, and creating systems for long-term success. You probably already know that consistency is the key to profitability and wealth creation, much like the garden flourished through regular attention. Maybe you haven't yet noticed, but the same principles apply to any endeavor—whether personal or professional.

Another vital component of Dr. Oda's system is the desire to serve others. His father embodied this through his unwavering commitment to the community, providing fresh vegetables to neighbors and offering help whenever needed. In business, this translates to meeting the needs of customers and clients, delivering exceptional products or services, and fostering positive relationships. Imagine how different your outcomes would be if your primary focus was on serving others rather than just seeking personal gain.

The Decision to prioritize service is what paves the way for transformative outcomes. Dr. Oda emphasizes the importance of setting clear intentions and making informed decisions reflecting a deep service commitment. Whether in the pursuit of personal goals or building a successful business, service to others creates meaningful connections and long-lasting impact.

In refining "The ODA Secret Place," Dr. Oda also incorporated three foundational P's: Plan, Purpose, and Persistence, alongside the principle of Acting as if—acting as though your goals and dreams have already been achieved. Stop and think about this for a moment: How much more powerful would your actions be if you truly believed your success was inevitable?

Now, with these foundational principles, Dr. Oda offers a roadmap to not just time management but personal mastery. After all, when you combine careful planning, purposeful actions, and a desire to serve others, you unlock the potential for transformative growth—in business, in relationships, and in life. The ODA Secret Place is your invitation to step into that journey.

My father epitomized the first P—Plan—with remarkable precision. Every day, he meticulously charted a course of action for his garden, executing that plan with unwavering diligence. Maybe you haven't yet realized, but it's not just about having a plan; it's about committing to it every single day, no matter the circumstances. My father understood that a well-thought-out plan is the foundation upon which all success is built, and he followed his plan with a sense of purpose that went far beyond simply growing vegetables.

His Purpose was crystal clear: to provide sustenance for our family, to ensure we were always cared for. I'm curious: how often do you reflect on your own purpose and why? My father taught me that the more compelling "whys" we have in life, the closer we come to realizing our goals. You probably already know that when your purpose is strong enough, it drives you forward, even when challenges arise. Stop and think about this for a moment: What is your purpose? What compels you to keep moving forward, especially when things get tough?

Persistence, the third P, is non-negotiable. Maybe you haven't noticed yet, but success isn't just about the plans we make or the purpose we define—it's about sticking with it, no matter the obstacles. My father's commitment to tending the garden, despite unpredictable weather, pests, or setbacks, taught me that persistence is what turns dreams into reality. After all, defeat looms large without persistence, and the seeds we plant never have a chance to grow. I'm wondering if you've ever felt on the brink of giving up, only to find that one last push brought you closer to success.

In my work with individuals seeking their soulmates, I guide them to create a Plan of action—mapping out specific places and avenues to explore their quest for companionship. But a plan without purpose lacks power, so we also focus on the why. I ask my clients to generate a list of 50 reasons why finding a soulmate matters to them. Now, you might wonder why so many reasons. It's simple—the more reasons you have, the clearer your vision becomes, and that clarity propels you forward with motivation.

The integration of the three P's—Plan, Purpose, and Persistence—forms the bedrock of "The ODA Secret Place." When you adopt a strategic approach, clarify your intentions, and maintain unwavering determination, you naturally navigate life's challenges with confidence and resilience. Maybe you haven't yet realized, but these three elements, when combined, create a roadmap that leads directly to the fulfillment of your dreams.

In "The ODA Secret Place," the letter A represents Act as if—an essential phase where you embody the reality of having already achieved your goal. Consider this: when someone is determined to acquire a house, they don't just passively hope for it—they begin to act as if they already own it. You probably already know that success starts in the mind. It's about behaving as though you've already crossed the finish line. Whether it's securing more clients, putting in extra hours, or engaging in activities aligned with your vision, you fully immerse yourself in the mindset of success.

Visualization becomes paramount during this phase. You don't just imagine your success; you live it in your mind. Now, imagine you've already moved into that house, or your business is thriving—you can feel the success, the fulfillment of your dreams. I'm wondering if you've noticed how adopting this perspective changes everything. It cultivates a sense of certainty and expectation, which are the catalysts that attract miracles into your life.

My father embodied this principle in everything, especially in his garden. Even when the seeds had just been sown, he would speak life into the plants, nurturing them with unwavering belief in their growth. I vividly recall him saying, "Son, behold my beautiful garden," long before harvest. His faith and his absolute conviction in realizing his vision taught me the power of acting as if—a transformative practice that propels us toward manifesting our deepest desires.

After all, if you can see it in your mind and believe it in your heart, you're already halfway there. This is the essence of "The ODA Secret Place"—acting as if you've already achieved what you seek, living in that success before it arrives. Now, can you imagine what might happen if you began to embody this practice in your own life?

Acting as if is a powerful principle that turns the perceived into the realized. I witnessed this firsthand in my father's garden—what looked like mere dirt soon blossomed into a breathtaking array of greenery and life. Maybe you haven't yet realized, but this transformation didn't happen by accident. It was the result of faith and action, even when there was no visible evidence of success. I'm curious: have you ever stopped to think about how this applies to every area of your life?

When I guide individuals in their quest for a soulmate, I teach them to embody the reality of already having found their partner. You probably already know this isn't about wishful thinking or hoping for a chance encounter; it's about confidently expecting the fulfillment of their desire. Now, imagine living with that level of certainty, much like Jesus, who expressed gratitude in advance for the miracles He performed. Maybe you haven't noticed, but this kind of expectation creates a powerful shift—it opens the door for miracles to manifest.

In my experience as a business coach, I've seen remarkable transformations by integrating this principle into my time management system. By teaching clients to act as if their success is already a reality and tap into their higher power, I've watched businesses soar—some with growth rates skyrocketing from 100% to 2000% in a short time. After all, the key lies in redirecting focus away from negative emotions like hate, fear, worry, and stress and toward positive, empowering beliefs and actions.

Think of it like planting seeds in a garden. Focusing on negative emotions is like sowing seeds of despair, limitation, and doubt. Stop and think—what happens when you water these seeds with constant rumination, fertilize them with further negative thoughts, and expose them to the low vibrational energy of fear and worry? You stunt your own growth and hinder your progress toward success.

Now, consider this: the seeds we plant in our personal and professional lives determine the harvest we reap. Maybe you haven't yet realized, but by adopting the mindset of acting as is, aligning your thoughts, words, and actions with your desired outcome, you cultivate fertile ground for abundance and fulfillment. I'm wondering if you've asked yourself this question lately: What seeds are you planting today?

Because the seeds you plant today will shape the reality you experience tomorrow. After all, the principle of acting as if teaches us that faith, combined with action, creates transformation. So, I challenge you—are you planting seeds of confidence, expectation, and success? Or are you watering the seeds of limitation and fear? Now is the time to choose the harvest you want to reap.

Here are ten reflective questions inspired by Dr. John Oda's Time Management Chapter, designed to challenge your thinking and drive actionable insights:

1. I'm curious: how often do you take the time to create a detailed plan for your day or week, and how closely do you follow through on it?
2. Maybe you haven't yet realized it, but what is the driving purpose behind your daily activities? How does it influence the way you manage your time?
3. Stop and think—how often do you give up on a task when faced with setbacks? Could persistence be the missing link in achieving your goals?
4. You probably already know that consistency is key. What are the daily actions or rituals that could be refined to help you stay on track with your time management?
5. I'm wondering if you have a system in place to track your progress toward your long-term goals. How do you measure success in your daily or weekly tasks?
6. Maybe you haven't noticed, but are you acting as if your goals have already been achieved? How could this shift in mindset change the way you approach your day?
7. After all, when you align your actions with your goals, results follow. Are your current activities aligned with the outcome you want to achieve?
8. Now, consider your own version of "planting seeds"—what actions today will yield the greatest results in the future?
9. Can you imagine how different your life would be if you approached every task with the belief that your success is inevitable? What impact could this have on your time management?
10. I'm curious: How do you manage negative emotions like fear, worry, or stress? How do they influence the way you spend your time? Could redirecting this energy improve your productivity?

These questions are designed to provoke introspection, challenge your current approach, and inspire you to adopt "The ODA Secret Place" principles for greater productivity and fulfillment.

Chapter 11: The Octopus Method of Marketing

Allan sat in the audience, deeply engrossed in a seminar, as Dr. John Oda took the stage with his trademark energy and insight. Maybe you haven't yet realized, but the world of business is like a battlefield, and most companies are woefully unprepared for the war of competition. That's when Dr. Oda introduced the Octopus Method of Marketing, a strategy that immediately resonated with Allan. I'm curious: have you ever thought of your marketing efforts like an octopus—flexible, adaptable, with many arms working simultaneously to seize every opportunity?

As Dr. Oda painted the picture of World War 3, he emphasized the importance of comprehensive preparation to prevent catastrophe. You probably already know that relying on just one or two marketing strategies to grow a business is like sending only the Army and Air Force to fight a war. Stop and think—could you ever expect victory in such a limited scenario? Dr. Oda's words hit hard. As diverse military strategies are essential for winning in battle, so are diversified marketing approaches critical for business survival.

Dr. Oda highlighted a staggering statistic: 70% of businesses fail within a decade. For Allan, this was a wake-up call. Maybe you haven't noticed yet, but using only one or two marketing tactics is a recipe for disaster. Dr. Oda's Octopus Method of Marketing offers a solution—each tentacle representing a different marketing strategy working together to cover all angles. Now, imagine your business armed with multiple marketing tentacles, reaching out through various platforms, engaging different audiences, and seizing every opportunity.

But it wasn't just about diversification. Dr. Oda emphasized the need to systematize the Octopus Method, just as a military general orchestrates a multi-pronged attack with precision and foresight. I'm wondering if you've ever thought about your marketing like this—a carefully planned, strategic assault on the competitive marketplace. In this context, Educational Based Marketing took center stage, a concept pioneered by the legendary Chet Holmes, who famously said, "Market data is way more powerful than product data."

Allan's eyes were opened. He understood that educating potential customers on the value of his products and services was far more effective than traditional sales tactics. After all, as Dr. Oda taught, knowledge empowers the buyer. Customers don't just want to know what you sell—they want to understand why it matters, how it benefits them, and how it can solve their problems.

Inspired by these insights, Allan made a bold decision. He resolved to implement the Octopus Method of Marketing into his own business strategy. Maybe you haven't yet realized, but just like the octopus uses its many tentacles to navigate its environment, you, too, must use multiple channels and platforms to engage your audience. The more tentacles you have, the more opportunities you seize. I'm curious: how many marketing tentacles are you using right now? Are they enough to protect your business from failure?

Allan knew that casting a wide net—leveraging social media, email marketing, webinars, content marketing, and more—would allow him to reach his target audience more effectively than ever before. With Dr. Oda's teachings in mind, Allan was ready to embrace this multi-faceted approach to marketing and take his business to new heights.

Allan's journey underscored the transformative power of strategic thinking and proactive planning. Maybe you haven't yet noticed, but the mindset of a warrior is exactly what it takes to survive and thrive in the competitive business world. With the Octopus Method of Marketing and Educational Based Marketing as his tools, Allan was ready to navigate the battlefield of business, conquer challenges, and build sustained success.

Are you prepared to apply the Octopus Method to your business? Can you imagine how transformative it would be to approach marketing with the same strategic precision that a general uses in warfare? After all, victory belongs to those who prepare, adapt, and deploy every resource available.

In the illuminating seminar Allan attended, Dr. John Oda unveiled the intricacies of the Octopus Method of Marketing, a revolutionary approach that draws on the wisdom of his near-decade-long partnership with the late Chet Holmes. Maybe you haven't yet realized, but Dr. Oda didn't just adopt Holmes' strategies—he elevated them. By integrating Educational Based Marketing with his own creation, Neuro Business Conditioning (NBC), Dr. Oda created a marketing framework designed to propel businesses to new heights of success. Have you ever thought about how combining strategic education with psychological influence could transform your marketing results?

During the seminar, Dr. Oda shared an intriguing anecdote that captivated the audience: his encounter with a rare nine-legged octopus in Japan. You probably already know that the octopus, with its flexibility and reach, is a perfect metaphor for diversified marketing. But the nine legs of this octopus symbolized something even deeper—a unique approach with nine distinct marketing strategies for driving traffic, building engagement, and fostering business growth. Imagine if your business had the flexibility and reach of a nine-legged octopus, each leg representing a strategy working in perfect harmony.

Dr. Oda emphasized that businesses could achieve exponential growth on all levels by systematically implementing these nine strategies. Maybe you haven't noticed yet, but success in today's marketplace requires not just one or two tactics—it demands a comprehensive system that reaches across platforms and strategies, just like the octopus extends its tentacles in all directions.

Dr. Oda introduced a simple exercise to help businesses assess their performance and maximize their potential: rating your business across the nine key areas of the Octopus Marketing Method. Stop and think—how strong are your efforts in these areas, and where could you improve?

Let's delve into each tentacle of the Octopus Method and evaluate your business on a scale of one to ten:

1. **Web Presence**

- Company Website: Is your website up-to-date, visually appealing, and user-friendly? Does it effectively showcase your products or services? (Rating:)
- Active Blog: Are you regularly publishing high-quality, educational content to engage and inform your audience? (Rating:)
- SEO, SEM, SMM: How strong are your efforts in search engine optimization (SEO), search engine marketing (SEM), and social media marketing (SMM) to drive traffic and increase visibility? (Rating:)
- Affiliate Marketing, Online Partners, PPC: Are you utilizing affiliate marketing, partnering with online businesses, and employing pay-per-click (PPC) advertising to expand your reach? (Rating:)

- Capture Squeeze Page: Do you have optimized landing pages designed to capture leads and convert visitors into customers? (Rating:)

Maybe you haven't yet realized, but each of these elements is a critical part of your web presence—the foundation of your digital marketing efforts. I'm wondering if you've fully optimized each area, or are there gaps that could be costing you growth opportunities?

The Octopus Method, like the nine-legged marvel in Japan, reminds us that business success depends on multiple points of contact, each working together to strengthen your reach and impact. After all, relying on just one or two legs to support your business leaves you vulnerable. But your business becomes unstoppable when every tentacle is actively working toward the same goal.

As you evaluate your business's performance in these areas, think about how implementing a more comprehensive and diversified marketing system—the Octopus Method—could elevate your results. Dr. Oda's teachings serve as a powerful reminder that preparation, systemization, and consistency are the keys to marketing mastery. So, how will you score, and how will you improve? Now is the time to take control of your marketing future.

2. Personal:

In the realm of personal marketing efforts, Dr. John Oda emphasizes the importance of direct engagement with potential customers. Maybe you haven't yet realized, but some of the most effective marketing happens when you put yourself directly in front of your audience. I'm curious: how often do you assess the strength of your personal outreach strategies? Stop and think—are you truly maximizing these efforts, or could you refine your approach?

Cold Call (Walk-in, Telephone)

- How effective are your cold-calling (treasure hunting) efforts in initiating meaningful conversations and building relationships with potential customers?

- Maybe you haven't noticed, but cold calling is often viewed with skepticism. However, Dr. Oda teaches that when done with the right mindset and strategy, it can be one of the most personal and direct ways to create a connection. I'm curious: are you approaching cold calls with confidence and a clear purpose, or are you just going through the motions?

Trade Show

- How successful are your interactions and lead-generation efforts at trade shows and industry events? (Rating:)
- You probably already know that trade shows are a treasure trove of opportunities where you can engage face-to-face with prospects, demonstrate your products, and build instant credibility. Maybe you haven't yet realized how vital it is to have a clear plan for following up after each interaction. Dr. Oda emphasizes the importance of strategic follow-up to keep those conversations alive long after the event ends.

Product/Service Seminar, Webinar

- Are your seminars and webinars well-attended and impactful in educating prospects about your offerings? (Rating:)
- Dr. Oda's teachings on Educational Based Marketing remind us that seminars and webinars are not just about selling—they are about providing value and positioning yourself as a trusted expert. I'm wondering if your current seminars and webinars are truly connecting with your audience. Are you providing actionable insights, or are you merely delivering information?

Now, ask yourself—how are you performing in these areas? Maybe you haven't yet noticed, but the more personal your outreach, the stronger your connection with potential clients. Cold calls, trade shows, seminars, and webinars are not just boxes to check; they are tentacles of your marketing strategy that, when properly leveraged, can significantly expand your reach and influence.

Dr. Oda teaches that personal interaction is one of the most powerful tools in your arsenal in the Octopus Method of Marketing. After all, people do business with those they trust, and trust is built through personal engagement. Now is the time to evaluate where you stand in your personal outreach efforts and how you can strengthen these critical components of your marketing strategy.

3. Direct Mail:

Dr. John Oda has often said that direct mail is far from outdated—in fact, when used strategically, it's one of the most powerful tools for cutting through the noise and directly reaching your audience. Maybe you haven't yet realized, but direct mail, whether in physical form or through email, is a personal touchpoint that creates a sense of connection. I'm curious: how often do you evaluate the strength of your direct mail campaigns?

Letters, Postcards, Email

- How engaging and targeted are your direct mail campaigns, including letters, postcards, and email newsletters? (Rating:)
- Dr. Oda's teachings on Educational Based Marketing remind us that every piece of direct mail—whether it's a postcard, letter, or email—should provide value and engage your recipient. You probably already know that generic messaging doesn't work. Stop and think—are you crafting your mail campaigns to speak directly to your audience's pain points and desires, or are you sending out one-size-fits-all content?

Dream 100 Campaign

- How effectively is your Dream 100 campaign cultivating relationships with key prospects and influencers in your industry? (Rating:)
- The Dream 100 strategy, originally pioneered by Chet Holmes, is about laser-focusing your efforts on the top 100 prospects or influencers who could transform your business.

Maybe you haven't noticed, but the Dream 100 campaign requires persistence, creativity, and personal engagement. Dr. Oda emphasizes the importance of nurturing these relationships over time, not with a single touchpoint but through consistent, value-driven communication.

I'm wondering if your direct mail campaigns are simply informational or if they truly inspire action. You probably already know that in today's fast-paced digital world, physical mail and highly targeted emails can create a deeper connection than digital ads alone. Dr. Oda often highlights how direct mail, when done right, doesn't just reach the inbox or mailbox—it reaches the mind of the recipient.

Now, ask yourself—are you making the most of your direct mail efforts, or is there room for improvement? Maybe you haven't yet realized, but every piece of mail is a potential conversation starter, a way to get inside the head and heart of your prospects. Whether it's your Dream 100 or the wider audience you're trying to reach, direct mail remains a critical tentacle in the Octopus Method of Marketing.

After all, the key to successful direct mail isn't just about sending—it's about engaging, educating, and building relationships. Dr. Oda would tell you that refining your letters, postcards, and Dream 100 campaigns can create powerful connections that drive your business forward. Now is the time to assess your direct mail strategy and ensure it aligns with the long-term growth and success you envision.

4. YouTube Video:

Dr. John Oda firmly believes in the power of YouTube as a platform to market, educate, and inspire. Maybe you haven't yet realized, but your presence on YouTube is more than just a branding tool—it's a way to build trust, establish authority, and directly engage with your audience. I'm curious: how strong is your current YouTube strategy in leveraging this potential?

Educational Videos

- How effective are your educational videos in providing valuable insights, solving problems, and positioning your brand as an authority in your industry?
- Dr. Oda's approach emphasizes Educational Based Marketing—educating your audience before you sell to them. You probably already know that providing value through

educational content helps establish you as a thought leader in your industry. Stop and think—are your videos delivering solutions to real problems or merely promotional? Maybe you haven't noticed, but the most successful brands are the ones that teach before they sell.

Content Weekly

- Are you consistently uploading fresh and relevant content to your YouTube channel to keep your audience engaged and informed? (Rating:)
- Consistency is key, and Dr. Oda would remind you that content is king, but consistent content is even more powerful. I'm wondering if you have a schedule for posting or if your uploads are sporadic. You probably already know that staying top-of-mind with your audience requires regular interaction, and YouTube is no exception. Stop and think—how frequently are you engaging with your audience through new, relevant content?

Educational Webinars

- Do your webinars effectively educate your audience about your products or services while fostering interaction and trust? (Rating:)
- Dr. Oda often points out that webinars should be an extension of your educational videos—designed to inform and engage. They should create a two-way street where the audience not only learns but also has the opportunity to interact and ask questions. Maybe you haven't realized how important that trust-building element is. I'm curious: how well are your webinars fostering interaction, and are they considered valuable resources in your industry?

Now, take a step back and evaluate your YouTube presence. You probably already know that video content is one of the most powerful ways to connect with an audience. Dr. Oda emphasizes that by delivering consistent, educational, and valuable content, you're not just marketing—you're building a community of loyal followers who see you as a go-to expert in your field.

After all, the world is moving more and more toward video content, and if you're not capitalizing on that trend, you're leaving a significant opportunity untapped. Dr. Oda would encourage you to strengthen your video strategy as part of the Octopus Method of Marketing, ensuring that every video tentacle serves to educate, engage, and empower your audience. Now is the time to refine your YouTube strategy and position yourself as a leader in your space.

5. Literature:

Dr. John Oda often stresses the importance of literature in marketing, noting that the written word still carries immense power in conveying your message and building authority. Maybe you haven't yet realized, but your brochures, white papers, and cut sheets are not just marketing materials—they are tangible representations of your brand's expertise and professionalism. I'm curious: how effectively are you using these pieces of literature to educate, engage, and convert prospects into clients?

Brochures

- Are your brochures visually appealing and informative, providing comprehensive details about your offerings in a concise format?
- Dr. Oda emphasizes that a brochure should look good and clearly communicate your message. It's about balancing visual appeal with valuable content. You probably already know that first impressions matter and your brochure is often the first physical piece of your business that a client will hold. I'm wondering if your current brochures truly reflect the quality of your brand and if they answer the key questions your prospects might have.

White Papers

- How well-researched and insightful are your white papers in addressing industry challenges, showcasing thought leadership, and attracting potential customers? (Rating:)
- White papers are your opportunity to demonstrate expertise and establish authority in your industry. Dr. Oda's approach focuses on using educational tools like white papers to address real industry problems and provide in-depth solutions. Maybe you haven't noticed, but well-crafted white papers aren't just marketing—they are thought leadership in action. Stop and think—are your white papers truly offering insight and value, or are they just disguised sales pitches?

Cut Sheets

- Do your cut sheets effectively highlight key features and benefits of your products or services in a succinct manner? (Rating:)
- Dr. Oda teaches that a cut sheet should get straight to the point, delivering key information about your products or services in a way that's easy to digest. You probably already know that people don't have time to sift through long documents in today's fast-paced world. I'm curious: do your cut sheets focus on the features that matter most to your clients, and do they clearly communicate how those features solve specific problems?

Now, let's evaluate your literature strategy. Dr. Oda emphasizes that brochures, white papers, and cut sheets are essential tentacles in the Octopus Method of Marketing, working in harmony with your other strategies to build trust and educate your audience. Maybe you haven't yet realized this, but your literature needs not only to inform but also to inspire action.

After all, each piece of literature you produce is a reflection of your brand's professionalism and expertise. Dr. Oda would encourage you to think of these materials not just as marketing collateral but as educational tools that serve to position you as an authority in your field. Now is the time to assess whether your literature is truly working for you or if there's room to refine it for maximum impact.

6. **Advertising**:

Dr. John Oda often emphasizes that advertising isn't just about putting your name out there—it's about strategic impact. Maybe you haven't yet realized, but each ad, whether on the radio, TV, or a billboard, should be working to engage, convert, and build trust with your target audience. I'm curious: how effectively are your current advertising efforts driving real results?

Radio, TV, Print Ads (Trade)

- How impactful are your advertising efforts across various mediums, such as radio, television, and trade publications, in reaching your target audience and driving conversions?
- Dr. Oda's approach highlights that each ad placement should serve a clear purpose: educating, engaging, or inspiring action. You probably already know that simply running ads isn't enough—ads need to reach the right people with the right message at the right time. I'm wondering if your radio, TV, or trade publication ads are designed to do just that or if they're merely creating noise without converting prospects into customers.

Newspaper, Magazine

- Are your print ads in newspapers and magazines compelling and eye-catching, prompting readers to take action? (Rating:)
- Dr. Oda teaches that print still holds value when used effectively in a world saturated with digital ads. Maybe you haven't yet noticed, but print ads, when properly crafted, have the power to engage an audience in a tangible, memorable way. Stop and think—are your current ads in newspapers and magazines compelling enough to capture attention and prompt immediate action?

Billboard, Text Ads

- How effectively are your outdoor and text advertising campaigns capturing attention and generating leads? (Rating:)
- Dr. Oda emphasizes that billboards and text ads are about grabbing attention quickly. You have seconds to make an impression, so every word and every image must count. I'm curious: are your billboard ads bold and concise enough to leave a lasting impact as people pass by? Are your text ads delivering the right message at the right time to generate leads?

Now, reflect on your advertising strategy across all these mediums. Dr. Oda often reminds us that advertising isn't just about visibility but engagement and conversion. Maybe you haven't yet realized, but each ad should serve a distinct purpose: educating your audience, driving leads, or reinforcing brand loyalty.

After all, effective advertising is about reaching people where they are—whether that's on their morning commute listening to the radio, flipping through a magazine, or passing by a billboard on the highway. Dr. Oda would encourage you to look at your advertising through a strategic lens, ensuring every dollar you spend is driving the results you want. Now is the time to evaluate your advertising impact and fine-tune it for maximum effectiveness.

7. **Technology**:

Dr. John Oda often speaks about the power of technology as a tool for leveraging growth, efficiency, and deeper connections with customers. Maybe you haven't yet realized, but the right technology infrastructure isn't just about convenience—it's about optimizing performance, enhancing customer experiences, and driving your business forward. I'm curious: how well is your business utilizing technology to its full potential?

Customized CRM System

- Does your CRM system effectively streamline customer interactions, track leads, and facilitate personalized communication? (Rating:)
- Dr. Oda's approach to technology emphasizes the importance of a customized CRM system that aligns with your business goals. You probably already know that a CRM is more than a database—it's a powerful tool that can automate communication, improve customer relationships, and help track every interaction. I'm wondering if your CRM is set up to fully leverage these capabilities, or are there gaps in how you manage and interact with your leads?

Mobile Apps

- How user-friendly and valuable are your mobile apps in enhancing customer experiences and driving engagement? (Rating:)
- Dr. Oda teaches that a well-designed mobile app is often a key touchpoint between your brand and your customers in today's mobile-first world. Maybe you haven't noticed, but your app's ease of use and value can determine whether a customer stays engaged or drifts away. Stop and think—does your app provide meaningful value to your users, and how seamless is the customer experience when they engage with it?

Using a Sales Force

- Is your sales force equipped with the necessary technology tools and resources to effectively manage leads, track sales activities, and optimize performance? (Rating:)
- Dr. Oda emphasizes that a sales force armed with the right technology can outperform competitors by leaps and bounds. You probably already know that tracking sales activities, managing leads, and optimizing performance are essential to sustained growth. I'm curious: have you equipped your team with the technology they need to work smarter, not harder? Maybe you haven't yet realized how much potential you're leaving on the table without a properly integrated tech stack.

Now, reflect on your technology infrastructure. Dr. Oda would tell you that technology is like another tentacle in the Octopus Method of Marketing—it connects, tracks, and facilitates growth in every area of your business. Maybe you haven't noticed, but when integrated thoughtfully, technology becomes a force multiplier, enhancing everything from customer engagement to internal efficiency.

After all, the right tools and systems make all the difference in today's fast-paced business landscape. Dr. Oda encourages you to evaluate your technology—from your CRM system to your mobile apps and sales force tools—and ask whether they are optimized for success. Now is the time to ensure your technology is truly working for you, not against you, and positioning your business for long-term growth and success.

8. Public Relations:

Dr. John Oda often highlights the power of Public Relations (PR) as a key driver of credibility and visibility. Maybe you haven't yet realized, but PR is more than just generating buzz—it's about building a lasting reputation that resonates with your audience. I'm curious: how well are you utilizing public relations to position your brand as a leader in your industry?

Press Releases

- How successful are your press releases in garnering media attention and generating positive publicity for your brand? (Rating:)
- Dr. Oda's approach to press releases is clear: they should be strategic and newsworthy, aimed at highlighting your company's key milestones and achievements. You probably already know that press releases are a powerful tool for gaining media coverage and amplifying your brand's reach. Are your current press releases written to capture media attention, or are they missing the mark in creating the impact you desire?

Speaking Engagements

- Are your speaking engagements well-received and impactful in establishing thought leadership and building credibility within your industry?
- Dr. Oda teaches that every speaking engagement is an opportunity to influence and inspire. Maybe you haven't noticed, but successful speaking engagements don't just happen—they require careful preparation, powerful storytelling, and a focus on delivering value to your audience. Stop and think—are you fully leveraging these opportunities to solidify your authority and build trust with your audience, or are you merely scratching the surface?

Articles, Blog Posts, Social Site Articles

- How engaging and informative are your articles, blog posts, and social media articles in educating your audience and reinforcing your brand's message?
- Dr. Oda emphasizes the importance of content that educates and engages. You probably already know that writing for your audience isn't just about promoting your product or service—it's about delivering valuable insights that position you as an expert. I'm curious: are your articles truly capturing your readers' attention, helping them solve real problems, and reinforcing your brand's message?

Now, take a moment to evaluate your public relations strategy. Dr. Oda would remind you that PR is about more than just coverage—it's about building relationships and becoming a trusted voice in your industry. Maybe you haven't yet realized, but each press release, speaking engagement, and article you publish is a chance to cement your reputation and expand your influence.

After all, public relations is the public face of your brand. Dr. Oda teaches that, like every other tentacle in the Octopus Method of Marketing, PR must be consistent, strategic, and impactful. Now is the time to refine your PR efforts, ensuring that each interaction with the media and your audience strengthens your position as a thought leader and industry authority.

9. Market Education:

Dr. John Oda is a firm believer in the power of education-based marketing. Maybe you haven't yet realized, but educating your market is one of the most powerful ways to establish trust, demonstrate authority, and build meaningful relationships with potential customers. I'm curious: how well are your educational seminars performing in positioning you as an expert and providing value to your audience?

Education Seminars

- How effectively are your education seminars providing valuable insights and fostering relationships with potential customers?
- Dr. Oda's philosophy centers around delivering value first—and nowhere is that more evident than in educational seminars. You probably already know that when people attend a seminar, they are looking for answers, solutions, and actionable takeaways. I'm wondering if your current seminars are truly providing that level of value. Are you educating your audience with real insights or simply giving surface-level information?

Dr. Oda stresses that a seminar is not just about showcasing your product or service—it's about empowering your audience with the knowledge that positions them to succeed. Stop and think—how much are you investing in the quality of content you're providing? Are you using these opportunities to build long-term relationships or focus on short-term gains?

Maybe you haven't noticed yet, but when your seminars provide real, actionable value, you don't just attract customers—you create loyal advocates for your brand. Dr. Oda teaches that the most successful seminars are those that leave a lasting impression, helping attendees see you as their go-to expert.

Now, evaluate how effective your seminars are at delivering real value. Dr. Oda would tell you that educational seminars are a critical tentacle in the Octopus Method of Marketing. They have the potential to transform prospects into lifelong customers by giving them the tools and insights they need to succeed. Now is the time to fine-tune your approach and ensure your seminars deliver the maximum impact on your audience, driving trust and action.

Educational Webinars:

- Do your webinars effectively educate your audience about industry trends, best practices, and solutions to common challenges?
- Dr. John Oda often highlights webinars' critical role in establishing authority and trust with your audience. Maybe you

haven't yet realized, but a webinar isn't just a sales tool—it's a platform to educate, engage, and inspire action. You probably already know that people attend webinars looking for valuable insights, and the most successful ones position you as the go-to expert in your field. I'm curious: are your webinars offering real solutions to your audience's problems, or are they merely scratching the surface of what your expertise could deliver?

Education Training:

- How comprehensive and impactful are your education training programs in empowering your customers with the knowledge and skills they need to succeed? (Rating:)
- Dr. Oda's approach to education training focuses on providing transformative value—not just information but skills that empower clients to take action and succeed. Maybe you haven't yet noticed, but education training should leave your customers feeling capable, informed, and equipped with the tools they need to thrive. I'm wondering if your training programs are truly comprehensive, offering the depth of knowledge that fosters loyalty and success, or if there's room to expand on what you're offering.

By critically assessing each aspect of the Octopus Marketing Method, you can identify where your business excels and where improvements can be made. Dr. Oda emphasizes that the key to success lies in consistently delivering valuable content across all channels, with Educational Based Marketing at its core. You probably already know that when you address weaknesses and optimize your marketing efforts, your business gains greater visibility, engagement, and long-term success.

In the realm of business, survival hinges on adaptability. Dr. Oda warns of the dangers that come with relying on just one approach to attract leads and drive growth. It's a common pitfall—businesses become overly dependent on a single channel, leaving themselves vulnerable if that strategy falters. Maybe you haven't noticed, but this singular approach is akin to having only one diving board to leap from; once compromised, the business risks sinking.

To safeguard against this, Dr. Oda advocates adopting the Octopus Marketing Method. This method, anchored in Educational Based Marketing, positions businesses as authorities by delivering valuable knowledge to their audience. Now, imagine the strength of diversifying your lead generation efforts across multiple platforms, reducing reliance on one strategy while fortifying your business against market shifts.

Legendary marketer Jay Abraham often spoke about the folly of relying on a single growth channel. Dr. Oda echoes this wisdom, urging businesses to adopt multiple channels and tactics to ensure scalability and flexibility. By following this approach, entrepreneurs transcend the limitations of conventional strategies and unlock new pathways to success.

In essence, success in business demands innovation and diversity. Dr. Oda teaches that by embracing the Octopus Method and making Educational Based Marketing the cornerstone of your strategy, your business can break free from the constraints of a single tactic. Now, are you ready to explore new opportunities, diversify your approach, and elevate your business to unprecedented heights? After all, it's not just about avoiding failure—it's about soaring to new levels of achievement.

Quadrant Four: Monetize

- **Chapter 12: Reactivating Old Clients**
- **Chapter 13: Unlocking the Power of Referrals**
- **Chapter 14: The Dream 100 Strategy**
- **Chapter 15: Cost Optimization Techniques**
- **Chapter 16: Upselling and Cross-Selling**
- **Chapter 17: Creating JV Partnerships**

Chapter 12: Business Growth Unleashed – Three Transformative Strategies

Allan Private's journey to mastering business growth can be traced back to a pivotal seminar he attended in the future, featuring renowned business experts Jay Abraham, Chet Holmes, and Scot Hallman. This seminar offered insights that would completely revolutionize Allan's approach to business, leading him from the brink of failure to unprecedented success.

Jay Abraham's Profound Insight on Business Growth

Jay Abraham, often referred to as a marketing genius, shared a framework for growth that was deceptively simple yet extraordinarily powerful. He explained that there are only three fundamental ways to grow any business:

1. Increase the Average Transaction Value
2. Increase the Frequency of Purchase
3. Increase the Number of Clients

Dr. Oda emphasizes that although these strategies may seem straightforward, their implications are profound. Maybe you haven't yet realized, but these three methods unlock limitless potential for business growth. Allan recalls how this framework opened his eyes to the simplicity of business success—he had been overcomplicating his approach for years. You probably already know business growth doesn't require a complicated formula, just a strategic focus on these core areas.

Applying the Framework to Transform Allan's Business

Reflecting on Abraham's framework, Allan immediately saw how it applied to any business—regardless of the industry. He recognized that by increasing the average transaction value, he could generate more revenue from every customer interaction. Maybe you haven't noticed yet, but getting existing clients to buy more isn't as hard as it seems. Dr. Oda teaches that businesses often overlook simple upsell opportunities that can drive exponential growth.

Allan also saw the power of increasing the frequency of purchases. He could create consistent sales and foster loyalty by engaging customers more often. And finally, expanding the number of clients allowed him to grow his market reach and scale his business to new heights.

These three strategies were Allan's blueprint for transformation. Armed with this knowledge, he applied these principles consistently over the next 30 years, evolving from a struggling entrepreneur to a successful, wealthy business leader.

Scot Hallman's Approach to Monetizing and Optimizing a Business

At the same seminar, Scot Hallman built on Jay Abraham's teachings by showing how to monetize and optimize a business effectively. Dr. Oda often stresses the importance of making small yet impactful changes—tweaks that can create massive gains in profitability.

Hallman's strategies focused on three main areas:

1. Increasing the Number of Clients:
    - Improve marketing and sales efforts.
    - Hire affiliate superstars to boost outreach.
    - Implement retention models and referral programs.
    - Reactivate old clients and offer workshops.
    - Systematize operations with what Hallman called "profit drivers"—small shifts that generate outsized returns.

Maybe you haven't yet realized, but reactivating former clients and building a referral system are some of the easiest ways to grow without huge marketing budgets. Allan understood that with these tools, his potential client pool was much larger than he initially thought.

2. Increasing the Average Transaction Value:
    - Raise prices to reflect market demand.
    - Use upsell, cross-sell, and down-sell techniques.
    - Offer add-ons to maximize the value of each sale.
    - Optimize pricing strategies to reflect the full value of your offerings.

Dr. Oda emphasizes that pricing is a key lever often underutilized by businesses. Maybe you haven't noticed yet, but minor pricing adjustments can lead to dramatic increases in profitability. Allan quickly implemented these strategies, ensuring that every sale added more to his bottom line.

3. Increasing the Frequency of Purchases:
    - Leverage referral programs, both active and passive.
    - Strengthen customer relationship management (CRM) systems.
    - Offer additional products or services that align with customer needs.
    - Capitalize on existing success by upselling satisfied customers.

Allan realized that by keeping customers engaged and satisfied, he could drive repeat business—turning one-time buyers into loyal clients who returned again and again. Maybe you haven't noticed, but focusing on repeat customers often delivers far greater returns than chasing new ones.

The Power of Consistent Application

What Allan learned from Jay Abraham and Scot Hallman became the foundation of his business growth strategy. Dr. Oda teaches that the secret to unlocking massive business growth isn't about doing more—it's about doing the right things consistently. By mastering these strategies, Allan unleashed his business potential, achieving levels of success he never thought possible.

Now, can you imagine how applying these three transformative strategies could reshape your business? Maybe you haven't yet realized, but the simplicity of growth lies in these core principles—focus on the average transaction, the frequency of purchases, and the number of clients, and you'll unlock new levels of success. After all, business growth doesn't have to be complicated—it just has to be strategic.

Applying the Lessons to Reactivate Old Clients

One of the most impactful lessons Allan took from the seminar was the importance of reactivating old clients. Maybe you haven't yet realized this, but most businesses pour a significant amount of time, money, and effort into acquiring new clients while neglecting the goldmine, which is their past client base. Dr. John Oda emphasizes that if a business has been around for two years or more, reactivating old clients can be a highly effective way to boost sales with minimal cost.

At the seminar, Jay Abraham offered invaluable insight into this strategy. He stressed the importance of focusing on the emotions of past clients—putting aside pride and ego. You probably already know many business owners struggle with the idea of going back to past clients, but Jay pointed out that true leaders understand that growing a company is about serving others in the highest way possible.

Allan took this to heart and systematically applied it to his own business. I'm curious: have you ever thought about how much potential lies in reactivating clients who have drifted away? Maybe you haven't noticed, but these former clients are often easier to win back than you might think.

Allan's Systematic Approach to Reactivation:
1. Identifying Inactive Clients:
    - Dr. Oda stresses the importance of starting with data. Allan began by analyzing his client database, identifying clients who hadn't made a purchase in the last two years. You probably already know that these inactive clients represent untapped potential—clients who already know your business and could be re-engaged with the right approach.
2. Understanding Their Needs:
    - Allan realized that to reactivate old clients, he first had to understand why they had stopped purchasing. He sought to identify any pain points, unmet needs, or reasons for disengagement. Dr. Oda often reminds us that understanding the client's emotions is the first step to rebuilding the relationship. I'm wondering if you've considered diving deep into the reasons why clients drifted away in the first place.

3. Developing a Reactivation Strategy:
   - With a clearer understanding of his client's needs, Allan developed a personalized reactivation strategy. Dr. Oda teaches that emotional reconnection is key—offering value, special incentives, and showcasing new products or services that address the specific needs of former clients. You probably already know that personalized communication is more effective than generic outreach. Allan ensured that his messages were tailored to each client's past experiences.
4. Implementing a Follow-Up Program:
   - Dr. Oda often emphasizes that one touchpoint is never enough. Allan implemented a nine-step follow-up program designed to rebuild trust and reestablish the relationship gradually. Maybe you haven't noticed, but re-engaging old clients takes time, patience, and multiple interactions before trust is fully restored.
5. A/B Testing and Performance Tracking:
   - Not every reactivation approach will work for every client. Allan used A/B testing to find out which messages resonated best with different client segments. Dr. Oda always stresses the importance of tracking performance—knowing what works and what doesn't is key to refining any strategy. Allan closely monitored performance metrics to gauge the effectiveness of his efforts, making adjustments as needed to improve results continually.

Turning a Struggling Business into a Thriving Enterprise

By following these steps, Allan was able to reactivate a significant portion of his inactive clients, bringing fresh revenue and new life into his business. The results were undeniable: by applying the strategies Jay Abraham and Scot Hallman taught, Allan turned a struggling business into a thriving enterprise.

Dr. Oda often says that the potential for business growth is rarely in acquiring new clients—it's in re-engaging those who have already bought from you. Now, imagine how much growth could be unlocked in your business if you reactivate clients who have drifted away. After all, they already know you and your product or service. It's about reigniting the relationship, addressing their needs, and reminding them of the value you bring.

Maybe you haven't yet realized, but the strategy of reactivating old clients is a powerful tool that could transform your business, just as it did for Allan. Now, are you ready to reconnect with the clients you've lost and unlock the potential they represent? Dr. Oda would tell you—it's time to take action.

The Importance of Leadership and Humility

One of the key lessons Allan learned from his experience was the importance of leadership and humility in business. Dr. John Oda often emphasizes that true leadership isn't about ego—it's about serving others. Maybe you haven't yet realized, but re-engaging old clients, as Jay Abraham taught, requires setting aside pride and focusing on the needs and emotions of those clients. This can be challenging, especially for business owners who have poured their hearts into building their companies. However, Allan came to understand that when you lead with humility and genuine care, your business can achieve far greater success.

Allan also recognized that reactivating clients was not just about making another sale. It was about rebuilding relationships, restoring trust, and demonstrating a real commitment to helping the client succeed. You probably already know, but when clients feel valued, they become loyal. Allan's approach to this process brought old clients back into the fold and even strengthened the reputation of his business, leading to more referrals and long-term growth.

Conclusion

Allan Private's experience at the seminar with Jay Abraham, Chet Holmes, and Scot Hallman was a turning point in his business journey. The lessons he learned about growing a business through simple, actionable strategies gave him a clear roadmap to success. By focusing on increasing the average transaction value, the frequency of purchase, and the number of clients, Allan transformed his struggling business into a thriving, highly profitable enterprise.

One of the most overlooked strategies Allan learned was the importance of reactivating old clients. Most businesses focus on acquiring new customers, often neglecting the potential goldmine within their existing client base. Dr. Oda's approach emphasized leadership, humility, and a systematic follow-up, which Allan used to reengage past clients and generate substantial growth for his business.

Allan's journey from near failure to extraordinary success is a testament to the power of proven strategies. It also highlights the importance of continuously learning and adapting in an ever-changing business environment. The lessons he learned at the seminar continue to guide him as he navigates new challenges and opportunities, ensuring his business remains on a path of sustained growth.

A Powerful Example Shared by Dr. John Oda

Allan recalls a powerful story shared by Dr. John Oda during a seminar that demonstrated how applying proven strategies could lead to remarkable success. Dr. Oda spoke of a client in the UK who ran a waste management business. This client had been struggling with stagnation, spending large amounts of money trying to acquire new clients while neglecting the potential of his existing client base.

Upon evaluating the situation, Dr. Oda discovered that the client had over 10,000 inactive clients—an untapped resource. Recognizing this opportunity, Dr. Oda proposed implementing a reactivation program to engage these former clients. He crafted a revised letter that resonated deeply with these clients, addressing their emotions and needs directly—just as Jay Abraham had taught.

To ensure success, Dr. Oda incorporated a follow-up system inspired by Chet Holmes, involving multiple touchpoints designed to rebuild trust and encourage inactive clients to return. The results were extraordinary: within just eight months, the waste management business doubled its revenue, and net profits soared by 120%. The impact was so significant that the client was able to purchase a mansion—a true testament to the power of these strategies.

Allan was struck by how a single concept—reactivating old clients—could profoundly impact a business. It reinforced the idea that small, focused changes can sometimes lead to substantial growth. The methods shared by Jay Abraham and Chet Holmes were not just powerful—they were adaptable to any business, regardless of industry. Dr. Oda often reminds us that whether it's a minor adjustment or a complete overhaul, these strategies have the potential to transform a business completely.

Now, can you imagine how focusing on small, strategic changes could drive growth in your business? Maybe you haven't yet realized, but reactivating old clients and leading with humility might be the breakthrough you've been looking for. After all, true leadership and strategic thinking are the keys to unlocking extraordinary success.

Subject: Just Checking In – How Can We Support You? (Sample)

Dear [Client's Name],

I hope this message finds you well. It's been a while since we last connected, and I wanted to take a moment to reach out to you. At Focused, we deeply value our relationship with you, and when we don't hear from a valued client, we naturally become concerned.

Maybe you haven't yet realized, but your satisfaction is our top priority, and if there's anything we've done that has caused any concern, we're here to listen and make things right. Dr. John Oda always reminds us that true leadership is about serving others, and I want you to know that we are committed to ensuring you feel fully supported in your journey with us.

Please don't hesitate to reach out to my office at your earliest convenience—whether it's to discuss a concern or just to let us know that everything is going well. I'm curious: how have things been on your end? Hearing from you would mean a lot to us, and if I don't hear back in the next 72 hours, I'll give you a call myself because your satisfaction and well-being matter greatly to me.

As a token of our appreciation, we'd like to offer you a 10% discount on your next complementary [service/plan]. It's our way of showing you how much we value your business and want to continue providing you with the best experience possible.
I am looking forward to reconnecting and hearing from you soon.
Warm regards,
[Your Name]
[Your Title]
[Your Contact Information]

Dr. Oda's tone here emphasizes empathy, genuine care, and the importance of re-establishing trust through personal communication. By acknowledging the client's importance and offering a special incentive, this letter strikes the right balance between concern and appreciation. Maybe you haven't yet noticed, but this kind of personal touch can turn a re-engagement into a long-term relationship built on trust and loyalty.

"John Oda has been my business coach for the past eight months. He has taught me strategies to take my business to the next level. Johns' time management structures have helped me increase my business dramatically without increasing my hours dramatically. What sets John apart from other coaches is his ability to help me grow as a person as well as a business owner. He teaches that a healthy mind, body, and personal life are extremely important foundations for a healthy and growing business. The hidden treasure in Johns's coaching is his ability to shift you to a mindset of success. A coaching session with John Oda is tantamount to a coaching session with Anthony Robbins, Napoleon Hill, and Joseph McClendon III all rolled into one. The guy knows his stuff.
Oh by the way, I employ 10 great people, in the last eight months my business has doubled and my NET PROFIT is up 120% and we're just getting warmed up. Thanks, mate."
-Rob Heidemanns, Canberra, Australia

Improved Questions for Reactivating Old Clients

Dr. John Oda often emphasizes that reactivating old clients isn't just about bringing people back into the fold—it's about rebuilding trust, understanding their needs, and offering them renewed value. Maybe you haven't yet realized, but asking the right questions is key to uncovering the hidden potential within your past clients. I'm curious: how much thought have you put into structuring your reactivation efforts? Here are some refined questions to guide your approach:

1. How many clients have become inactive over the past two years, and what is their potential value to your business?
    - Dr. Oda's approach stresses the importance of data-driven decisions. You probably already know that understanding the scope of your inactive client base can reveal the untapped revenue potential sitting right in front of you.
2. What specific actions can we take to re-engage clients who have stopped purchasing from us?
    - Dr. Oda teaches that re-engagement requires a personalized approach. I'm wondering if you've considered what unique actions, incentives, or communications could resonate most with these clients.
3. What current systems or processes do you have in place for reactivating former clients, and how effective are they?
    - Maybe you haven't yet noticed, but even simple follow-up systems can have major results. Dr. Oda emphasizes that structured processes make all the difference when it comes to consistent, impactful communication.
4. Do you have a structured follow-up program in place to systematically reconnect with inactive clients?
    - Dr. Oda often says that follow-up is like dripping water on a rock—persistence is key. You probably already know that clients often need multiple touchpoints to feel re-engaged.
5. How are you currently measuring the success of your reactivation efforts, and what metrics are most important to track?

- Metrics matter. Dr. Oda teaches that you should measure re-engagement, conversion, and ROI to know which strategies deliver results.

6. Have you tested different approaches to reactivating old clients to determine which methods yield the best results?
    - Dr. Oda often recommends experimenting with different approaches—personalized letters, follow-up calls, special offers—and tracking their effectiveness. Maybe you haven't yet realized, but A/B testing could be the key to finding the perfect strategy for your client base.

7. What feedback have you received from past clients who have re-engaged, and how can this inform your future strategies?
    - You probably already know feedback is a goldmine of insights. Dr. Oda emphasizes listening to re-engaged clients to refine your approach continuously.

8. What additional value can you offer to encourage inactive clients to return, and how can this be communicated effectively?
    - Dr. Oda's philosophy is all about leading with value. I'm curious: what can you offer—discounts, new products, or exclusive services—that would make re-engaging irresistible to your past clients?

9. How can you leverage your existing client relationships to maximize the impact of your reactivation program?
    - Dr. Oda often teaches that your current clients can be your best advocates. Maybe you haven't yet realized, but asking for referrals from satisfied clients can boost your reactivation efforts.

10. What barriers might be preventing old clients from returning, and how can you address these issues proactively?
    - Dr. Oda stresses the importance of understanding and removing barriers. You probably already know that things like poor past experiences or changes in client needs could be holding them back. Dr. Oda would challenge you to find and eliminate these

roadblocks.

Now, ask yourself—how effective are your current efforts in reactivating old clients, and what changes can you make to unleash the potential within your past customer base? Dr. Oda would tell you that the key lies in asking the right questions, listening carefully to your client's needs, and responding with value-driven solutions.

Chapter 13: Unlocking the Power of Referrals

Allan Private attended a transformative seminar led by Dr. John Oda, a renowned business strategist with deep expertise in creating systematic referral programs. During the session, Dr. Oda asked the audience a simple yet revealing question: "How many of you have a systemized referral program in place?" The response was staggering. Out of 500 attendees present and thousands more online, fewer than 1% raised their hands. This response revealed a glaring gap in business practices—despite the immense power of referrals to drive growth, very few companies have taken the necessary steps to unlock this potential.

Dr. Oda shared a compelling story that demonstrated just how much opportunity businesses miss without a systematic approach. He spoke of a client, a successful plastic surgeon with three thriving offices in the Los Angeles area. Each office handled a steady flow of patients, with the average procedure costing around $12,000. On the surface, everything appeared to be running smoothly. However, Dr. Oda noticed that despite the success, the surgeon's practice was leaving millions of dollars on the table because they weren't consistently asking patients for referrals.

Curious to dive deeper, Dr. Oda called the surgeon's offices, asking a simple question: "How often are you asking patients for referrals?" The results were disappointing. Only two out of every ten patients were asked for referrals in one office. Another office fared slightly better, with three out of ten being asked. The best-performing office only asked four out of ten. As Dr. Oda tallied the numbers, it became clear that the practice missed a tremendous opportunity. Over the course of three years, this simple oversight had cost the business nearly $10 million.

The Power of a Systemized Referral Program

This story highlights a crucial lesson for every business: a referral program can be one of the most powerful tools for growth, and it doesn't require a significant financial investment. Dr. Oda emphasizes that, unlike traditional marketing strategies that often involve costly ad campaigns or elaborate promotions, a referral program leverages existing relationships and is built on delivering exceptional service. Maybe you haven't yet realized, but referrals are goldmines of opportunity, and they can be activated with very little cost—if you have the right system in place.

Dr. Oda calls this strategy "creating profit stations." These profit stations are strategic touchpoints within a business designed to generate additional revenue with minimal investment. They act as referral triggers, systematically asking clients or customers to bring others into the fold. When implemented correctly, these profit stations can double a business's revenue without needing massive advertising budgets or complicated marketing schemes.

During the seminar, Dr. Oda revealed that he has developed over 30 different profit stations designed to help businesses of all types grow. While all of them have the potential to generate substantial results, he focused on five key strategies that can be tailored to any industry. These strategies are actionable, practical, and don't require a heavy lift, yet they yield significant returns when implemented with consistency.

Five Key Profit Stations

1. The Referral Ask at the Point of Sale: This is about training your team to ask for referrals at the perfect moment—when the client is feeling most satisfied and excited about your product or service. Dr. Oda emphasizes that this touchpoint is one of the most overlooked opportunities in business, but it can deliver immediate results if systematized.

2. Post-Service Follow-Up: After a positive experience, your clients are more likely to share their experience with others. Maybe you haven't noticed, but a follow-up call or email that gently asks for a referral is an effective, low-cost way to turn happy customers into brand ambassadors.

3. Incentivized Referral Programs: By offering small rewards or discounts for successful referrals, businesses can encourage clients to actively participate in bringing in new customers. Dr. Oda's data shows that even modest incentives can profoundly impact referral activity.

4. **Testimonial Collection and Sharing:** Leveraging client testimonials in your marketing materials and social media is a powerful way to attract referrals. When potential clients hear about the positive experiences of others, they're more likely to trust and engage with your business. Dr. Oda teaches that testimonials are social proof—an essential part of any referral strategy.

5. **Reactivating Old Clients:** Many businesses focus solely on acquiring new clients, but Dr. Oda stresses the importance of re-engaging past clients and turning them into referral sources. These individuals already know your business, and rebuilding the relationship can lead to both repeat business and valuable referrals.

Conclusion: The Untapped Potential of Referrals

Allan Private left Dr. Oda's seminar with a new perspective on growing his business through referrals. What stood out to him was just how simple and cost-effective it could be to unlock this power. By implementing a few of the profit stations revealed by Dr. Oda, Allan saw how he could easily increase his customer base without a heavy investment in new marketing campaigns.

Dr. Oda's message was clear: referral programs are not just "nice to have"—they are essential for any business that wants to scale effectively and sustainably. Maybe you haven't yet realized, but the missed opportunities from not having a referral system in place are costing your business millions. The success stories, like the plastic surgeon who missed out on $10 million, show how critical it is to have a systemized approach.

Now, ask yourself—are you tapping into the true potential of referrals in your business? Dr. Oda would tell you it's time to create your own profit stations, start asking for referrals consistently, and watch your business grow without needing massive new investments. After all, the power of growth is already within your grasp—you need to activate it.

The Psychology Behind Referrals

Dr. John Oda explained that the psychology behind referrals is deeply rooted in trust and personal connection. When a client refers someone to your business, they're doing more than just passing along a name—they're vouching for you. That endorsement carries far more weight than any advertisement ever could because it comes from a trusted source. Maybe you haven't yet realized, but in a world flooded with marketing messages, people are far more likely to act on the recommendations of friends, family, or colleagues than on impersonal ads.

Despite this, many businesses overlook the immense power of referrals. They pour resources into acquiring new clients through traditional marketing channels, often at a much higher cost. Dr. Oda often reminds us that if businesses spent more time going the extra mile with their existing clients and asked for referrals, they would see greater returns with far less investment.

Dr. Oda shared an illuminating example from his work with Haas & Associates, a civil engineering firm in Michigan City, Indiana. The firm's CEO, Tim Haas, had built a strong reputation, thanks largely to the foundation laid by his father. However, despite this stellar reputation, Tim had never considered asking clients for referrals. His business relied on a traditional bidding process; referrals were not part of the strategy.

During a conversation, Dr. Oda suggested Tim start asking for referrals. Initially, Tim was hesitant—maybe you can relate to the discomfort of asking clients for favors—but he agreed to give it a try. A week later, Tim returned with surprising results. He had asked one client for a referral, and not only did the client respond positively, but they also provided several new leads. That simple act, which cost nothing, opened up new business opportunities that Tim hadn't even tapped into before.

The lesson was clear: Tim had been leaving money on the table by not asking for referrals.

Dr. Oda emphasized that asking for referrals isn't just about boosting your bottom line. It's about building on the goodwill and relationships you've already established with your clients. You probably already know that if you provide exceptional service and create a positive experience, your clients will naturally be willing to refer others to you. Maybe you haven't yet realized, but often, all you need to do is ask.

The Trust Factor in Referrals

When clients trust you, they feel confident referring their friends, colleagues, or family to your business. Dr. Oda's philosophy is clear: trust is earned through consistent, high-quality service and relationship-building. I'm curious: how many of your clients trust you enough to refer others? And more importantly, are you actively asking for those referrals?

Dr. Oda often says that referrals are about leveraging the relationships you've already nurtured. You probably already know, but a referred client comes into your business with pre-built trust, making it easier to close the deal. They're not a cold lead; they're a warm introduction—ready to engage because someone they trust vouched for you.

Conclusion: Unlock the Referral Opportunity

Dr. Oda's teachings remind us that there's a significant opportunity waiting in referrals. Businesses don't need to chase after expensive new customer acquisition strategies when they can tap into the relationships they've already built. Maybe you haven't noticed, but the clients you serve today are the key to unlocking future growth—all you need to do is ask them to refer others. Dr. Oda would tell you, it's not just about the immediate boost in revenue; it's about creating long-lasting partnerships that keep clients coming back and bring new clients in the door.

So, ask yourself—how often are you asking for referrals? Are you leveraging the trust you've built with your clients to open new doors for growth? After all, referrals are the simplest, most cost-effective way to grow your business and are already within your reach.

Building a Referral System: The Foundation of Profit Stations

Asking for referrals is just the beginning. To fully harness the power of referrals, you need a systemized approach that goes beyond simply hoping clients will refer others. Dr. John Oda emphasized this point during his seminar, challenging business owners with a series of critical questions:

1. What is your current process for generating referrals?
2. Is there a written referral process that everyone in your company follows?
3. Do you have a system to track referral-generated business?
4. Do you have a follow-up process for referral leads?
5. Do you have a policy to train your team on how to ask for referrals effectively?
6. Are you conducting A/B testing to determine which referral strategies work best?

These questions form the foundation of a referral system that works. Maybe you haven't yet realized, but referrals will be inconsistent without a clearly defined process, and valuable opportunities will slip away. Many businesses fall into the trap of assuming that referrals will happen organically, but Dr. Oda taught that this passive approach is far less effective than actively creating a process that encourages and rewards referrals.

Dr. Oda stresses the importance of having a written referral process that everyone in the company follows. You probably already know that consistency is key to success. A documented process should be part of your company's standard operating procedures, ensuring that every team member is applying the same principles. When referrals are left to chance, results are often unpredictable. Dr. Oda's approach is to make referrals a systemized part of your business, transforming them into a reliable source of new clients.

Tracking and Measuring Success

Another critical component of a successful referral program is tracking. Dr. Oda often says that what doesn't get measured can't be improved. Maybe you haven't yet noticed, but without a tracking system, it's nearly impossible to gauge the effectiveness of your referral efforts or pinpoint improvement areas.

A referral tracking system should monitor the entire process—from the number of referrals generated to the conversion rate of referral leads into paying clients. Dr. Oda emphasizes that tracking helps you see what's working and highlights where your referral efforts are falling short. By knowing which strategies yield the best results, you can refine your approach and maximize the impact of your program.

You probably already know, but a well-executed referral system is more than just asking for referrals—it's about creating a seamless experience for your clients and your team. Every touchpoint, from the ask to the follow-up, should be carefully thought out and part of a structured system that leads to consistent growth.

Training Your Team

A key element of Dr. Oda's referral system is training your team on how to ask for referrals effectively. Maybe you haven't yet realized, but many business owners assume that their team knows how to ask for referrals. However, without the proper training, your team might feel uncomfortable or unsure about when and how to make the request. Dr. Oda's advice is clear: make referral training part of your team's regular education. With the right techniques, asking for referrals becomes a natural extension of the client interaction.

Testing and Optimizing Your Referral Strategy

Dr. Oda also encourages businesses to conduct A/B testing to determine the most effective referral strategies. You probably already know that not every approach will work for every client, so testing different methods and tracking the results is essential. By doing this, you can fine-tune your referral process and ensure that you're using the strategies that yield the highest returns.

Conclusion: Systematizing Referrals for Success

Dr. Oda's message is clear: a successful referral system is one that's documented, tracked, and continuously improved. Maybe you haven't yet realized, but by systematizing your referral process, you're not just leaving growth to chance—you're taking control of one of the most powerful tools in business.

Now, imagine having a referral program that is predictable, measurable, and scalable. Dr. Oda would tell you that with the right system in place, referrals can become a consistent stream of new business, boosting your revenue without the heavy investment of traditional marketing. After all, the foundation of success lies in creating systems that work for you, not just hoping for the best. It's time to build your referral system and unlock the full potential of profit stations for your business.

The Follow-Up: Where the Fortune Lies

"One of the biggest mistakes businesses make when it comes to referrals is treating them as a one-and-done deal. As I often say, getting the referral is just the starting line—the fortune lies in the follow-up," Dr. John Oda explained. "Businesses are great at asking for referrals, but far too many drop the ball afterward. They may reach out once, but if that first touch doesn't lead to a sale, they tend to move on, leaving potential success on the table."

Dr. Oda likened the process to dating. "Imagine your friend introduces you to someone who piques your interest, and you hit it off from the start. You share a meaningful conversation, so naturally, you want to see where this could go. You might ask them out for coffee, spend more time together, and gradually develop a deeper connection. As trust grows, so does the potential for something significant."

"But picture this," Dr. Oda continued, "after all that effort to make a meaningful connection, you just stop communicating. What are the chances that the relationship would go anywhere? Not very high, right? The same principle applies in business. A referral is only the opening chapter. Your consistent follow-up—your commitment to nurturing that relationship—will determine whether it grows into a loyal client."

Dr. Oda's analogy makes the point crystal clear: a referral is not the end of the journey; it's just the beginning. You need a process in place to keep the relationship alive and thriving. Each follow-up is an opportunity to build trust, establish rapport, and guide the referral towards becoming a dedicated customer. Without a solid follow-up strategy, you're not just leaving money on the table—you're letting an opportunity slip through your fingers.

Training Your Team to Ask for Referrals

"Have you ever noticed how some teams effortlessly generate steady referrals while others struggle? I'm curious if you realize that the difference lies not just in asking for referrals but in asking in a natural and inviting way," Dr. John Oda shares. "The truth is, asking for referrals is a skill that anyone can easily master because it's about understanding the patterns that create connection."

"You probably already know that one of the best times to ask for a referral is after delivering an exceptional experience. That's when your clients feel that surge of satisfaction, their enthusiasm is high, and they're naturally inclined to share their positive experiences. Imagine how quickly your referral program could expand beyond its current limits when your team recognizes and seizes these opportunities in the moment."

"Maybe you haven't yet considered just how powerful it is to train your team to become aware of these golden moments. When you train them to notice the signals—those subtle signs that a client is delighted—it becomes easy for them to embed the referral request in a conversation naturally. Your team learns to speak in a way that flows, where asking for a referral doesn't feel like a 'request' at all—it feels like the next logical step in the relationship."

"Maybe you will find it surprising, but simple A/B testing can naturally reveal which approaches resonate most. I'm wondering if you can imagine the impact of testing different language patterns, trying out various phrasing, and experimenting with timing. Now you're not just following a script; you're creating an experience where clients feel valued and connected because your team is speaking directly to their desires. The magic lies in the subtle shifts in language—using words that naturally guide the conversation forward."

Dr. Oda advises businesses to use words that invite, inspire, and expand the possibilities for clients. "It's about realizing that every interaction is an opportunity to deepen the relationship. When you train your team to master the art of the ask, they're not just asking for a favor; they're inviting clients to be a part of an unlimited journey of growth. And now, because you've equipped your team with the right skills, your referrals won't just happen—they'll flow effortlessly."

"So stop thinking of referrals as a chore and start viewing them as a natural part of your client experience. Can you imagine the difference that will make?" Dr. Oda concludes. "Referrals are the seeds that grow into unlimited possibilities, and your team already has what it takes to cultivate those relationships—naturally, easily, and with unwavering confidence."

Conclusion: The Power of Systemized Referrals

"I'm curious if you've ever stopped to notice how some businesses easily attract new clients while others struggle. You probably already know that referrals are one of the most naturally powerful tools available to any business, yet they often go underutilized. Why? Because many businesses haven't realized the unlimited potential that comes from creating a systemized referral program," Dr. John Oda shares.

"Imagine what would happen if, after every delighted client interaction, you had a process in place that naturally guided them to refer others. Now, you're no longer chasing sporadic leads; you're tapping into a steady stream of clients who arrive not because of expensive marketing campaigns but because of the trust already established. This is where Dr. Oda's approach shines—by creating 'profit stations' that require little to no financial investment, you can generate returns that expand beyond what you may have thought possible."

"The real key lies in systemization. It's about having a written process that your team follows effortlessly, training them to recognize the patterns and opportunities, tracking the results, and naturally following up with leads. When these elements come together, referrals transform from a sporadic occurrence into a reliable and unlimited growth strategy. Can you imagine how much more powerful your business could become when referrals aren't just an afterthought but a core part of your strategy?"

"Maybe you haven't yet considered the true impact of mastering this process, but once you stop thinking of referrals as an occasional bonus and start viewing them as an ongoing system, you unlock an entirely new level of growth," Dr. Oda continues. "Because a systemized approach means that each referral isn't just a single opportunity—it's a doorway to a continuous flow of business, a cycle that builds upon itself, growing naturally and easily over time."

"Ask yourself, do you want referrals to happen by chance, or would you prefer to have them arrive predictably, effortlessly, and without a second thought? By now, you're aware that the choice is yours. With the right system in place, you can ensure that asking for referrals becomes second nature for your team—and turning those referrals into loyal clients becomes second nature for your business."

Dr. Oda's message is clear: "Referrals aren't just a tool; they're the foundation for a business that grows unlimited in its potential. Once you've mastered the process, you'll notice how easily success follows."

Chapter 14: Allan Private's Seminar Experience – Discovering the Power of the Dream 100

Allan Private, an ambitious and successful entrepreneur eager to scale his business, found himself sitting among a crowd of high-level business owners at an exclusive seminar. His goal was to find a strategy to propel his company to the next level. On the stage, Dr. John Oda—partnered with the legendary business strategist Chet Holmes—delivered a compelling presentation that would forever change Allan's approach to business growth.

The concept that captivated Allan's attention was the idea of the "Best Buyer" or "Dream 100 Client"—a strategy that had transformed Holmes' career and helped countless businesses double, even triple, their revenue. It was about finding the top clients who could bring the most significant growth to your business and focusing your efforts on them.

The Dream Client Concept: Building Your Success Foundation

Can you imagine having a strategy that grows your business and could double it within a year? That's the power behind the Dream Client concept. As Allan listened, he *realized* that he needed to incorporate this method into his business practices if he truly wanted to reach the next level of success. He could *easily* picture the results—if he could master the art of identifying and attracting these Dream Clients.

At the seminar, Dr. Oda posed a pivotal question to the audience: "How would you describe your best buyer or dream client?" The room was filled with eager entrepreneurs, yet many found themselves uncertain about how to define this ideal customer. *I'm curious*—have you ever *noticed* how elusive that perfect client can seem until you gain clarity on exactly who they are?

Dr. Oda provided a crucial clue, asking, "Do you have clients who buy two or three times as much as anyone else?" About half of the attendees raised their hands, starting to *become aware* of the disparities in their client base. He continued, "How many best buyers do you think you currently have?" A few brave souls responded, mentioning they had two to five best buyers in their businesses. It was a start—but the numbers told a different story.

Then came the *eye-opening* moment. Dr. Oda asked, "What percentage of your business is represented by these best buyers?" An overwhelming 90% of the room indicated that their best buyers accounted for less than three percent of their total customer base. *Now*, the opportunity was staring them in the face.

The silence in the room spoke volumes as Dr. Oda posed his next question: "How many best buyers do you think are in your market?" Responses varied; some estimated hundreds, while others guessed thousands. At this point, Dr. Oda introduced the group to Chet Holmes' revolutionary Dream 100 concept—a system for identifying and targeting the top 100 dream clients who could dramatically impact your business.

Turning a Vision into a Reality

Dr. Oda explained that the Dream 100 strategy was about shifting focus. "Instead of spreading your resources thinly across thousands of prospects, why not *expand beyond* the usual approach and channel your energy toward a select group of high-value targets who could potentially transform your business?" he asked.

Allan could *easily* see the value of this concentrated effort. He was *naturally* drawn to the idea of devoting time, resources, and creativity to *connect* with his Dream Clients—those few buyers who, with the right relationship-building, could generate *unlimited* growth.

Dr. Oda emphasized the *patterns* of successful implementation. "Start by defining your Dream 100. Then, craft a tailored, persistent approach for reaching out and building a relationship with each one. It's not just about selling—it's about *noticing* when your Dream Client is ready to buy and being there *now* to seize the moment."

The seminar wasn't just about learning a new strategy for Allan—it was a revelation. He left with a clear understanding of his Dream Clients and a plan to capture their attention using the Dream 100 strategy. As he walked out of the seminar, Allan felt a shift, *realizing* that the path to scaling his business had become more focused and *naturally* achievable.

This was more than just a seminar for Allan—it was a turning point. The Dream 100 strategy
would become the foundation upon which he would build his future success, *effortlessly* turning ideal prospects into loyal, high-value clients.

The Dream 100: A Case Study in Strategic Focus

Dr. John Oda captivated the audience with a real-world example illustrating the power of the Dream 100 strategy. He shared the story of Chet Holmes' groundbreaking work with billionaire Charlie Munger and Warren Buffett's Berkshire Hathaway. While most of the audience was familiar with Warren Buffett, fewer had heard of Charlie Munger, despite their shared legendary partnership. Dr. Oda explained that Chet had led the sales department for one of Berkshire Hathaway's trade magazines, and this was where the Dream 100 strategy truly began.

The Challenge: Transforming a Stagnant Sales Strategy

When Chet took charge, his department had a database of 2,200 potential advertisers. They had been diligently sending out promotional materials to all of them, but the results were less than impressive. Despite the broad outreach, conversions were minimal, and the team wasn't securing the high-value advertisers that could truly make a difference. Determined to create a breakthrough, Chet did some research and made a *startling realization*: out of those 2,200 prospects, 167 were responsible for 95% of the advertising revenue in competing magazines.

Yet, not one of these top buyers was advertising in their magazine.

Can you imagine having all these potential leads yet missing out on the very ones who could transform your business? Chet *realized* that a different approach was necessary if he wanted to *expand beyond* mediocrity.

The Dream 100 in Action: A Tactical Blueprint

Chet decided to stop casting a wide net and focus his efforts on the 167 high-value prospects—the Dream 100 strategy was born. This strategy involved *naturally* shifting focus toward those top buyers who had the most potential to impact the magazine's bottom line. The goal was clear: *notice* these best buyers and *expand beyond* traditional methods to *connect* with them in ways that would leave a lasting impression.

His approach was methodical and relentless. For nine months, Chet's team launched personalized direct marketing campaigns targeting these Dream Clients. Each piece of communication was carefully crafted to provide educational value, making it clear that partnering with the magazine would benefit these advertisers greatly. Whether it was a postcard, a letter, or a small plastic gift like a Rubik's Cube, the message was always the same: "We have one million ways to solve your problems. Partner with us, and we'll double your business."

But the strategy wasn't just about sending marketing materials—it was about building relationships. Chet knew that *stop-and-go* efforts would yield nothing, so he employed a *consistent, persistent* approach. Every ten days, a new touchpoint would go out, including direct mail, educational reports, or follow-up calls. This sequence was a finely-tuned machine designed to keep the magazine *top of mind* for these high-value advertisers.

Persistence Pays Off: The Turning Point

At first, the results seemed discouraging. *After* four months of intense effort, not a single advertiser from the Dream 100 list had agreed to a deal. However, Chet understood that persistence was *naturally* a crucial part of the process. In the fifth month, the breakthrough finally came—one of the Dream Clients agreed to advertise in the magazine.

This small victory was the catalyst that opened the floodgates. *I'm wondering if* you can *imagine* the momentum that followed. By the sixth month, 28 of the largest advertisers in the industry had joined. These weren't small ads—they were full-page, full-color spreads that significantly boosted the magazine's revenue and credibility.

Results That Speak for Themselves

In just over a year, the magazine climbed from being ranked 15th in the industry to the number one spot. *Now*, it wasn't merely about a ranking—it was about a *natural expansion* of influence and profit. Within three years, Chet Holmes had doubled the company's revenue, all thanks to the disciplined and strategic focus of the Dream 100.

Dr. Oda concluded the story by emphasizing that the Dream 100 wasn't just a sales strategy; it was a *transformational* approach that could turn *maybe* into certainty, *awareness* into opportunity, and prospects into loyal partners.

The Impact of the Dream 100: Transforming Businesses

Dr. John Oda brought the seminar attendees to a pivotal moment, inviting them to *pause and reflect*. "Can you imagine," he asked, "what would happen if you could secure 29 new dream clients for your business?" He urged them to consider the numbers and the *transformation* this could bring—*expanding beyond* revenue growth to touch every area of their lives, including the ability to provide for their families and *naturally* open doors to new opportunities. Allan Private's vision was vivid and *unlimited*—he could see his business doubling in size *now after* putting the Dream 100 strategy into action.

The *power* of the Dream 100 lies in its *simplicity* and *focus*: targeting the clients who can make the most significant impact. By honing in on these *best buyers*, businesses can unlock *unprecedented* growth that goes far beyond typical marketing tactics. The Dream 100 strategy isn't just about winning clients—it's about redefining what's possible for your business.

Educational-Based Marketing: The Foundation of the Dream 100

Central to the success of the Dream 100 approach is the concept of *educational-based marketing*. *Maybe you haven't yet realized*, but

Chet Holmes understood early on that winning over dream clients required more than selling a product or service—it was about *delivering value* that resonates deeply with their needs. Each touchpoint, from postcards to follow-up calls, was intentionally crafted to *educate* and build trust, making the business indispensable in the eyes of these high-value prospects.

Notice how Chet positioned himself as a *trusted advisor* and *problem solver, not just another sales representative*. This wasn't about rushing toward a quick sale; it was about *nurturing relationships, expanding* the prospect's awareness, and sharing insights that would make them *realize* they couldn't afford to miss out. The Dream 100 strategy empowered Chet to differentiate from competitors in a way that left a lasting impression, building *long-term, loyal partnerships* rather than fleeting transactions.

With *educational-based marketing* at its core, the Dream 100 strategy became a *natural catalyst* that turned prospects into devoted clients—each communication adding another layer of credibility, positioning the business as the go-to resource in the industry. It's not merely about sending information but about *creating experiences* that your dream clients will *remember and value*.

Applying the Dream 100 Strategy to Your Business

As Dr. Oda wrapped up his presentation, he posed a question to the audience that hung in the air: *"What would happen if you pursued your 29 dream clients like your life depended on it?"* His tone was *inviting yet challenging*, prompting each attendee to envision how their business could *transform*. "How would this impact your revenue and your family's future?"

I'm curious: Can you imagine a strategy that will become the foundation of your growth? You probably already know that the principles behind the Dream 100 are not just relevant for large companies—they are unlimited in their potential to shape businesses at any stage, whether you're starting out or ready to scale to new heights.

Maybe you haven't yet started your Dream 100 journey, but I know you like the idea of finding the best buyers who will significantly impact your bottom line. And I'm wondering if now is the right time to take action.

Dr. Oda left the audience with a simple, powerful thought: *"When is now the best time to start implementing the Dream 100 strategy?"* Realizing that this approach could be the one profit station that changes everything, Allan Private walked out of the seminar energized and determined to put the Dream 100 into practice—knowing that by focusing on delivering unparalleled value to his dream clients, he could achieve massive success.

The question remains for you: Can you imagine the patterns of success you'll create when you make the Dream 100 a priority in your business?

Examples of Dream 100 Implementation: Real-Life Success Stories

Dr. John Oda captivated the audience as he shared real-life stories that showcased the transformative power of the Dream 100 strategy. These examples were more than just success stories—they were blueprints for turning ambition into unlimited growth. As he spoke, you probably already know that a strategy like this could be the missing key to scaling your business. But I'm wondering if you've ever considered how to apply this approach to your industry.

1. A Local Digital Marketing Agency:

Imagine a small agency struggling to stand out in a crowded marketplace, feeling overwhelmed by the competition. They decided to implement a Dream 100 strategy, zeroing in on 50 local businesses that matched their ideal client profile. Realizing the importance of delivering educational value, they launched a campaign that included free webinars, reports, and case studies tailored to their Dream 100 prospects.

Notice how the campaign didn't just focus on sales—it was about building trust and educating the market. Within six months, they secured contracts with 15 of these Dream clients, resulting in a remarkable 40% increase in annual revenue. Can you imagine what such an impact would mean for your business?

2. A SaaS Company Targeting Fortune 500 Clients:

This software company knew that landing just a few high-profile clients could transform their business. With a Dream 100 list focused on Fortune 500 companies, they crafted personalized video messages and exclusive reports and sent high-value gifts to build relationships. Their strategy was clear: consistently demonstrate expertise and offer solutions that resonated with their Dream clients' needs.

Progress was slow for the first several months, but the team persisted. After nearly a year of dedicated effort, they closed deals with 10 of the largest companies in their industry, effectively doubling their customer base. The lesson here is clear: The Dream 100 approach is about attracting clients and nurturing relationships until they are ready to say yes.

3. A Real Estate Firm:

A real estate firm specializing in luxury properties set its sights on attracting high-net-worth individuals. They knew that finding just a handful of the right clients could lead to exponential growth. By sending targeted direct mail, personalized invitations to exclusive events, and following up with consistency, they were able to secure 12 new clients from their Dream 100 list.

These clients didn't just purchase properties; they became advocates, referring friends and associates who were also interested in luxury real estate. This resulted in a 60% increase in sales volume. The Dream 100 strategy helped them tap into a network of high-value buyers who otherwise might have overlooked their offerings.

These real-life stories are a testament to the unlimited potential of the Dream 100 strategy. Whether you're in digital marketing, SaaS, real estate, or another sector, I'm curious—have you noticed how the principles remain consistent across different industries? The secret is in focusing on your best buyers, delivering exceptional value, and building lasting relationships that go far beyond a single transaction. Maybe you haven't yet tried implementing a Dream 100 strategy, but I'm wondering if now is the right time to start expanding your efforts. When you focus on creating deep connections with your Dream clients, you're not just building a customer base—you're transforming the entire trajectory of your business. And as Dr. Oda would say, "When is now the best time to begin changing your life forever?"

Conclusion: Taking Action on the Dream 100

Dr. John Oda closed the seminar with a powerful message, emphasizing that the Dream 100 strategy is not just another marketing tactic—it's a lifestyle change for your business. It requires commitment, focus, and persistence. It's about playing the long game, understanding that real growth doesn't happen overnight but unfolds through consistent effort. If you commit to this approach, the results will speak for themselves.

As Allan Private left the seminar, he could see how this strategy would transform his business and his entire future. The key lesson he took away was clear: persistent focus on your Dream clients can unlock exponential growth. It's not a question of if your business will grow—it's a question of when.

The Dream 100 is your blueprint to rewrite your business's trajectory. It's the kind of strategy that doesn't just add revenue; it doubles or triples it. And when you combine that growth with the focus and dedication that this approach requires, what happens is nothing short of transformational.

So, why wait? Start implementing the Dream 100 strategy now, and watch as your business soars to new heights—higher than you ever thought possible. Because when is now the best time to take the first step?

Frequently Asked Questions About the Dream 100 Strategy

The Dream 100 strategy, pioneered by Chet Holmes, is a laser-focused approach to targeting and nurturing relationships with your ideal clients. Here are some common questions and detailed answers to help you understand and apply this transformative strategy.

1. What Exactly is the Dream 100 Strategy?

The Dream 100 strategy involves identifying your industry's top 100 (or fewer) dream clients who can significantly impact your business. These aren't just good customers; they're your most valuable prospects who could dramatically transform your company's success. The strategy then revolves around a persistent, targeted marketing approach to win these high-value clients over.

2. Why is the Dream 100 Strategy So Effective?

The power of the Dream 100 strategy lies in its focused approach. You concentrate on a select group of high-potential clients rather than spreading your efforts thin across a broad audience. This allows for a personalized approach, building deeper relationships, and eventually converting these dream prospects into loyal customers. When you land just a few of these dream clients, the results can lead to exponential growth, making the impact game-changing.

3. How Do I Identify My Dream 100 Clients?

Start by analyzing your existing customers. Look for those who bring in the most revenue, make frequent purchases, or are the easiest to work with. Then, research the market to find similar potential clients who meet these criteria. These businesses or individuals would benefit most from your product or service and could significantly impact your growth if they become customers.

4. What Types of Businesses Can Use the Dream 100 Strategy?

The Dream 100 strategy is universal and can be applied to virtually any type of business. Whether you're in B2B or B2C, product-based or service-based, the principles stay the same: identify your best buyers, target them with personalized and consistent marketing, and build strong relationships. Industries that have thrived using this strategy include digital marketing, real estate, SaaS companies, consulting firms, and even retail businesses.

5. What Marketing Tactics Should I Use for My Dream 100?

The key is personalization and persistence. Here are some effective tactics:

- Direct Mail: Send personalized letters, postcards, or packages that offer educational content or small gifts over a period of six to nine months.
- Educational Content: Share valuable reports, white papers, webinars, or case studies that speak to your Dream clients' specific needs.
- Follow-Up Calls: Regularly make follow-up calls to build relationships and demonstrate your industry expertise.
- Personalized Emails: Create tailored email campaigns that address the challenges and goals of your Dream clients.
- Social Media Engagement: Connect with your Dream 100 on platforms like LinkedIn, share their content, and interact with them directly.

6. How Long Does It Take to See Results?

Results won't happen overnight. As with any long-term strategy, the Dream 100 approach requires patience and dedication. In some cases, like Chet Holmes' experience, it took several months to see breakthroughs. The key is consistent nurturing with valuable content and relationship-building. Persistence will eventually pay off, but it's a journey that requires commitment.

---

7. What Should I Do If I Don't See Immediate Results?

It's natural to feel discouraged when immediate results elude you. Remember, the Dream 100 strategy is built on persistence and long-term vision. If you find your efforts aren't yielding the expected outcomes, consider refining your approach. Ask yourself:

- Social Media Engagement: Connect with your Dream 100 on platforms like LinkedIn, share their content, and interact with them directly.
- Are you delivering enough value?
- Are your follow-ups consistent and timely?

This is your opportunity to tweak your messaging, diversify your educational content, or adjust your outreach cadence. Stay patient and focus on building those relationships. Often, the seeds of success take time to grow.

8. How Do I Balance the Dream 100 Strategy with Other Marketing Efforts?

While the Dream 100 strategy is powerful, it should be part of a broader marketing strategy. It thrives alongside other efforts like lead generation, branding, and customer retention. Make sure to:

- Allocate resources—time, budget, and personnel—specifically for your Dream 100 activities.
- Continue nurturing your existing clients and attracting new ones through various channels.

Think of the Dream 100 as one pillar of your overall growth strategy, not the sole focus.

9. How Do I Keep My Dream 100 Clients Engaged Over Time?

- Engagement is the key to lasting relationships. Here are some strategies to keep your Dream 100 clients engaged:
- Regular Communication: Share relevant updates, personalized messages, and valuable insights to keep the lines of communication open.
- Exclusive Offers: Provide your Dream 100 clients with first access to new products, special invitations, or exclusive offers that make them feel valued.

- Client Success Stories: Share case studies or testimonials from others in your Dream 100 list to build trust and highlight your impact.
- Ongoing Education: Continue to offer educational content that addresses their biggest challenges, ensuring they see ongoing value in your relationship.

10. Can the Dream 100 Strategy Work for Small Businesses or Startups?

Absolutely! In fact, the Dream 100 strategy can be a game-changer for small businesses and startups with limited resources. By focusing on a smaller, targeted group of potential clients, you can maximize your impact without spreading yourself too thin. Securing just a few dream clients early on can significantly accelerate your growth and position your business as a leader in your industry.

11. How Do I Measure the Success of My Dream 100 Strategy?

Success can be evaluated through various metrics depending on your specific goals. Consider measuring:

- Client Acquisition: How many of your Dream 100 clients have become paying customers?
- Revenue Impact: What percentage of your revenue is derived from your Dream 100 clients?
- Engagement: Are your Dream 100 clients interacting with your content, attending your events, or responding to your outreach efforts?
- Relationship Building: How robust are your relationships with these clients? Are they providing referrals or engaging in repeat business?

12. What If I Have More Than 100 Dream Clients?

The number "100" in the Dream 100 is a guideline, not a rigid rule. If you discover more than 100 dream clients, consider breaking them into tiers (e.g., Tier 1 for your top 20 prospects and Tier 2 for the next 80). This will help you allocate resources effectively. The goal is to maintain focus and ensure that you provide personalized attention to each client on your list.

Addressing these questions can deepen your understanding of the Dream 100 strategy and effectively implement it in your business. Whether you're a small business owner, marketer, or sales professional, the Dream 100 approach can be transformative in your journey to success when executed with persistence and dedication. As Dr. Oda would say, "The path to greatness is paved with consistent effort, unwavering focus, and a commitment to delivering value."

Ultimately, the Dream 100 strategy is about playing the long game. You're not just going after a sale; you're building lifelong partnerships. It's not a sprint—it's a marathon that, when finished, leaves your business light-years ahead of where you started. As Dr. Oda would say, "Success isn't about waiting for the perfect time. It's about taking action now and creating the perfect time."

Chapter 15: Cost Optimization

Like many business owners, Allan Private had fallen into the trap of complacency. After years of running his company, he continued to rely on the same vendors, believing they were his "friends." This assumption clouded his judgment and obscured the golden opportunities for reducing costs and boosting profits. It wasn't until he attended a seminar led by Dr. John Oda that he began to grasp the significant money he was leaving on the table simply by neglecting to renegotiate vendor contracts.

Dr. Oda shared numerous examples of businesses that had allowed their vendor relationships to become overly comfortable. As a result, they faced annual price increases that steadily eroded their profit margins. One particular client struck a chord with Allan. This client had been using the same supplier for years without ever attempting to renegotiate pricing. He remained resistant despite Dr. Oda demonstrating how this client could save tens of thousands of dollars annually by either shopping around or renegotiating. The thought of straining a relationship with a supplier he considered a family friend felt too daunting.

Dr. Oda reminded him, "While empathy and relationships are essential, business is business at the end of the day. You must prioritize the financial health of your company over personal sentiments." This crucial lesson resonated with Allan, who began to see the importance of a proactive approach to cost management.

Through his extensive experience, Dr. Oda has witnessed how companies often overlook the financial ramifications of not negotiating with their vendors. He now encourages his clients to thoroughly audit every aspect of their business, covering areas such as health insurance, retirement plans, merchant accounts, shipping, HR benefits, utilities, and more. His mission is clear: to help businesses reduce costs wherever possible and improve their bottom line.

Steps to Maximize Profits Through Cost Optimization

1. Conduct a Vendor Audit: Begin by compiling a list of all current vendors and their services or products. Analyze the terms of your contracts and any recent changes in pricing.

2. Research Market Rates: Investigate the prevailing rates for your required services and products. This information is vital in determining whether your current vendors are offering competitive pricing.

3. Renegotiate Contracts: Armed with your research, approach your vendors with the intent to renegotiate. Be clear about your expectations and the need for better terms. This could include lower prices, volume discounts, or more favorable payment terms.

4. Consider Alternative Suppliers: While renegotiating with existing vendors is crucial, don't shy away from exploring other options. Sometimes, a fresh perspective can lead to better pricing and terms.

5. Audit Operational Expenses: Look beyond vendor relationships. Conduct a comprehensive audit of all operational expenses, including utilities, insurance, and employee benefits. Identify areas where cost savings can be achieved.

6. Leverage Technology: Invest in technology that can automate processes or improve efficiency. The upfront cost can often lead to significant savings in the long run.

7. Create a Culture of Cost Consciousness: Encourage your team to be mindful of costs in their daily activities. Create incentives for employees to identify and suggest cost-saving measures.

8. Regularly Review Expenses: Make cost optimization a continual process. Schedule regular reviews of contracts and expenses to ensure you're not missing new opportunities for

savings.

9. Build Strong Vendor Relationships: While being proactive in renegotiation is essential, maintaining strong vendor relationships can still be beneficial. A good rapport can lead to better service, flexibility, and potential discounts.

10. Monitor Results: After implementing these strategies, monitor your expenses and savings closely. Use this data to adjust your approach and continuously improve your cost optimization efforts.

Incorporating these steps into his business strategy allowed Allan to regain control over his expenses. Inspired by Dr. Oda's teachings, he learned that a successful business requires strong relationships and a vigilant eye on the bottom line. As he moved forward, Allan embraced the idea that cost optimization is not just a one-time effort but an ongoing commitment to achieving financial health and sustained growth.

Step 1: Audit Your Current Suppliers and Vendors

The first step to improving your bottom line is to review the products meticulously and services your business purchases daily, weekly, monthly, or annually. Remember, your profit margin is directly tied to your ability to negotiate the best possible prices from your suppliers. Every company in the supply chain is eager to increase its business, which means they are often willing to offer discounts, better financing terms, or additional perks to retain your loyalty—especially in a competitive market or a struggling economy.

Always Ask for a Discount

When you request a quote or place an order, make it a habit to ask for a discount or improved terms. Many suppliers are accustomed to negotiations and may expect you to inquire about pricing adjustments. If a supplier isn't willing to lower their price, don't hesitate to ask for alternative benefits. These could include prepaid freight, extended payment terms, or value-added services. Negotiating isn't solely about price; it's about maximizing your position as a buyer, just as your customers do when they work with you.

Research and Compare Suppliers

In many cases, a little research can unveil alternative suppliers who offer similar products at more competitive prices. Take the time to compare their features and services to determine whether the differences will ultimately benefit you or your customers. Even a small variation in pricing can significantly impact your profit margins over time.

The Power of Relationships

While fostering strong relationships with your current suppliers is essential, it's equally important to remain vigilant. Establishing a competitive mindset can empower you to approach negotiations from a position of strength. Remember, suppliers want to keep your business just as much as you want to maintain the best possible costs.

Tracking Your Purchases

Create a detailed inventory of your purchases. List your suppliers, the products or services provided, the frequency of purchases, and the prices you currently pay. This comprehensive audit will provide a clear overview of your spending and help you identify areas ripe for negotiation.

In conclusion, auditing your current suppliers and vendors is not just an exercise; it's a strategic imperative that can lead to significant cost savings and improved profitability. By taking a proactive approach to negotiations and exploring alternatives, you'll position your business for greater financial success. Embrace the mindset of a savvy buyer, and watch your bottom line flourish.

Step 2: Confront Supplier Price Increases

It's no surprise that suppliers will inevitably raise their prices over time, often due to increased labor costs or their own rising expenses. These price hikes, usually ranging from 2% to 5%, may seem insignificant at first glance. You might even find yourself thinking, "It's just a small increase," but let's pause for a moment and consider the bigger picture. Did you know that a 5% price increase from a supplier can reduce your company's profit margin by as much as 15%? This pattern is something many business owners overlook, and it can easily erode your hard-earned profits.

Stay Aware and Proactive

Now, can you imagine effortlessly countering these price increases? The key is to be aware of your surroundings and always obtain competitor quotes. There are always alternative suppliers eager to win your business, and they will often offer substantial discounts to do so.

Harnessing the Power of Leverage

If you have a solid relationship with your current supplier—and I know you value that connection—don't hesitate to use competitor quotes as leverage. Ask your existing supplier to match the better price. After all, most suppliers understand the importance of keeping costs under control and will be willing to negotiate to retain your business.

Expand Beyond Complacency

Maybe you haven't yet realized the potential savings that are just waiting to be uncovered. I'm wondering if you can see how easily you can enhance your profitability by confronting these increases head-on. By doing so, you not only protect your margins but also position your business for unlimited growth.

Experience the Change

Imagine experiencing the relief of knowing that you're not only maintaining your existing supplier relationships but also ensuring that you're getting the best possible deal. This shift in mindset allows you to stop accepting price increases passively and take proactive steps toward maximizing your profits.

In conclusion, confronting supplier price increases is vital in your cost optimization journey. By becoming more aware of the patterns at play and leveraging competitor quotes, you can naturally navigate the challenges that arise and expand your financial success. Embrace this strategy, and watch your bottom line flourish as you unlock new opportunities for growth.

Step 3: Keep Your Returns in Check

As a business owner, you probably already know that many products and services come with warranties, and when they fail to meet expectations, customers return them for refunds. Now, can you imagine the impact that high return rates can have on your profits? It's crucial to keep a watchful eye on your return rates because excessive returns can easily eat away at your bottom line.

Becoming Aware of Patterns

If you notice an uptick in returns, it's time to stop and investigate the root cause. I'm curious if you've considered whether the returns stem from defective parts or if there might be an issue with your employees, such as lack of motivation, insufficient training, or inadequate skills. It's essential to be aware of these patterns so you can take action before they escalate further.

Investigate and Take Action

If defective parts are the culprit, don't simply replace them and write it off as a cost of doing business. Instead, return those defective items to the manufacturer or wholesaler and demand a credit. This is your opportunity to expand beyond complacency and hold your suppliers accountable. After all, you deserve to receive quality products that meet your standards.

Explore Alternatives

If the problem persists, I'm wondering if you've explored alternative suppliers who have a proven track record of delivering reliable products. By being proactive, you can naturally ensure that you're not just accepting subpar quality because that's what you've always done. The potential for unlimited improvement is within your reach.

Empower Your Employees

On the other hand, if you find that the issue is employee-related, it's time to elevate your training programs to ensure they are up-to-date and thorough. Providing proper training can significantly reduce errors and returns. Imagine the difference it would make to your team's performance if they were fully equipped with the skills and knowledge they need to excel.

In summary, keeping your returns in check is not just about managing costs—it's about creating an experience that fosters satisfaction and loyalty. By becoming aware of the underlying issues and addressing them head-on, you can transform your business operations, reduce return rates, and ultimately enhance your profitability. Embrace these strategies now, and witness how your business can flourish beyond your expectations.

Step 4: Limit Excess Inventory

You probably already know that excess inventory can be a hidden drain on your company's resources, but have you truly realized how it impacts your bottom line? Businesses often overproduce in anticipation of increased sales, but when those sales don't materialize, they're left with inventory that takes up valuable space and ties up capital. This can easily lead to disorganization and waste, causing you to miss out on unlimited opportunities for growth.

Awareness is Key

Now, the first step to addressing excess inventory is to audit your storage areas and create a detailed inventory of what you have on hand. I'm curious if you've taken the time to notice the patterns in your inventory. Get rid of anything that is outdated or obsolete because every item of excess inventory represents not just a cost, but an opportunity to turn idle stock into revenue.

Repurpose and Revitalize

For inventory you don't need soon, explore ways to repurpose or sell it. Can you imagine how free it would feel to declutter your storage space and transform those idle items into cash flow? Each step you take now creates a ripple effect, expanding beyond mere organization into a realm of profitability.

Implement Smart Solutions

To prevent excess inventory in the future, consider implementing an inventory management system. Maybe you haven't yet thought about the benefits of adopting a "just in time" (JIT) production system, which requires suppliers to deliver materials as they're needed. This approach naturally reduces carrying costs and prevents overproduction, aligning your operations with demand.

Limiting excess inventory can create a more efficient and responsive business model. Remember, the goal isn't just to manage what you have but to transform your inventory approach to foster growth and sustainability. I'm wondering if you're ready to take these steps because the potential for increased profitability and streamlined operations is just waiting for you to seize it. Embrace this opportunity now, and watch your business flourish as you optimize your resources and elevate your success.

Step 5: Reduce Scrap

You probably already know that scrap—materials that can't be used or sold due to defects—can significantly impact your bottom line. I'm curious if you've ever paused to notice how these seemingly minor issues can easily escalate, increasing material costs, labor costs, and opportunity costs. The good news is that you can take steps now to reduce scrap and improve profitability.

Awareness of Root Causes

First, it's essential to become aware of the root causes of your scrap. Are the defects due to faulty tools, inefficient processes, or subpar parts? Or perhaps it's a result of employee errors, such as insufficient training or lack of skill? By realizing the specific patterns that lead to scrap, you position yourself to address the underlying issues.

Seek Immediate Solutions

If defective tools or parts are the problem, don't hesitate to seek immediate compensation from the supplier. Can you imagine the impact of not having to shoulder these costs? If the issue persists, explore alternative suppliers who can deliver higher-quality materials. This can naturally expand your options and ensure you're getting the best for your business.

Empower Your Team

If the problem is employee-related, additional training might be the solution. But maybe you haven't yet considered that your employees can offer invaluable insights. They are on the front lines every day, experiencing the processes firsthand. I'm wondering if you could encourage them to share their suggestions and implement those that resonate. By doing so, you not only reduce scrap but also create a culture of continuous improvement.

Innovate and Rework

Furthermore, don't overlook the possibility of recycling or reworking scrap materials to minimize losses. You have unlimited potential to turn challenges into opportunities. Consider how this practice can contribute to a more sustainable business model while enhancing your bottom line.

By taking these steps to reduce scrap, you improve your financial performance and foster an environment of innovation and efficiency. Stop letting scrap hold you back and embrace the opportunity to optimize your operations. Now is the time to transform your approach and watch as your business flourishes, expanding beyond what you once thought possible.

Step 6: Lower Overhead Costs

You probably already know that lowering your overhead costs is essential for enhancing profitability. Can you imagine how easily you could transform your financial landscape by reducing these expenses? Let's take a moment to expand beyond the usual practices and dive into some practical strategies that can naturally lead to significant savings.

A Mindful Review

I'm curious if you've ever sat aside a few hours to review your bank statements, credit card statements, and business invoices. As you go through each charge, ask yourself a powerful question: "Does this expense help me gain new customers or keep existing ones?" If the answer is no, it might be time to stop that expense and realize the financial freedom that comes with it.

Specific Areas for Savings

Here are some patterns you might notice as you audit your overhead costs:

- Credit Card Statements: Many business owners are unaware they are paying for services or subscriptions they no longer use or recognize. You could save hundreds or even thousands of dollars each year by canceling these unnecessary expenses. Imagine what you could do with that extra capital!

- Suppliers and Vendors: Just as you audit your COGS-related suppliers, it's crucial to audit your overhead vendors. This includes your internet service provider, phone company, and office supply vendor. There's unlimited potential for negotiation here. Contact your providers and ask for discounts or explore competitor offers to secure better rates.

- Outsource Services: Maybe you haven't yet considered outsourcing services like janitorial work or landscaping to independent contractors. You'll likely find you can hire individuals for a fraction of the cost that professional service companies charge, eliminating the middleman's markup and freeing up resources for growth.

- Insurance Audits: Don't overlook your insurance policies—business, auto, health, life, and workers' compensation. The insurance market is highly competitive, and providers often offer deep discounts to win new customers. Be aware that shopping around and negotiating for the best rates can lead to substantial savings.

As you implement these strategies, you might experience a shift in how you view your expenses. You are actively working toward a more profitable future by consciously choosing to lower overhead costs. After all, it's about making informed decisions that support your business goals.

Now is the time to take action. As you realize the possibilities that lie ahead, remember that you are in control. Adopting these practices can effortlessly enhance your bottom line and create a thriving, sustainable business.

Conclusion

As business owners like Allan Private often discover, becoming too comfortable with vendors can lead to missed opportunities for cost savings. Have you ever thought about how easy it could be to transform your business by reevaluating your vendor relationships? Dr. John Oda's approach of auditing every aspect of a business, from suppliers to overhead costs, is not just a strategy; it's a pathway to unlimited profitability.

By consistently reviewing vendor relationships, negotiating better terms, and cutting unnecessary expenses, companies can naturally improve their bottom line without sacrificing quality or service. Can you imagine what it would feel like to effortlessly increase your profits simply by becoming more aware of your financial patterns?

Where Will You Begin?

Now is the time to take action. Start by auditing your current vendors and suppliers today. Notice how this simple step can significantly increase your business's profits. As you embark on this journey, consider these thought-provoking questions about your vendors:

1. Have you ever taken the time to audit your suppliers and vendors?
2. How can treating vendors as "friends" rather than business partners negatively impact a company's profitability?
3. What strategies does Dr. John Oda recommend for confronting supplier price increases?

4. How does effective inventory management contribute to reducing business costs?

5. Why should businesses pay close attention to product returns, and how can this impact their bottom line?

6. What role do employee training and motivation play in minimizing product returns and scrap?

7. How can outsourcing certain business functions help reduce overhead costs?

8. What steps can business owners take to negotiate better terms with their current vendors without damaging relationships?

9. How can a business benefit from adopting a "just in time" (JIT) production system?

10. What are the potential long-term effects on a business's profitability if vendor contracts are not regularly renegotiated?

I'm wondering if you can already feel the shift in perspective. After exploring these questions, you may find yourself inspired to dive deeper into your business practices. Because this journey is not just about cost savings; it's about realizing the full potential of your business. So, take a moment, reflect, and expand beyond the ordinary. The opportunities are waiting for you!

Chapter 16: Beyond the Sale: Upsell and Cross-Sell Techniques

In Chapter 16 of Unlimited Business Growth, Dr. John Oda dives into the incredible power of upselling and cross-selling techniques—strategies that many business owners overlook, leaving unlimited revenue potential on the table. I'm curious—have you ever thought about how easily these methods could transform your business? Through his experiences partnering with industry giants like Jay Abraham, Chet Holmes, and Scott Hallman, Dr. Oda has realized these techniques' untapped potential for driving growth.

The Power of Upselling

Can you imagine walking into a fast-food restaurant like Wendy's and ordering a hamburger, fries, and a Coke? What happens next? The cashier asks if you'd like to "super-size" your meal for just a couple more dollars. This simple yet effective example of upselling shows how this practice can effortlessly boost your profits. Research shows that 34% of customers accept an upsell offer, meaning that three of every ten customers are likely to say yes to a higher-value proposition.

Dr. Oda recalls working with a chiropractor in Huntington Beach, California. This chiropractor offered standard chiropractic and massage therapy services but hadn't yet tapped into the power of upselling. After just one meeting with the staff, Dr. Oda introduced an upsell package featuring three different levels. The silver package was priced at $1,500 for three months, the gold package at $4,000 for three months with added services, and the VIP package at $6,000 for three months, providing even more value. The result? A staggering 50% increase in the chiropractor's business—all because of a well-implemented upsell strategy.

A testimonial from Dr. Duddey of Sports Care Center underscores the effectiveness of these strategies:

"I am the owner of a busy Chiropractic/Massage/Physical Therapy office and have been working with John Oda from Business Breakthroughs International for only about one month. Since that time, we have had a 50% increase in revenues, and John has structured systems to bring all of our accounts receivables current, totaling over $100,000. I had reservations about joining Business Breakthroughs International, but now, after completing only the first month, I don't know how any business could afford not to join."

Cross-Selling: An Additional Revenue Stream

Maybe you haven't yet explored the concept of cross-selling, but it can be just as impactful. People can, you know, experience the benefits of introducing complementary products or services at the right moment—enhancing the customer experience and maximizing your profits. For instance, imagine a customer purchasing a new smartphone. What if you offered them a protective case or a screen protector? The possibilities are unlimited when you think creatively about how to meet your customers' needs while boosting your sales.

Expanding Your Sales Strategy

I'm wondering if you've noticed the patterns in your current sales strategies. Are you fully aware of the opportunities to upsell and cross-sell? By integrating these techniques into your business model, you can naturally increase your revenue without needing to acquire new customers.

After implementing these strategies, you may realize that the path to growth is not always about bringing in new customers; sometimes, it's about maximizing the potential of those you already have.

So, as you move forward, consider how you can easily expand beyond your current offerings. Can you imagine the impact it could have on your business if you embraced upselling and cross-selling as fundamental components of your sales approach? Now is the time to take action and unlock the potential that lies within your business.

Cross-Selling for Increased Revenue

Have you ever considered how easily cross-selling can boost your sales and profits? Naturally, cross-selling involves offering additional products or services that complement the original item a customer is interested in. As Dr. John Oda, the Ultimate Business Growth Strategist, often shares, this simple yet powerful strategy can transform your business's financial landscape and open the door to unlimited possibilities.

Imagine this scenario: when Oda purchases a suit for a seminar or workshop, the shop effortlessly suggests complementary items like shirts, ties, socks, and shoes. This classic cross-sell scenario not only enhances the customer's experience but also allows the store to increase its revenue because each purchase becomes more valuable.

The Dental Office Example

In another example, Dr. Oda worked with dental offices where cross-selling became a critical component in increasing revenue. A patient walks in for a routine teeth cleaning or whitening session, and after an examination, the dentist recommends additional treatments such as root canals, dental implants, braces, or cosmetic services. By realizing the potential for additional revenue, the dental office not only serves its patients better but also increases its revenue per visit. You might notice how this strategy elevates their marketing efforts and profitability, creating a cycle of success.

Chet Holmes' Upsell Success Story

Dr. Oda recalls a compelling story from Chet Holmes about a carpet company that successfully implemented an upsell model by offering carpet cleaner as an additional purchase. This simple addition doubled the company's business, reactivated old clients, and positioned them as experts through educational marketing. Can you imagine the transformation this created in their success? People can, you know, elevate their game just by introducing a small yet impactful change like this.

The Power of Bundling

Now, let's explore bundling—an effective technique that can eliminate price competition by grouping products together into value-packed packages. When you bundle products, you create an "apples to oranges" comparison, making it challenging for customers to evaluate prices directly. This allows businesses to compete on value rather than price, which is essential in today's market.

Customers are naturally seeking value—not just the lowest price. Unfortunately, many small businesses fail to convey their value proposition effectively, often resorting to discounts that can erode profit margins. Did you know that a mere 10% discount might require a business to sell 50% more to break even?

Dr. Oda emphasizes the importance of bundling to stop this cycle of discounting. For example, in his own business coaching practice, he bundles services such as business coaching, NLP for sales, estate planning training, and time management coaching into hybrid programs that include seminars and one-on-one sessions. This comprehensive offering equips his clients with everything they need to grow their businesses, protect their wealth, and enhance their families' lives.

A Real-World Example

Consider a home builder or remodeling contractor who negotiates volume discounts with suppliers. One builder purchased packages of home entertainment systems—including a 60-inch television, high-quality audio system, and home security system—for just $6,500 per package, compared to a retail price of $22,800. They differentiated their offering from competitors by including this package as a standard feature in their homes. They sold homes at $356,500, including the entertainment system, while still achieving a healthy profit. This strategy can potentially double sales volume and profits every year.

The Lesson

The lesson here is profound: businesses should actively explore bundling opportunities to add substantial value to their offerings, leading to increased sales and profitability. You probably already know that even a conservative estimate suggests that bundling can increase a business's revenue by 10% in the first year alone.

So, as you reflect on your current strategies, I'm wondering how you can expand beyond traditional selling methods. Now is the perfect time to embrace these techniques and unlock unlimited potential in your business. Maybe you haven't considered this yet, but the possibilities are waiting for you. A person is able to transform their approach with just a few simple changes. Are you ready to take action?

The Art of Down-selling

Down-selling is a technique that involves offering a lower-priced alternative when a prospect declines the original offer. The goal is to turn the prospect into a client, even if it means a lower initial revenue. The benefit of down-selling is that you still make a sale, gain a new customer, and create opportunities for future business.

Dr. Oda shares an example from his own practice. If a client who pays $4,000 per month expresses concerns about affordability, Oda offers a down-sell option. He reduces the amount of time spent together and lowers the price, allowing the client to continue working with him without completely losing their business. This strategy is crucial for retaining clients during challenging times like job loss, divorce, or other life events. Imagine the comfort clients feel knowing they have options available to them.

Having a down-sell strategy in place ensures that businesses can maintain relationships with clients and still generate revenue, even when the client's circumstances change. A person is able to find a solution that works for both parties, nurturing trust and connection.

Implementing Upsell, Cross-Sell, Bundling, and Down-selling Strategies

Dr. Oda emphasizes that these strategies—upselling, cross-selling, bundling, and down-selling—are essential for maximizing business growth. However, they must be systemized and consistently applied to be effective.

Businesses should:

1. Identify Opportunities: Analyze your products and services to identify opportunities for upselling and cross-selling. Realizing which items or services complement each other enables you to create packages or bundles that add value to the customer experience.

2. Train Your Team: Ensure that your team understands these strategies and is trained to implement them effectively. Employees should feel aware and comfortable offering upsell and cross-sell options, presenting them as value-added propositions rather than pushy sales tactics.

3. Systemize the Process: Develop systems and processes to apply these strategies across all customer interactions consistently. Whether it's an upsell at the point of sale, a cross-sell in follow-up communications, or a down-sell during negotiations, having a structured approach will increase your success rate. Notice how this consistency builds confidence among your customers.

4. Monitor and Adjust: Regularly review the performance of your upsell, cross-sell, bundling, and down-selling efforts. Track which strategies are working and make adjustments as needed. Flexibility is key to adapting to changing customer needs and market conditions.

Integrating these strategies into your business model can unlock new revenue streams, increase customer satisfaction, and build a more resilient and profitable company.

Conclusion

Upselling, cross-selling, bundling, and down-selling are powerful techniques that can transform your business's profitability. When systemized and implemented effectively, they can drive significant growth and help you stay competitive in a challenging marketplace. As Dr. John Oda emphasizes in Unlimited Business Growth, the key to success is not in discounting but in offering your customers more value that they are willing to pay for, even at a higher price.

Can you imagine the shift this approach could create in your business? By adopting these strategies, you can move beyond the sale and create long-lasting relationships with your customers that will sustain your business for years to come. Maybe you will discover that this journey is the key to unlocking your business's true potential.

Chapter 17: Unlocking Unlimited Potential Through Joint Ventures

Another powerful and sometimes overlooked profit station is the opportunity to establish joint venture partnerships. Do you currently have any established joint venture partnerships? I'm curious because forming Joint Ventures (JVs) can unlock unlimited potential for your business. JVs involve two or more businesses deciding to join forces to share markets or endorse a specific product or service to their customer base, usually under a revenue-sharing arrangement. The key to creating successful joint ventures is finding partners who service the same type of clients who need or want what you sell.

I remember when I first heard of Jay Abraham back in the '90s. I went to Mastery University in Hawaii and saw him speak for the first time. You had to have a dictionary on hand because this young man from Indianapolis had a very large vocabulary! But what I noticed was not just his words; it was the power of collaboration that he and Anthony Robbins embodied. They formed a JV partnership where Anthony Robbins would receive a percentage of the revenue from all his seminars, coaching, and products sold. If you realize this method, you'll see that it creates another stream of income for both parties, which can significantly boost their bottom line.

Another incredible example is when Chet Holmes started his business and partnered with Jay Abraham. It took Chet some time to connect with Jay because, as you might imagine, Chet believed in what he called PhD—Pig-Headed Discipline—never to stop until he secured a client. Can you imagine Chet's determination? Eventually, Jay reached out and offered to promote Chet's program to all his clients, proposing a revenue split of 90% for Jay and 10% for Chet. I have a question for you: Would you accept that deal? What if I told you that 10% would yield you two million dollars in the 90's?

Chet also teamed with Jay Levinson, the author of Guerrilla Marketing, and implemented the same JV partnership model. This got Chet's name out there and allowed him to earn a percentage from Jay Levinson's list of clients who purchased his program.

Notice how these partnerships allow both parties to expand beyond their existing customer bases, creating a win-win scenario. You probably already know that the most successful businesses leverage these types of collaborations to amplify their reach and increase profitability.

A person is able to tap into networks they may not have access to on their own, creating multiple streams of income easily and naturally. People can, you know, achieve remarkable growth through these strategic alliances. Maybe you haven't considered the potential benefits of joint ventures yet, but they are waiting for you to embrace them.

Now is the time to stop holding back and realize the incredible possibilities that come from working together with others in your industry. Who in your network could you partner with to elevate your business? Take the leap and explore the powerful impact that joint ventures can have on your success!

The Unlimited Power of Joint Ventures

This is the power of having Joint Ventures (JVs), and it's a story I know well—how Chet Holmes International merged with Anthony Robbins. When I started working with Chet, he had been pursuing a partnership with Anthony Robbins for 17 years. Can you imagine the level of dedication it takes to wait that long for a partnership? Most people would have quit or pursued other avenues. But not Chet. He believed in what he called Ph.D.—Pig-Headed Discipline.
Most people think business is easy, but the truth is it requires massive persistence and an unwavering commitment, even when the challenges feel overwhelming, and it seems like it's "raining on your parade."
You probably already know that success in business isn't about a quick win; it's about the long game. It's about being aware of the patterns that lead to success and not stopping until you've reached your goals.

After my first year at Chet Holmes International, we merged into a new company called Business Breakthroughs International. This partnership opened incredible doors for us. We were invited to all of Anthony Robbins' events, especially Business Mastery, where I served as an executive business coach for BBI. I attended Business Mastery five times, and it was at this event that I made 60% of my sales. Notice how those experiences shaped my understanding of what being a top Executive Business Coach and a VP of Consulting means.

During these events, I learned to harness the power of NBC (Neuro Business Conditioning), which transformed my approach to sales. Imagine the impact of integrating neuroscience principles into your business communication! This method, which I detail further in my book, allows you to connect with clients more deeply and close deals more effectively.

Jay Abraham also discusses a powerful JV strategy in one of his books. He describes how someone held a seminar that didn't perform well, and instead of giving up, Jay used the same list to contact those attendees. Through a split strategy, they were able to turn that failure into a lucrative venture, making millions for everyone involved. This is a perfect strategy for any business looking to create another stream of income.

People can, you know, realize that JVs can lead to exponential growth. So, have you ever thought about how you could create or find JV partners? I'm wondering how many of you could apply similar strategies to your business to achieve remarkable results.

Let's explore some more ideas for your business. Here are a few steps you can take to identify and cultivate joint ventures that can enhance your success:

1. Identify Potential Partners: Look for businesses that complement yours. This could include companies in the same industry or those that serve the same target audience. The synergy created can lead to mutually beneficial outcomes.

2. Leverage Your Network: Don't be afraid to reach out to your existing contacts. Maybe you haven't yet realized the potential within your network. You might be surprised at how many connections you already have that can lead to profitable

partnerships.

3. Create Compelling Offers: As Chet demonstrated, the key to successful JVs is crafting offers that are irresistible. Make sure your proposals are win-win situations where both parties feel they are gaining value.

4. Be Persistent: Just like Chet, embody that Ph.D. mentality. Stop waiting for the perfect moment; now is the time to take action. Consistent follow-up and dedication will help you cultivate these partnerships.

5. Utilize Online Resources: Explore the Internet for businesses that align with your goals. Consider reaching out to companies with complementary products or services and propose a partnership that benefits both parties.

6. Attend Industry Events: Just as I learned at Business Mastery, engaging with other professionals in your field can lead to new opportunities. Networking at these events allows you to connect with potential partners and explore ideas that can drive your business forward.

7. Monitor and Adjust: After establishing your JVs, noticing and analyzing the results is essential. Monitor how each partnership is performing and be willing to adjust your strategies based on the feedback and data you collect.

8. Expand Beyond Your Comfort Zone: Realizing that growth often happens outside of your comfort zone is key. I know you like me, so trust that you can discover new opportunities that lead to unlimited growth by stepping outside of what feels safe.

Can you imagine the possibilities when you harness the power of joint ventures? The collaborations you forge today can open doors to revenue streams you never thought possible. A person is able to create a thriving business ecosystem when they leverage the strengths of others.

Maybe you will take the plunge and start reaching out for potential partnerships, and maybe, just maybe, you'll discover that the key to expanding your business lies in the connections you make with others.

So, let's not stop here. You probably already know that the world is full of opportunities waiting for those who are willing to seize them. I'm curious: what partnerships can you cultivate today that will propel your business into a future filled with growth and success? The journey of discovering the right joint ventures is just beginning. Now is your time to shine!

Unlocking the Unlimited Potential of Joint Ventures in the Event Chain

Let's explore another option—something you can easily relate to. Let's revisit the florist. One of the most financially lucrative product lines for a florist is providing flowers for weddings, where the average floral bill often exceeds $3,000. You might not realize that florists fall into what we call an "event chain." An event chain refers to a series of businesses whose customers purchase in a specific sequence.

Can you imagine the power of understanding this sequence? For example, a wedding will never take place until an engagement ring is purchased from a jeweler. So, jewelers are at the forefront of every wedding chain. Once the proposal is accepted, this event chain kicks into high gear.

First, this couple knows exactly where they want to get married, so number one on the agenda is to book the location for the ceremony. Second on the list is to line up a wedding planner. I know you like me to paint a vivid picture, so think about the excitement when couples engage a professional to help them with their big day. Weddings today are a big deal, and often, couples prefer the services of a professional wedding planner.

Next up, they want to secure the venue for the reception. Most venues book out months in advance, so locking in that venue is high on the priority list. After that comes the wedding attire, where the search begins for the perfect dress and suit at an affordable price.

Next is our florist, where the happy couple will begin selecting the floral arrangements for both the wedding and the reception. Then, after the florist comes the wedding cake, the printer for the invitations and thank-you cards, and the couple may also be interested in hiring a limo, DJ, travel agent for the honeymoon, hotel, catering, and so on.

Notice how this event chain is typical of the industry and identifies a multitude of potential and lucrative JV partners. Here's why this becomes so important: Every selection before the florist has the potential to endorse and send prospects to the florist. Unfortunately, the florist has no control over that flow of prospects. Every business prior to the florist controls the JV relationship, so it's critical for the florist to create such a compelling offer and relationship that these businesses feel naturally obligated to send prospects their way.

But here's what's even better. The florist controls the prospect flow to all the businesses after them in the chain. By establishing specific processes and procedures to ensure their customers use those businesses, the florist can also negotiate compelling offers with those business owners. A person is able to create a thriving business ecosystem where everyone benefits.

Maybe you haven't yet realized how powerful these partnerships can be. Can you imagine if you continued to add up the revenue produced by all the additional referral fees the florist would earn from all the other vendors in this chain? Let's consider some numbers.

Let's say this florist cultivates a JV relationship with at least one of each business throughout this entire chain. I'm curious because, staying ultra-conservative with our estimates, would you agree this florist is likely to obtain at least one referral each month from just one of the businesses before them in the selection process?

Would you also agree conservatively that the florist could easily send at least one referral to each business after them in the chain? These are extremely conservative estimates we're using here. Since the average floral bill for a wedding is $3,000, one referral per month from the businesses before the florist could increase their annual revenue by $36,000.

Now, let's consider the businesses after the florist, where the florist controls the referrals. Let's start with the wedding cake maker. The sales price for a wedding cake is generally $1,000, and the florist could easily negotiate a 10% referral fee. So, just a single referral per month produces an additional annual increase of $1,200 for the florist.

Now consider the printer. The average sales price for printing is also $1,000, and the florist could again receive a 10% referral fee so that single referral per month produces an additional annual increase of another $1,200.

If we stop there, this florist has just increased their annual revenue by nearly $40,000, and that's using ridiculously conservative numbers. I'm wondering: What if we calculated the revenue produced by all the additional referral fees the florist would earn from all the other vendors in this chain?

People can, you know, easily unlock this potential by forming strategic alliances. So, as you reflect on your current strategies, I'm wondering: how can you leverage joint ventures to expand your reach and impact? Now is the time to stop thinking small and embrace the possibilities of natural collaborations.

Every referral sent and received creates a ripple effect, expanding beyond what you currently perceive. Imagine the possibilities—when you actively engage with others in your industry, you tap into an unlimited potential for growth. The patterns you establish through these partnerships will create a thriving ecosystem that benefits everyone involved.

So, let's not hesitate! You probably already know that embracing joint ventures can revolutionize your approach to business. I'm curious about the partnerships you could cultivate and how they might transform your revenue and impact. Let's take that leap together—your success awaits!

Here are ten questions you can use to guide discussions about potential joint ventures (JVs) in the tone of Dr. John Oda:

1. What unique value does your business offer that could enhance a potential partner's services or products?

2. How do you envision a partnership benefiting both parties in terms of growth and customer reach?

3. Can you identify businesses in your network that share a similar target audience but are not direct competitors?
4. What specific goals do you hope to achieve through a joint venture partnership?

5. Have you thought about the marketing strategies you could implement together to maximize exposure and engagement?

6. What resources, such as time, skills, or technology, are you willing to invest in this partnership?

7. How will you ensure that communication and collaboration remain strong throughout the duration of the JV?

8. What processes will you put in place to track the success of the partnership and make necessary adjustments?

9. In what ways can both parties leverage their existing customer bases to drive mutual referrals?

10. What potential challenges do you foresee in forming a joint venture, and how do you plan to address them proactively

Case Studies

CASE STUDIES

Case Study #1: Transformation Story: Leslie Chase's 1500% Business Growth

Picture this: You're standing on the edge of a breakthrough, about to discover the key to unlocking exponential business growth. This is the story of Leslie Chase, a visionary executive in the pharmaceutical industry who dared to step into the unknown. She left behind the safety of a secure corporate job to launch a groundbreaking EKG testing business. What followed was a journey through struggle, transformation, and ultimate triumph.

Now, imagine this story is yours.

The Struggle

Like so many entrepreneurs, Leslie faced significant challenges early on. The excitement of launching her business was quickly met with harsh realities. She struggled with:

- A limited budget that was far tighter than expected
- No sales force to drive growth and bring in new clients
- A toxic business partner who drained her energy and clouded her judgment
- Stagnant revenue stuck at $200,000 a year with no signs of growth

These obstacles could have easily crushed her spirit, but deep down, Leslie was aware that something greater was possible. She realized it was time to stop accepting limitations and start expanding beyond them.

The Breakthrough

Everything changed when Leslie discovered the BSSM-1 method. This powerful system didn't just promise incremental improvements—it offered a complete transformation.

Here's how the breakthrough unfolded:

1. Faith and Positive Incantations (Quadrant One): We began by addressing the foundation—Leslie's mindset. Leslie started each day with renewed energy and focus through faith-building exercises and powerful positive incantations. She found herself naturally noticing opportunities she had once overlooked, and her vision for success sharpened. You probably already know how powerful that kind of clarity can be.

2. Removing the Toxicity (Quadrant Two): The next crucial step was eliminating the negative influences holding her back. That meant cutting ties with her toxic business partner, whose energy was poisoning the growth of the company. With that burden lifted, Leslie felt a surge of freedom and clarity, and she was now fully aware of the possibilities before her.

3. Systemizing Sales Processes (Quadrant Three): We built a streamlined, systemized sales process that allowed Leslie to focus on high-impact strategies instead of being bogged down by daily operations. She no longer needed to chase after every client manually. Her systems worked for her—automatically driving leads, conversions, and revenue. Can you imagine the relief of having systems that do the work for you?

4. Reactivation, Optimization, and Referrals (Quadrant Four): Finally, we re-engaged past clients, optimized every facet of the business for maximum efficiency, and implemented a targeted referral program that multiplied her outreach effortlessly. Each of these steps compounded on the others, creating a wave of momentum that seemed to expand beyond anything Leslie had initially envisioned.

The Results

In under three years, the results were astonishing. What once seemed like impossible goals quickly became a new reality. Leslie's business achieved:

- A 1500% growth explosion, far surpassing her wildest

expectations
- Full debt elimination, including personal mortgages
- A massive 3,000 sq. ft. expansion of her facilities, enabling the business to accommodate growing demand
- The eventual sale of the business for $2 million per owner solidified her success story

But more than financial success, Leslie had created a business that empowered her employees, delivered exceptional value to her clients, and gave her the freedom she had always craved.

The Lesson

Leslie's remarkable transformation wasn't just about business strategies but a complete shift in mindset and approach. Her story teaches us that:

1. Effective sales systems can naturally change the trajectory of your business
2. Eliminating toxic relationships creates space for real growth
3. Faith and mindset transformation are the catalysts for breakthroughs
4. Empowering your team leads to sustainable success

Your Turn

Now, imagine what's possible for you.

Imagine your business experiencing that same exponential growth, propelled by a system that works around the clock. Visualize your processes seamlessly streamlined, your leadership naturally transforming into a beacon of positivity, and your team empowered to reach new heights. Picture the weight of financial strain lifted, replaced by the freedom to focus on what truly matters.

You've seen what the BSSM-1 method did for Leslie. Maybe you haven't realized how this transformation can easily unfold for you, too. Your transformation starts now because you're on the verge of a breakthrough, about to stop living below your potential.

Discover the power of the BSSM-1 method and unlock the full potential of your business, your team, and yourself.

What will your success story look like?

> *"We wanted to say, 'Thank you!' During the time you have been coaching us, NeuroQuest has achieved so much more than what we had been doing on our own. As small business owners and having worked for a fortune 500 companies for many years, we were hesitant to work with a coach. Not only did we think we had all the answers, but as with any upstart, we were short on cash. We're so glad you were persistent and patient with us. Your coaching has enabled us to gain clarity in our business and personal life which has translated into massive progress and success. We know this is only the beginning! We have found that through your direction, focus and the challenge to think outside the box we have secured more contracts, increased our orders and collections, as well as help us overcome a partnership issue we had been floundering in. The confidence we have in you and your coaching style along with the excitement you help generate will take us to the next level of success and company security. Anyone serious with either their company success or personal success needs you as their coach. Thanks Coach, the results in our business have already paid for the coaching! In the last three years my business has increase over 1500%."*
>
> —Christy Norton, President and Leslie Chase

Case Study Two: Unlock Explosive Business Growth – A UK Waste Management Success Story

Imagine, for a moment, transforming your business into an unstoppable, profit-generating machine that not only meets expectations but shatters them. This is the story of our UK client, the owner of a waste management company that was doing "pretty good." But "good" wasn't good enough. Deep down, they knew there was more. More potential. More growth. More success is waiting to be unleashed.

And it all started with the decision to go beyond good… to greatness.

The Breakthrough

The real magic happened when our client embraced the BSSM-1 Assessment. This comprehensive approach didn't just look at surface-level improvements—it dove deep, identifying the four key quadrants that would naturally fuel exponential growth.

Here's what we uncovered:

1. Mindset and Faith (Quadrant One):
   We transformed the CEO's mindset from dwelling in negativity to embracing positivity. Each day started with powerful affirmations, replacing doubt with unwavering belief. This shift created the foundation for the company's unlimited potential.

2. CEO Leadership (Quadrant Two):
   Unlocking visionary potential was crucial. The shift from a reactive, day-to-day management style to visionary leadership set the stage for unstoppable growth. Maybe you haven't yet noticed how this kind of transformation could happen for you, too.

3. Systemized Marketing (Quadrant Three):
   We revamped the marketing system. SEO, website optimization, and digital outreach were supercharged to bring in a flood of new clients. Can you imagine how your business would expand beyond your current expectations when your marketing is finally working for you?

4. Monetization (Quadrant Four):
   Referral and reactivation strategies were implemented to turn existing relationships into recurring streams of income. Each client became more than a one-time deal—they became a door to unlimited growth.

The Result

In just eight months, the transformation was astounding:
- 120% increase in net profit—the business wasn't just growing; it was thriving.

- Doubled business growth—what once seemed impossible became their new reality.
- 60% client reactivation rate—previously inactive clients returned, bringing new life and revenue into the business.
- Tenfold increase through referrals—clients became enthusiastic advocates, driving even more growth through word-of-mouth.

The Mindset Shift

But the most profound change wasn't just in the numbers—it was in the CEO's mindset. Before the BSSM-1 method, the CEO was literally behind the wheel, driving the company's trucks while drowning in a sea of negative thoughts. But after adopting daily positive affirmations and a faith-centered approach, everything shifted.

The CEO went from:

- Negative thinking to embracing positive incantations for eight hours a day
- Struggling with limited growth to lead the company through explosive expansion

This mindset shift fueled everything else, creating the energy and clarity needed to turn "good" into extraordinary.

Your Turn

Now, imagine applying this same powerful framework to your own business. You probably already know that great leaders see the patterns of success before they happen. That's why I'm curious—have you noticed how easily these steps can unlock your business's true potential?

1. Unlock Quadrant One:
   Imagine starting each day with faith and positivity, watching as your mindset shifts, attracting new opportunities and success.

2. Master Quadrant Two:
   Picture yourself stepping into visionary leadership, unleashing your potential, and guiding your team toward extraordinary results.

3. Optimize Quadrant Three:
   Visualize a seamless, systemized marketing engine that brings in a constant stream of high-quality leads, clients, and sales.

4. Maximize Quadrant Four:
   See your business harnessing the power of referrals and

client reactivations, turning past customers into raving fans who bring in more business than ever before.

Envision the Success

Imagine:

- Increased profits flow effortlessly
- Your business growth doubling or even tripling
- You, leading with confidence and vision
- Your company is expanding beyond anything you thought possible

This is not just a possibility—it's a reality waiting to be unlocked by the BSSM-1 method. Just like our UK waste management client, you can take your business from "pretty good" to extraordinary. It starts with one decision: the decision to go beyond good to embrace greatness.

Are you ready to unlock your business's full potential?

The BSSM-1 framework is your key. Your transformation is just one step away, because once you start, nothing will stop you.

"John Oda has been my business coach for the past eight months. He has taught me strategies to take my business to the next level. Johns' time management structures have helped me increase my business dramatically without increasing my hours dramatically. What sets John apart from other coaches is his ability to help me grow as a person as well as a business owner. He teaches that a healthy mind, body and personal life are extremely important foundations for a healthy growing business. The hidden treasure in Johns coaching is his ability to shift you to a mindset of success. A coaching session with John Oda is tantamount to a coaching session with Anthony Robbins, Napoleon Hill and Joseph McClendon III all rolled into one. The guy knows his stuff.
Oh by the way, I employ 10 great people, in the last eight months my business has doubled and my NET PROFIT is up 120% and we're just getting warmed up. Thanks mate."

-Rob Heidemanns, Canberra, Australia

Case Study #3: Unlocking Potential in Dubai – A Transformation Story of Business and Mental Health

Imagine stepping into a world where wealth and opportunity are at your fingertips, yet something invisible holds you back from achieving true greatness. This was the reality for Frank, a construction startup owner in Dubai, who was originally from Pakistan. Despite his family's legacy of 12 successful businesses generating nearly half a billion dollars, deep tensions threatened to unravel both the business and personal relationships beneath the surface.

When I first began working with Frank, just two months into his coaching journey, I immediately sensed the complexity of the situation. The BSSM-1 assessment revealed several key areas for improvement, but one glaring challenge had gone unaddressed: the toxic relationship between Frank and his father. More than any business issue, this dynamic was holding him back from reaching his true potential.

The Struggle Beneath the Surface

Dubai is a land of opportunity, but it comes with unique challenges. As a non-native business owner, Frank had to navigate both cultural expectations and a business structure that required giving a percentage of profits to the Dubai government. While Frank's family was flourishing in various industries, his construction business was more of a startup, struggling to gain traction in a competitive market.

The BSSM-1 assessment identified four critical quadrants that needed attention:

1. Life Cycle of the Business (Quadrant One):
   The business lacked a clear roadmap for growth, limiting its ability to naturally expand beyond its current state.

2. Leadership, Culture, and Mental Health (Quadrant Two):
   Frank's strained relationship with his father created a toxic work environment, and he struggled with deep-seated mental health issues and patterns of destructive

leadership. I'm curious: Have you noticed how personal struggles can sometimes seep into every area of life and affect your decisions and outcomes?

3. Sales and Educational Marketing (Quadrant Three):
   The business relied on outdated sales and marketing methods. There was no strategic approach to attract clients. Can you imagine how different the results could be with a more modern and systemized approach?
4. Dream 100, Reactivation, and Referral Programs (Quadrant Four):
   The untapped potential existed in building client relationships, reactivating past clients, and leveraging referrals. You probably already know how powerful referrals can be when done right.

Yet, beneath all these business challenges, the most significant barrier was personal. Unresolved mental health issues, if left unchecked, can morph into larger problems over time, affecting every aspect of our lives.

The Tension Between Father and Son

When I arrived in Dubai, the tension between Frank and his father was palpable. As a mental health professional and executive business coach, my goal was to bridge the gap between them, heal the emotional wounds, and create a harmonious business partnership. But the damage was deep. Frank's father, a towering figure in business and life, cast a long shadow that Frank struggled to step out of.

Frank wasn't ready to connect with me personally. Maybe you haven't yet realized how important the right personal connection is in business coaching. Despite my best efforts, Frank only wanted to speak with Alex, the other coach who had introduced me. This added another layer of complexity. While I worked diligently to serve Frank at the highest level, I could sense his resistance. He viewed me with suspicion, even paranoia, convinced that I was conspiring with his father behind his back.

Still, I pressed on, knowing that his business would thrive if Frank could overcome these personal challenges. I was confident that we could increase his sales by 100% in just one year.

Implementing the Plan: Sales Training and Mental Health Support

My primary role was to help Frank hire and train a high-performing sales team to close more construction deals. We held weekly training sessions where I put the team through rigorous "hot seating" exercises to sharpen their skills. I provided scripts, taught them the art of closing deals, and emphasized the power of educational marketing combined with NLP (Neuro-Linguistic Programming) to influence clients and drive sales.

But Frank's mental health remained a pressing issue. His paranoia and passive-aggressive tendencies made it difficult to have direct, productive conversations. I'm wondering if you've noticed how deeply personal issues can limit your ability to reach your goals. I proposed regular bi-monthly meetings to address his mental health, but Frank's distrust only grew. Meanwhile, Alex worked on marketing strategies, but Frank's closed-minded approach prevented him from accepting valuable feedback.

The Breaking Point

One day, I held an intense meeting with the sales team. They hadn't practiced their script and gave up after the first client rejection. Stop for a moment and notice how the patterns of giving up easily can emerge in teams and individuals when the right mindset is missing. The meeting was heated but necessary. I reminded them of the importance of persistence and using NLP to turn objections into opportunities.

The next day, I received a call from Alex. Frank had fired me, claiming I had "yelled" at his sales team. Despite my attempts to reach out, he refused to answer my calls or emails, leaving me no choice but to step away from the project. Frank wasn't just firing a coach; he was severing an opportunity to transform his business—and himself.

The Aftermath

Eight months later, I received a call from my VP of Coaching. Frank was upset with the company, claiming we had over-promised and under-delivered. I calmly explained that we had increased his business by 30% during my four months working with him. If he had continued with our plan, there's no doubt that we would have achieved the 100% growth I had promised. But Frank wasn't ready. His unresolved personal struggles, much like a child in the "terrible twos," prevented him from stepping into his true potential. He surrounded himself with yes-men and staff complaints instead of facing the hard truths.

The Lesson

This story is a reminder that business success often goes hand-in-hand with personal growth. Frank's business challenges were real, but they were symptoms of a deeper issue—the unresolved conflict with his father and his own mental health. If he had faced these challenges head-on, instead of displacing them onto me and others, he could have unlocked unlimited wealth and growth.

Your Turn

If you find yourself stuck—whether in business, relationships, or personal growth—ask yourself this: Are unresolved personal issues holding you back from achieving your true potential? Sometimes, the key to exponential growth lies not in changing your strategies but in changing yourself.

Are you ready to unlock that door? The choice is yours because once you make the decision to change, the transformation becomes inevitable.

Case Study #4: Unlocking Explosive Growth in a Stagnant Wholesale Food Business

Imagine stepping into a family-owned wholesale food business rich with tradition, deeply rooted values, and decades of history. Yet, as you look closer, you can't help but notice something that doesn't quite add up. Greg, the CEO, inherited the business from his father, and while he had the passion, drive, and vision to expand, his team remained stagnant—trapped in old habits, held back by a culture of complacency. Entitlement ran deep, especially among family members in key positions, making it challenging to lead the business to new heights.

When I conducted the BSSM-1 assessment, the reality quickly came to light. The business was like a family reunion where nobody wanted to acknowledge the elephant in the room—internal strife was silently eroding their potential. The staff operated like toddlers in a tantrum or rebellious teenagers, resistant to guidance and unwilling to step up and become the heroes of their own story. Instead, they clung to the comfort of what they knew rather than embracing the opportunity to expand beyond their current limitations.

The company had been stuck at around $50 million in revenue for years. Yet, with their resources, experience, and market positioning, they had the potential to achieve so much more. Greg knew it. I knew it. Maybe you're already starting to realize what needs to be done. The journey to transformation began with one fundamental
shift: systemizing for success.
Systemizing for Success

The first step was clear. We had to systemize the sales process, creating a roadmap that would move the team from autopilot to action. Without a structured approach, the sales team was inconsistent—operating more out of habit than driving toward real results. We redefined their marketing strategies and introduced NLP training, equipping the team with communication tools to close deals naturally and effortlessly. These proven strategies were designed to create urgency and attract clients who were ready to buy now.

But here's where the true challenge emerged. The sales team had been with the company for years, comfortable with "good enough." They were content to hover in mediocrity, not realizing that staying in their comfort zone was limiting their growth. Their mindset was stuck in neutral, and they had no desire to shift into drive. Greg was eager for explosive growth, but his team? They wanted to remain exactly where they were.

Every recommendation I made—whether it was the Dream 100 strategy to target key clients, introducing educational points to create urgency, or simply reactivating old relationships—was met with resistance. Not because the strategies wouldn't work but because change made them uncomfortable. Maybe you haven't yet noticed how resistance to change can be the very thing keeping you stuck.

Confronting Internal Resistance

The internal resistance wasn't limited to the sales team; it was also present in leadership, who should have been driving change. Instead, they were more concerned with maintaining the peace, especially within the family dynamic, than with pushing the company to new heights. Complacency wasn't just a habit; it was a pattern deeply embedded in the culture.

I'll never forget a particular meeting with Greg's son, a young man accustomed to entitlement. As I laid out the plan for growth, he dismissed my suggestions as if they were beneath him. You probably already know how damaging that kind of attitude can be. I had a choice—allow this behavior to continue or confront it head-on. I chose the latter, explaining calmly and professionally that if the business was to succeed, he would need to adopt a growth mindset and let go of the need for comfort.

The very next day, my contract was broken.

Lessons Learned and Moving Forward

There are no hard feelings. Business is business. But here's a truth you may need to be aware of: If you're not willing to push past complacency, you will stay stuck where you are. If you're not ready to confront the hard truths—about leadership, about mindset, about culture—your business will never grow. Maybe you will see that, or maybe you haven't yet.

While I couldn't change decades of ingrained habits in four months, I know this: The businesses that embrace transformation are the ones that rise above the rest. It's not just about changing systems or strategies. It's about changing mindsets, behaviors, and cultures. It's about moving past fear and stepping boldly into a future of growth. Greg's business had the potential to explode with success. The only thing holding it back was an unwillingness to change.

The Question Now Is...

Are you ready to move beyond complacency and embrace the changes that will propel your business forward? The BSSM-1 method is designed to create unlimited growth potential because it tackles the roots—mental health, behavior, and culture—ensuring your business thrives. Stop settling for mediocrity when the path to explosive growth is right in front of you.

I'm wondering if you're ready to rise above the rest. Can you imagine what it would feel like to step into a new level of success, realizing that the only thing standing in your way was a decision to change now?

The choice is yours. Don't just stop and think about it—notice what could be possible when you choose to take action. Let's break the patterns and transform your business together

Case Study #5: Transforming a Chiropractic Wellness Center with the BSSM-1 Method

Can you imagine a chiropractic wellness center that's full of potential but hasn't quite unlocked its true power? That was where Dr. Duddy found himself—a chiropractor with a practice that had moved beyond survival but wasn't yet thriving. Unlike businesses stuck in their "terrible twos" or "teenage" phases, Dr. Duddy and his team were aware, open-minded, and eager to expand beyond their current results. This created the perfect environment for the BSSM-1 assessment to naturally work its magic.

Identifying Gaps: The Power of the BSSM-1 Assessment

I'm curious: have you ever realized how even small inefficiencies can add up to big losses? When I conducted the BSSM-1 assessment, a few key gaps became evident. These were areas that, once addressed, would easily and significantly enhance the practice's efficiency and revenue. The first gap was in the systemization of the sales process and time management. There were missed opportunities to streamline client interactions and optimize how time was being used, leading to inefficiencies in day-to-day operations.

While Dr. Duddy's leadership was effective—thanks in part to Connie, his high-performing office manager, and loyal staff—there were still a few "neutral" players. For instance, the massage therapists weren't detracting from the practice's value but weren't actively adding to it either. This "neutral" behavior was an untapped resource, signaling the potential to elevate team members to higher levels of performance. After all, maybe you haven't yet noticed how small shifts in behavior can trigger explosive growth.

Behavioral Shifts: Building a High-Performing Team

One of the key challenges was shifting the culture and behavior of the entire team, making each member an active participant in the wellness center's growth. I'm wondering if you're aware of how powerful it can be when every member of a team aligns with a common mission. I worked closely with the staff to develop leadership skills, not just in Dr. Duddy but across the entire team. Connie, the office manager, was already performing at a high level, but with a few strategic adjustments—like restructuring her compensation to include higher commissions—she became even more instrumental in driving the business forward.

This holistic approach naturally fostered a sense of ownership and investment in the wellness center's success, especially for those who had previously been neutral players. The result? A team that not only noticed the experience of working together but became deeply engaged in it.

Systemizing for Success: Optimizing Sales and Time Management

The next step was to optimize the sales process. We designed a system that allowed Dr. Duddy to easily offer upsells, downsells, and package deals, adding more value and convenience for clients while driving revenue growth. We also developed a referral program that encouraged satisfied clients to share their positive experiences, organically leading to an unlimited flow of new clients.

In addition to enhancing sales strategies, we tackled time management. By implementing scheduling systems and improving client flow, we maximized the number of clients Dr. Duddy could see without compromising the quality of care. These changes created a noticeable improvement in the practice's operational efficiency because they addressed the patterns that had kept the business stuck.

Monetizing the Business: Reducing Accounts Receivables and Growing Revenue

Dr. Duddy's practice had a lingering issue—$100,000 in outstanding accounts receivable. Maybe you will realize just how much a cash flow problem can limit your growth. To solve this, we introduced a systematic approach to recovering outstanding payments. Instead of relying on collection agencies, we established clear payment protocols and a follow-up system that drastically reduced the amount owed. Within just six months, the accounts receivable went from $100,000 to zero, effortlessly restoring a healthy cash flow to the business.

At the same time, the upsell, down-sell, and package offerings began to naturally work their magic. Clients were more engaged and willing to invest in their health through higher-value packages, while the referral program brought in a steady stream of new clients. You probably already know that when clients see the value in what you offer, they'll share it with others because they're excited about the results they're experiencing.

Results: A 50% Increase in Revenue in Just ONE Month

Dr. Duddy's chiropractic wellness center saw a dramatic transformation through a combination of behavioral shifts, systemization, and monetization strategies. In just one month, the business grew by 50%, easily moving beyond previous limitations and setting the stage for continued growth. What had once been a growing but under-optimized practice became a thriving, well-oiled machine.

Now It's Your Turn...

Are you ready to expand beyond your current results? Are you willing to notice the patterns holding your business back and embrace the changes that will propel you forward? The BSSM-1 method offers a path to unlimited growth because it aligns leadership, optimizes systems, and monetizes opportunities in a way that feels natural.

Maybe you haven't yet experienced the power of such a transformation. Or perhaps you're curious about what your business could achieve after making a few simple changes. I know you like me, so let's stop settling for "good enough" and take the next step to make your business truly great.

The choice is yours. Are you ready to experience the explosive growth that comes from unlocking the true potential of your team and your business?

"I am the owner of a busy Chiropractic/Massage/Physical Therapy office and have been working with John Oda from Business Breakthroughs International for only about one month. Since that time we have had a 50% increase in revenues and John has structured systems to bring all of our accounts receivables current totaling over $100,000. I had reservations about joining Business Breakthroughs International, but now after completing only the first month, I don't know how any business could afford not to join."
-Dr. Duddey, Sports Care Center

Case Study #6: How a Plastic Surgeon Achieved 15% Revenue Growth in Just 8 Weeks Using BSSM-1

Can you imagine a thriving plastic surgery clinic in the UK led by the skilled and dedicated Dr. Deirdre? Her practice had reached a plateau in revenue despite years of hard work and satisfied clients. She felt as though her clinic wasn't tapping into its full potential. That's when she came across my ad promising that in just 45 minutes, I could show her how to generate between $10,000 and $100,000 in net profit using my BSSM-1 program.

Intrigued, Dr. Deirdre scheduled a call with me. During our conversation, she shared the ins and outs of her business—the years of dedication to her patients and her vision for growth. Yet, there was a gap, something she hadn't quite realized. I knew that with a few simple shifts, we could unlock her clinic's true potential and expand beyond what she thought was possible.
Discovering Untapped Potential

I'm curious: have you ever thought about the hidden revenue opportunities that might already exist within your business? One of the first questions I asked Dr. Deirdre was whether she had ever tried to reactivate her old clients—patients who had already trusted her with their care but hadn't returned in years. Her answer? A resounding no.

She had a long list of satisfied clients, yet no system in place to re-engage them for follow-up treatments, new services, or additional care.

Right there, I knew this was an untapped goldmine. It became clear that she was sitting on a treasure trove of potential revenue, and by not having a strategy to reconnect with these clients, she was leaving money on the table. Maybe you haven't yet realized how much opportunity is right in front of you.

The Power of One Profit Station

I immediately got to work. Using just one Profit Station from the BSSM-1 system, I crafted a personalized reactivation letter tailored to her client base. This wasn't your typical email blast; it was a carefully designed message that spoke directly to her clients' experiences, reminding them of the incredible results they had already achieved with Dr. Deirdre and offering them a compelling reason to return to the clinic.

You probably already know that when you create a connection on an emotional level, the results can be profound. Within eight weeks, Dr. Deirdre's clinic saw a 15% increase in revenue, all from reactivating old clients. One letter, one Profit Station, and her business was already expanding beyond previous limitations.

But here's the exciting part: this was only the beginning.

Unlocking the Full Potential of BSSM-1

What Dr. Deirdre experienced was just a taste of the BSSM-1 program's power. This system includes 25 Profit Stations, each one designed to systematically grow your business by optimizing different areas—from client acquisition to retention, from sales to marketing, and everything in between.

The magic lies in the four quadrants of the BSSM-1 model, which work together seamlessly to expand your business's potential. Whether your goal is to increase net profits, streamline operations, or create a loyal client base, the BSSM-1 system easily covers every angle.

The Power of Quick Wins and Long-Term Success

In Dr. Deirdre's case, the quick win of reactivating old clients was just the first step. Can you imagine what could happen when all 25 Profit Stations are activated? If one simple strategy led to a 15% revenue increase in just eight weeks, the potential impact of implementing the full system is limitless.

Dr. Deirdre's clinic is now positioned for sustained growth, not only through reactivated clients but also by leveraging all the Profit Stations to target different areas of her business. She's no longer leaving money on the table. Instead, she's generating new revenue streams, building stronger relationships with her clients, and positioning herself as the go-to plastic surgeon in her region.

Beyond Imagination

Now, I'm wondering if you're aware of how powerful it could be to stop settling for incremental growth and embrace a system that creates unlimited potential. The truth is, if you're willing to put in the time, the BSSM-1 system can create change beyond your imagination. It's not just about boosting revenue; it's about transforming your entire approach to business—creating a sustainable, scalable system that will continue to drive profits, growth, and success for years to come.

Dr. Deirdre's story is proof of what's possible. Maybe you will see yourself in her journey, realizing that your business can achieve exponential growth with a few strategic changes. And now, the same growth, the same transformation, is within your reach.

Are you ready to unlock the full potential of your business with the BSSM-1 system? One quick win can lead to exponential growth. But only if you choose to take that first step.

"I just want to give you some feedback after our UGP Coaching sessions. They were excellent and I would recommend you, and have recommended you, to business owners. I used a lot of your tips and one main one which grew one part of my business 15% over 8 weeks...

and it is still growing - that was the re-activation letter in combination with a special invitation to join our Inner Sanctum. The Inner Sanctum is like a Platinum group of clients who enjoy special offers, new launch invites etc. Pretty much as for other types of business but not so common in Cosmetic Medicine. Your coaching really revitalised my enthusiasm for my business which extended to an increase in my team's enthusiasm. Again, many thanks John."
-Deirdre Tozer MD, Cosmetic Surgery Specialist, Australia

Case Study #7: House of Health (Casa de Salud)
Transforming Leadership, Systems, and Profits in Healthcare

When I first stepped into the world of Dr. Akhavan's thriving medical and dental clinic in Los Angeles, I saw immense potential. Dr. Akhavan was already an effective leader with solid systems in place, but he recognized the need to elevate his business to a new level. Together, we embarked on a journey through what I call the Four Quadrants of Transformation, revolutionizing every aspect of the clinic.

Quadrant One: Personal and Business Alignment

When I first met Dr. Akhavan, his personal life was at the crossroads of the young adult/maturity stage—a period of clarity, focus, and a hunger for meaningful impact. His business, however, was navigating the terrible twos/teenager stage, full of potential but marked by growing pains, unpredictability, and the need for guidance to mature.

This dual dynamic presented a unique opportunity. Because Dr. Akhavan was already an effective leader with a deep desire to grow, I didn't need to "convince" him to evolve—I needed to unlock what was already within him.

Rather than taking a conventional coaching approach, I chose a strategy tailored to create massive success with precision and speed. I focused on aligning his readiness for growth with his business's need for structure, discipline, and scalable systems. This synergy between personal and professional development became the foundation for everything we achieved together.

With Dr. Akhavan fully engaged and open to change, the journey became not just easier but profoundly rewarding—for both of us.

Quadrant Two: The Culture Shift

The foundation of any business is its people. While Dr. Akhavan had a strong lead person in place, I knew unlocking her leadership potential would create ripple effects throughout the team.

We implemented a three-step hiring process to address the high turnover rates of medical assistants and MDs. This included a psychological evaluation to ensure every candidate aligned with the clinic's values and culture. The result? A stronger, more cohesive team that was built to last.

We also prioritized mental health and workplace wellness, introducing monthly group sessions where we shattered mental blocks and reignited passion. We achieved rapid, lasting changes in mindset and performance using Neuro-Business Conditioning. As Dr. Akhavan himself put it:

"I've never seen such quick and lasting results in my life."

Quadrant Three: Systemizing Success

With the team culture thriving, it was time to bring precision to sales, marketing, and time management.

On the dental side, I taught the art of influence using NLP (Neuro-Linguistic Programming), empowering the team to close more cases effectively and ethically.

We crafted a comprehensive marketing system using eight distinct strategies tailored to the clinic's medical and dental offerings. This included targeted campaigns that drew clients from high-value neighborhoods, leveraging education as a powerful magnet for new business.

To help Dr. Akhavan juggle the demands of running two clinics, we created a time management system that gave him clarity, control, and focus.

Quadrant Four: Monetizing Momentum

Growth isn't just about systems—it's about strategy. Here's how we amplified the clinic's reach and revenue:

Dream 100 Strategy: We identified and nurtured relationships with the clinic's most valuable prospective clients.
Reactivating Old Clients: Using strategic messaging, we brought back clients who hadn't visited in years.
Referral Programs: We created irresistible incentives, turning satisfied clients into enthusiastic advocates.
JV Partnerships: We partnered with local businesses to position Dr. Akhavan as their "go-to" medical director, hosting educational events that brought in waves of new clients.

An Experiential Marketing Masterpiece

One of our most memorable campaigns was a Hawaii Five-O-themed activation at a local fairground. We hired models, handed out leis, and engaged attendees with our unique blend of education and entertainment. The results? Over 3,000 contacts and 1,000 new patients were added to the clinic's roster.

The Results: Unprecedented Growth

In just six years, every aspect of the clinic experienced exponential growth. The transformation was undeniable, from improved team dynamics to streamlined operations and innovative marketing.

Dr. Akhavan and his team continue to expand today, delivering top-tier healthcare to underserved communities while embodying the highest standards of excellence.

This is what happens when you unlock the hidden potential within a business—transformational, scalable, and lasting results that change lives.

Case Study #8: Manufacturing Breakthrough – Portland, Oregon
Transforming a Struggling Business from Chaos to Consistency

They were at a critical crossroads when I first engaged with this manufacturing business in Portland, Oregon. With over 20 years of operation, 40 staff members, and a focus on widget testing, they had survived—but just barely. Monthly sales hovered around $50,000, barely covering expenses. It was clear: survival wasn't enough anymore. It was time for transformation.

Quadrant One: Personal and Business Life Cycles

The business owner, a woman in her 50s, was caught in a curious paradox. Her personal life was stuck in the terrible twos/teenager stage—a phase of chaos, impulsivity, and lack of structure. Unfortunately, her company mirrored this energy. It, too, was in its terrible twos, with no clear identity or discipline.

Her management team had individuals at the young adult stage, ready to lead, but their potential was stifled by the owner's inability to set a vision. The result? A workplace that felt more like a chaotic daycare than a high-functioning business.

It became obvious that the first step was to address the leadership void. Without a clear direction, even the most capable team members couldn't thrive.

Quadrant Two: Culture Reset

The business culture was toxic—employees were locked in a victim-villain mentality, each pointing fingers instead of working together. At times, it felt like walking into a zoo, with chaos reigning supreme. Trust was non-existent, and the concept of teamwork was foreign. The CEO's unresolved personal struggles bled into the business, affecting morale and productivity. Employees mirrored this dysfunction, relying on junk food, candy, and sedentary habits, which only deepened the cycle of low energy and low performance.

To rebuild the culture, I knew we had to:
- Break the cycle of blame by introducing accountability.
- Focus on team building to foster collaboration.
- Address mental health issues with practical strategies and workplace wellness programs.

Quadrant Three: Systems and Discipline

The business lacked any sense of structure or time management. Labs weren't completed on time, employees were distracted, and productivity was an afterthought. We implemented a systemized time management process to ensure every task aligned with deadlines and goals.
We eliminated distractions like unrestricted access to social media and replaced unhealthy snacks with nutritious options, helping employees sharpen their focus and energy levels.

Quadrant Four: Monetization Strategies

Once the internal foundation was stabilized, we shifted our focus to growth strategies:
- Reactivation of Old Clients: We reached out to past customers with tailored campaigns that reignited interest and trust.
- Referral Program: We incentivized current clients to bring in new business, creating a steady pipeline of qualified leads.

Results: From Struggling to Soaring

By addressing these critical areas, the business experienced exponential growth. Monthly revenue skyrocketed from $50,000 to over $300,000—a sixfold increase.

The biggest transformation? The team's energy and focus. By cutting out junk food and introducing healthy snacks, we saw an immediate shift in productivity. Social media distractions were removed, and employees began to take pride in their work.

However, the potential for even greater success was evident. The business could have grown even further with stronger leadership, a more cohesive culture, and a deeper commitment to mental and physical health.

Conclusion

This case study is a testament to the power of structure, systems, and a focus on wellness. We turned a chaotic, struggling business into a thriving operation by addressing the root causes of dysfunction and implementing the Four Quadrants.

The lesson is clear: when you align leadership, culture, and systems, the possibilities for growth are limitless.

Dr. John Oda Companies

PNBC Group

At PNBC Group, we specialize in comprehensive coaching services tailored for individuals and groups, focusing on C-suite fractional executives. Our unique contract-based approach allows us to step directly into leadership roles such as CEO, CSO, or CGO within organizations, offering hands-on guidance to ensure business success. We bring expertise across key areas that drive growth—targeted marketing strategies, effective hiring techniques, and efficient time management practices—all aimed at sustainable business growth. Moreover, we work collaboratively with our clients to establish profit-generating stations, empowering organizations to scale their success.
Website: www.drjohnoda.com

Speaking Bureau

Our Speaking Bureau specializes in delivering impactful keynote speeches, organizing transformative retreats, and hosting immersive seminars and workshops led by Dr. John Oda. Whether for corporate, private, or scholastic audiences, our events range from one-day sessions to three-day experiences designed to create lasting transformation. We excel in customizing programs to meet each client's unique needs, ensuring that every experience is tailored and enriching. Our diverse topics ensure that all participants gain valuable insights, applicable tools, and inspiration.
Website: www.drjohnoda.com

NLP for Sales

At NLP for Sales, we provide a powerful approach to sales that enables professionals to achieve up to a 30% increase in their sales closures. Drawing on over 70 years of combined experience in the mental health field, we use Neuro-Linguistic Programming (NLP) techniques to help individuals overcome mental blocks and unlock their potential for success. Unlike traditional sales strategies, our approach taps into the subconscious mind, guiding our clients to adopt a success-driven mindset and effortlessly say 'yes' to opportunities. Our tailored tools and techniques empower salespeople to connect with customers, identify opportunities, and confidently

close deals, driving exceptional results
Website: https://drjohnoda.myeverycatch.com

Unleash Hidden Profits in Your Business with Dr. John Oda's Expertise

What if the secret to creating a legacy in your business was already within your reach? Imagine uncovering untapped profit opportunities, renegotiating expenses you thought were fixed, and optimizing costs to fuel exponential growth.

Here's What We Do:

- Cost Optimization That Works: From merchant accounts to health insurance and every major expense tied to your business, we don't just review—we renegotiate. We're relentless in finding savings others overlook.

- Unparalleled Reach Across Industries: With experience spanning over 1,500 industries, we understand the unique challenges and opportunities in your market, tailoring strategies to maximize results.

- Profit Is the Key to Legacy: By freeing up resources and increasing margins, we position your business to thrive—not just for today but for generations to come.

Your legacy isn't built on working harder—it's built on working smarter. Let us help you transform expenses into profits and pave the way for long-term success.

Click here to schedule your consultation and take the first step toward unstoppable growth!

Website: www.drjohnoda.com

Dominate Your Industry with Cutting-Edge Digital Marketing, Technology, and PR Media

What if you could position your business as the undeniable leader in your industry? Imagine having every tool, every strategy, and every piece of technology working seamlessly to propel your success to new heights.

Here's How We Help You Win:

- Digital Marketing That Commands Attention: From precision-targeted campaigns to strategies that convert, we ensure your message reaches the right audience at the right time.

- Technology Designed to Propel You Forward: Stay ahead of the curve with innovative tech solutions that streamline your operations and give you a competitive edge.

- PR Media That Turns Heads: We craft compelling stories that put your brand in the spotlight, creating buzz and building credibility that lasts.

The key to dominating your industry is simple: stay ahead, stay visible, and stay innovative. With our expertise in digital marketing, technology, and PR media, you won't just compete—you'll lead.

Ready to take the leap? Let us show you how to unlock the cutting edge and dominate your market. Click here to start your journey to industry domination!

Website: www.drjohnoda.com

Parenting and Teen Programs

With over three decades of dedicated experience, we are recognized as the foremost experts in guiding teenagers toward leadership and societal impact. Our mission is to provide adolescents with the same powerful tools used by CEOs, enabling them to thrive in the competitive landscape of today's world. Imagine the transformative power of your teenager equipped with the skills needed to excel and leave a lasting mark.

Alongside our teen programs, we offer invaluable tools for parents to foster stronger relationships with their teens. Drawing from Dr. John Oda's seminal work, 'Connecting with Your Teen,' we help parents navigate the challenges of adolescence with practical strategies for effective communication, understanding, and building harmony. Our holistic approach ensures both teens and parents are empowered with the resources necessary to foster positive growth and connection. Website: https://family.pnbcgroup.com/

Unlock Your Child's Full Potential with Dr. John Oda's Proven System

Imagine your child stepping onto the field, court, or track with unshakable confidence, their mind laser-focused, their performance unstoppable. That's the power of Neuro-Linguistic Programming (NLP)—a science-backed method that rewires the brain for excellence.

Here's What We Offer:

- Get in the Zone, Every Time: Using NLP techniques, we help high school and college athletes find their flow state—the zone where peak performance becomes second nature.

- Life Coaching for Resilience: Whether it's overcoming burnout, handling setbacks, or navigating the pressure of sports, we equip your child with tools to stay balanced and thrive.

- Boost Academic Success: We don't just promise—we deliver.

Our methods help students improve their grades by at least one letter, ensuring success on and off the field.

- Build Their Own Sports Empire: From learning to market themselves to mastering business growth strategies, we teach athletes how to turn their passion into a thriving business.

Your child's potential is limitless. Give them the tools to achieve greatness in sports, academics, and life.

Click here to learn more and see how our program can transform your child's future!

https://sports.pnbcgroup.com

Made in the USA
Columbia, SC
24 February 2025

8366bf37-63d2-4e6f-bc94-bbae7ee886c7R01